The Origins and Development of the European Community

Edited by
David Weigall and Peter Stirk

Leicester University Press
Leicester and London
*Distributed in the United States and Canada by
St. Martin's Press, New York*

Leicester University Press
(a division of Pinter Publishers)
25 Floral Street, Covent Garden, London WC2E 9DS, United Kingdom

Editorial offices
Fielding Johnson Building, University of Leicester,
Leicester LE1 7RH

Trade and other enquiries
25 Floral Street, London WC2E 9DS, UK
and Room 400, 175 Fifth Avenue, New York, NY 10010, USA

First published in 1992

Distributed exclusively in the United States and Canada by St. Martin's Press, Inc., 175 Fifth Avenue, New York, NY 10010, USA

British Library Cataloguing in Publication Data

A CIP catalogue record for this book is available from the British Library.

ISBN 0 7185 1428 9 (hb)
ISBN 0 7185 1461 0 (pb)

Library of Congress Cataloging-in-Publication Data

A CIP catalog record for this book is available from the Library of Congress.

Typeset by Mayhew Typesetting, Rhayader, Powys
Printed and bound in Great Britain by Biddles Ltd., Guildford and King's Lynn

The Origins and Development of the European Community

Contents

Preface

The editors are grateful for permission to quote from sources in copyright, as listed at the end of the book. They are also grateful to Diana Gonzalez for all her help in preparing the typescript.

In the following pages the terms 'European Community' and 'European Communities' are both used. In 1967 the institutions of the European Coal and Steel Community (ECSC) the European Economic Community (EEC) and the European Atomic Energy Community (Euratom) were merged. Since that time the first term has come to be used more and more often. Other terms are 'Common Market' (sometimes the 'ECM') and 'EEC'. These occur frequently in the history of the Community, not least during the protracted debate for and against Community membership in the United Kingdom. However they are used misleadingly if they are meant to suggest the Community as a whole. The term 'European Common Market' in any case has no legal basis.

David Weigall
Peter Stirk
1 May 1992

List of acronyms

ACP	African, Caribbean and Pacific members of Lomé
ACUSE	Action Committee for a United States of Europe
AOC	Associated Overseas Countries
BENELUX	economic grouping of Belgium, the Netherlands and Luxembourg
CAP	Common Agricultural Policy
CCC	Commodity Credit Corporation
CCT	Common Customs Tariff
CEEC	Committee for European Economic Cooperation
CET	Common External Tariff
CFP	Common Fisheries Policy
CMEA	Council for Mutual Economic Assistance
COREPER	Committee of Permanent Representatives
CSCE	Conference on Security and Cooperation in Europe
D-G	Directorate-General
EAEC	European Atomic Energy Community
EAGGF	European Agricultural Guidance and Guarantee Fund
EBRD	European Bank for Reconstruction and Development
ECOSOC	Economic and Social Committee
ECB	the idea of a European Central Bank
EC	European Community
ECE	Economic Commission for Europe
ECJ	European Court of Justice
ECSC	European Coal and Steel Community
ECU	European Currency Unit
EDF	European Development Fund
EDC	European Defence Community
EEA	European Economic Area
EEC	European Economic Community
EIB	European Investment Bank
EFTA	European Free Trade Association
EM	European Movement
EMS	European Monetary System

EMU	Economic and Monetary Union
EP	European Parliament
EPC	European Political Cooperation
EPU	European Payments Union
ERASMUS	European Community Action Scheme for the Mobility of University Students
ERP	European Recovery Programme
ESC	Economic and Social Committee
ESF	European Social Fund
EUT	Draft Treaty establishing the European Union
ESPRIT	European Strategic Programme for Research and Development in Information Technology
EURATOM	European Atomic Energy Community
EUREKA	European Research Coordination Agency
GATT	General Agreement on Tariffs and Trade
GDP	Gross Domestic Product
GNP	Gross National Product
MECU	Million ECUs
MEP	Member of the European Parliament
MTN	Multilateral Trade Negotiation
NTB	Non-tariff Barrier
NATO	North Atlantic Treaty Organisation
OECD	Organisation for Economic Cooperation and Development
OEEC	Organisation for European Economic Cooperation
SEA	Single European Act
SEM	Single European Market
The Six (EC6)	the original members of the EC, France, Italy, the Federal Republic of Germany, Belgium, Netherlands and Luxembourg
The Nine (EC9)	the original members plus Denmark, Ireland and the United Kingdom
The Ten	EC9 plus Greece
The Twelve	EC10 plus Spain and Portugal
UEF	European Union of Federalists
VAT	Value Added Tax
VER	Voluntary Export Restraint
WEU	Western European Union

Introduction

The purpose of this book is to introduce students and other readers interested in contemporary history, politics and economics to the origins and development of the European Community. We examine the evolution of the EC in its historical context through a wide range of documents and texts in the belief that something which may often appear forbiddingly complex and, in spite of its everyday effects upon our lives, somewhat remote, is more easily comprehensible if it is related to the history of which it is a part.

Particular care has been taken to relate this process of integration to wider historical developments, for instance the Cold War and decolonisation and the prominent encouragement of the Community by the United States. The first two chapters examine the proposals for, and discussion of, European integration during the interwar period and World War II. Chapter 10 explores some of the implications for European integration and the Community of the dramatic course of events in Eastern Europe since 1989.

The introductory sections relate the texts to their historical backgrounds. There is particular emphasis on the variety of motives behind the development of the Community, on individual national interests as well as common interests, on the reasons for the uneven pace of its evolution and on the debates which it has generated, and which still continue.

The texts have been selected for the light they throw on these issues, debates and arguments. Why have some strategic choices been preferred to others? Why this option rather than another? Why, for instance, did the United Kingdom not apply to join until five years after the Six signed the Treaties of Rome? Why did the French National Assembly ratify these treaties as founder members but not, after four years of debate, the plan for a European Defence Community which their Premier, M. Pleven had proposed in 1950? Why did the Soviet Union from the interwar years right through to recent times display such hostility to the Community? These are just some of the many questions considered.

Our concentration on the development of, and debate over, the Community means that we have included only a selection of the articles from the key treaties. However the essentials are covered and explained, as are the roles of the EC institutions. As well as the memoranda, comments and speeches of major figures in the history of the Community, such as Jean Monnet and Paul-Henri Spaak, we have also included the views of less well-known figures where they offer an interesting perspective.

During the late 1970s and early 1980s there was considerable gloom about the state of the Community and the future competitiveness of the Western European economies. The word 'Eurosclerosis' was coined. The second half of the 1980s and the early 1990s have brought a new dynamism. This is not to say that important changes had not come about in the years up to the Single European Act of 1986 and the commitment to '1992', the completion of the internal market through the abolition of non-tariff barriers. After all, the Community had doubled its membership. Following long delays, direct elections had been introduced for the European Parliament and the European Monetary System had been instituted. Moreover important agreements had been drawn up with developing countries. Nevertheless the goal of the single market has necessarily brought with it some changes in the decision-making processes and compelled a reassessment of the role of the institutions. The agreements reached at Maastricht at the time of writing still have to be ratified by the parliaments of the Member States. As this goes to press, we have just had the results of the referenda in Denmark and Eire on Maastricht. The rejection by a small majority in Denmark poses considerable problems. In Eire a substantial majority were in favour. Although they have not removed the so-called 'democratic deficit' of the Community as much as many MEPs would like, the commitment to monetary union, if honoured (and even if the United Kingdom has reserved the right to opt out of the process), would be a very considerable advance.

Equally importantly, the revolutions in Eastern Europe have opened up or re-opened (if we consider the debates over integration which took place in the interwar years and during World War II) the whole question of the extent of integration. Could the Community cope with the incorporation of all those states which are currently expressing a wish to join? These changes also, of course, pose questions for other organisations as well, such as NATO. One question raised is whether the Community itself will, or should, develop a defence capacity.

In the light of such changes and the questions they present, an understanding of the growth of the Community is even more necessary than before. As the documents here illustrate, there was nothing inevitable or self-evident about the extent of European integration, the aims which a European union might pursue, or the institutions which developed.

As we can see, some of the fundamental arguments, over national sovereignty, over the balance between politically-prescribed integration and commercially-led integration are nothing new. Others, like the question of the transition from centrally-planned to market economic systems are.

What stands out particularly prominently now, though, is that there is a European Community which has its own voice, one not simply reducible to the sum of its Member States.

1 From the Treaty of Versailles to the outbreak of World War II

Introduction

Though the idea of European unification had been periodically raised since the end of medieval Christendom and the emergence of the early modern State, it was not until after World War I that it attracted prominent consideration. The destruction of a war, which many came to view as a European civil war, and the growth of American power, as well as revolution in Russia, shook European confidence to an unprecedented degree. This led statesmen and other observers to take seriously ideas which had previously been regarded as simply utopian. One of these ideas was European unity. Another was that of a global organisation. It was the latter which seemed to triumph with the creation of the League of Nations on 1 January 1920, with its seat at Geneva.

The choice between a regional institution and a global one was one of several dilemmas which appeared clearly in the interwar period and was to haunt the cause of European unification. Amid the immediate enthusiasm for the new diplomacy of President Woodrow Wilson of the United States and for the League a few voices were raised in favour of a strictly European solution to the threat of renewed conflict. (See Document 1.1.)

One of those who expressed the hope for a new peaceful global order was Count Richard N. Coudenhove-Kalergi. Born into the Habsburg aristocracy, he was well-placed to observe at first hand the realities of the new international order. He quickly concluded that the Wilsonian promise of a new order was not being fulfilled. Moreover, instead of evolving towards greater unity, Europe had in fact undergone a process of fragmentation. In the place of the multinational empires which had dominated East–Central Europe, there were now the Successor States. They were proud of their nationhood yet with substantial minority populations within their borders. The potential vulnerability and instability of these states presented a major threat to peace.

In the West the central problem of Franco–German enmity and distrust remained unresolved. French attempts to maintain their wartime victory against the much more populous and potentially stronger Germany collapsed with the failure of their occupation of the Ruhr in 1923. By then Coudenhove-Kalergi had launched himself as a publicist and organiser for the unification of Europe (see Documents 1.2 and 1.9). The years between the establishment of his Pan-European Union and the end of the 1920s were the highpoint of what has been called the 'first wave' of European integration. Organisations and publications in favour of integration proliferated to an extent which is now largely forgotten. At issue was not only the scope of a united Europe – should it embrace the United Kingdom?; should it be a Pan-European order?; was Russia to be considered part of Europe? – but also the ideological complexion of Europe.

Supporters of European unification could be found across the entire political spectrum. Authoritarians with strong Fascist sympathies as well as Communists incorporated European integration into their proposals (see Document 1.3). One of their few common sentiments was an apprehension of the United States. Despite Woodrow Wilson's sponsorship of the League of Nations, the United States refused to ratify it. Politically, traditional isolationism appeared to revive, and to revive strongly. In one way this allowed Europeans to recover some of their self-confidence. Economically, though, the United States could not be disregarded. The United States presented both an economic challenge and a model of political unity for a very heterogeneous population, as well as a promise of prosperity, which Europe could well imitate once she was united.

Among those who agreed on the desirability of European unification there was disagreement over the means to this end. It was not always assumed that politicians were the most credible guides for all too often they seemed to be far too beholden to their nationalistic peoples. A good number of 'Europeanists' placed their faith in business leadership. The prospects of business-led integration improved with the wave of economic rationalisation and the formation of cartels in the mid-1920s. The creation of the International Steel Cartel in 1926 expressed the hopes of those who looked forward to a Europe united by economic interests. This was not integration by means of open and free competition but integration by means of regulation, self-regulation by business (see Documents 1.4 and 1.5).

The mid-1920s saw some progress on the political front. Franco–German hostility abated as Gustav Stresemann for Germany and Aristide Briand for France concluded the Locarno Pact in 1925. This agreement, whereby Germany voluntarily accepted her Western borders as established at Versailles, left open the question of the Eastern frontiers of Germany. At the end of the decade Briand put forward the first proposal by a European government this century for a 'United States of Europe'. In this proposal the unresolved problems were very evident. Was political union to precede economic union, or vice versa? How much sovereignty would European States have to surrender to construct a viable union? Would federation properly resolve the conflict of interest between France and Germany? What would the relationship be between a European union and the League of Nations? Briand sought a way between all these difficulties, but by the time he presented his memorandum Germany had embarked on another course – to revise, if necessary by force, the postwar settlement in the East, whose territorial clauses particularly offended German nationalist sentiment.

With the ignominious collapse of Briand's initiative and the onset of the Depression prospects of peaceful integration receded. The idea, however, did not disappear and came to be used by ideologies which seemed to be inherently incompatible with European integration. Fascists and Nazis appropriated aspects of the idea of European unity and sought to turn them to their own purposes. Prominent now was the slogan of a new crusade against Europe's supposed ideological and racial enemies (see Document 1.7). With the outbreak of war in September 1939 the idea of international integration, both on a global and regional level, once again enjoyed a revival. Looking back with the benefit of wisdom after the event, the Versailles Settlement seemed to embody the folly of encouraging nationalist sentiments which would lead inevitably to international anarchy. To the advocates of European integration on a democratic basis the sacrifice of the idol of national sovereignty seemed a self-evident necessity (see Document 1.8).

Documents

DOCUMENT 1.1

Giovanni Agnelli and Attilio Cabiati, 'European Federation or League of Nations?', 1918

Towards the end of World War I Giovanni Agnelli, founder of the Italian Company of FIAT, and Attilio Cabiati, an economist, firmly rejected the projected League of Nations in favour of a European union with a strong central government. In posing the question, European federation or League of Nations?, they set out a strategic choice which was to bedevil attempts to forge a European union (see also Documents 1.4, 2.6 and 2.8).

Without hesitation we believe that, if we really want to make war in Europe a phenomenon which cannot be repeated, there is only one way to do so and we must be outspoken enough to consider it: a federation of European states under a central power which governs them. Any other milder version is but a delusion.

. . . The typical example which shows how one community, for its very survival, has had to change from a league of sovereign and independent states to a more complex form of a union of states ruled by a central power, is given with unsurpassable clarity by the history of the United States of America. As is well known, they went through two constitutions: the first, drawn up by a Congress of 13 states in 1776 and approved by these same states in February 1781; the second, approved by the national Convention of September 17th 1787 and which came into force in 1788.

A comparison between the two documents explains why the first failed, threatening the independence and freedom itself of the young Union, while the second has created a Republic, which we now all admire.

The 1781 constitution started by affirming the sovereign independence of the individual states. Article 2 states: 'each State retains its Sovereignty, Freedom and Independence, and every Power, Jurisdiction and Right. . .' It is true that Article 13 decreed that the states must 'abide by the Determinations of the United States in Congress assembled': but . . . Article 13 was in constant conflict with Article 2. The essence of sovereignty is legal omnipotence and it cannot acknowledge a higher sovereignty without destroying itself. . . The preface of the 1788 Constitution – which is basically the one currently in force – states solemnly: 'We, the Peoples of the United States, in Order to found a more perfect Union, establish Justice, ensure domestic tranquillity, provide for the common Defence, promote the general Welfare and secure the Blessings of Liberty to ourselves and our Posterity, do ordain and establish this Constitution for the United States of America.'

And in fact it sets up a central government, with legislative and executive power. . .

We also wish to dwell for a moment on another of the great benefits that only the creation of a federal Europe can bring with it: the setting up of the whole European Continent into one production market. . .

In Europe we had reached this level of absurdity, that every factory that arose in one state was a thorn in the side for every other state: that while the superb inventions of steam applied to land and sea transport, of electricity as motive power, of the telegraph and telephone had by then cancelled distance and made the world one single large centre and international market, little men strove with all their might to cancel the immense benefits of the big discoveries, artificially creating isolated markets and small production and consumption centres. . .

Only a federal Europe will be able to give us a more economic realization of the division of labour, with the elimination of all customs barriers. . .

DOCUMENT 1.2

Richard N. Coudenhove-Kalergi, 'Three Years of Pan-Europe', 1926

Count Richard N. Coudenhove-Kalergi was one of the most active publicists of European union in the interwar period. His book, Pan-Europa *was published in 1923. In the same year he launched the Pan-European Union, a movement intended to promote the cause of European union, with the backing of the Austrian Chancellor, Ignaz Seipel, among other leading figures. 'Three Years of Pan-Europe' is a supplement to the 1926 edition of* Pan-Europa.

This book appeared in 1923, the year of the Ruhr occupation, the darkest and most discouraging year that Europe had known since the World War.

The following year, 1924, passed under the sign of the French May elections, of the Dawes Plan, and of the London Conference. The road was opening to a European understanding.

The year 1925 was the year of Locarno, which led to the first practical step toward European understanding and unification. Thus Pan-Europe was a utopia in 1923, a problem in 1924, and a program in 1925.

The world–political tendency of these first three years of the Pan-European movement was:

(1) The stabilisation and liberation of the new Europe grown out of the World War. . .
(2) Increasing weariness of Europe on the part of America, Asia, Russia and England. . .

Asia is striving more and more for emancipation from Europe. Hand in hand with the cultural Europeanisation of this continent goes its political de-Europeanisation. . .

Russia is supporting this anti-European policy and is itself becoming more and more an Asiatic Great Power. . .

Following the victory of the Conservatives the imperial idea is fortifying itself in England. . .

The greatest differences of opinion prevail regarding the English Question: that is, whether England without risking its world position can become a federal state of Europe. England alone can answer this question of destiny. Its answer might be a compromise, as Locarno indicates. For the negotiations left no doubt regarding the fact that this security pact was the most extreme guarantee England could assume with respect to Europe without jeopardising its Empire.

Hence British policy with respect to Pan-Europe is affiliation, but not membership; understanding, but not federation.

DOCUMENT 1.3

Leon Trotsky, 'Perspectives of World Development', 1924

Trotsky was the most important advocate of a United Socialist States of Europe. His fall from power and exile were closely associated with the decline of the idea in Communist circles.

For what does America need? She needs to secure her profits at the expense of the European toiling masses and thus render stable the privileged position of the upper crust of the American working class. . .

The further this development unfolds along this road, all the more difficult will it be for the European Social Democracy to uphold the evangel of Americanism in the eyes of the European working masses. All the more centralised will become the resistance of European labour against the master of masters, against American capitalism. All the more urgent, all the more practical and warlike will the slogan of the all-European revolution and its state form – the Soviet United States of Europe – become for the European workers.

What is the Social Democracy using to benumb and poison the consciousness of the European workers? It tells them that we – the whole of Europe, dismembered and sliced-up by the Versailles Peace – cannot get along without America, but the European Communist Party will say: You lie, we could if we wanted to. Nothing compels us to remain in an atomised Europe. It is precisely the revolutionary proletariat that can unify Europe, by transforming it into the proletarian United States of Europe.

DOCUMENT 1.4

Elemér Hantos, 'The European Customs Union', 1926

Elemér Hantos, a Hungarian economist, wrote extensively on aspects of European integration. He was a member of the International Committee for a European Customs Union, founded in 1924. In the extract printed below, however, he asks whether a customs union is the most promising road towards integration (see also Document 1.5).

The victory of the Pan-European idea in the intellectual world of contemporary Europe has given new life, in economically oriented minds, to the idea of a European customs union. . . Why is the Pan-European idea carried over into the economic realm, appearing above all in the form of a European customs union? Is it perhaps that customs barriers most strongly thwart the free circulation of economic forces? In the times before the war one could answer this question affirmatively. To conduct trade policy meant, at that time, to utilise customs. Custom rates were the most important mechanism in trade policy. The arsenal of postwar trade policy worked with more comprehensive armaments; new weapons appear alongside the old. Exchange rate fluctuations, transfer difficulties, obstacles to transport, import and export bans, sales taxes and railway tariffs are barriers which exceed the highest customs dues in their effectiveness. Yet a European currency union or a European transport union is scarcely discussed: a trading union, on the other hand, is presented as the be all and end all of economic cooperation. The cause of this phenomenon is perhaps to be sought in this, that despite the inflation of currency advisers and theorists of money, there are yet more people who have an insight into, and trust their own opinion on, customs matters than is the case with financial policy or the technical problems of transportation. Moreover, the logic of things leads more easily from the well-known starting point of unpopular tariffs to general conclusions which are intelligible to broad circles. The syllogism, persuasive to every layman runs: the maintenance of customs dues means higher prices; higher prices bring a reduction in purchasing power; a reduction of purchasing power produces a shrinking market; a shrinking market leads to a reduction of production; a reduction of production creates poverty and misery. The European customs union, on the other hand, brings, through the abolition of customs dues, cheaper prices; lower prices create higher purchasing power; higher purchasing power produces an expansion of the market; expansion of the market leads to higher production; higher production creates prosperity and wealth. . .

However well one may agree about borders, however convinced one may be of the correctness of the goal of a European customs union, the difficulties of managing the transition from today's divisions to a unified economic region are not thereby overcome. Even the most enthusiastic defender of the idea shrinks back from a leap out of the current situation into the desired one and wants to allow far-reaching transitional measures. The sudden abolition of customs borders would condemn part of Europe's stock of factories and produce great unemployment. The considerable number of enterprises that are kept viable only by the customs tariffs of their homeland would be the first victims. Also, those factories which today can dump exports because of the high prices within their protected domestic markets, would be condemned to go under. Hardship could scarcely be avoided in the economic transformation, it could, however, be mitigated through a planned reduction which would set the date, for each branch of industry and for each customs area, at which customs must be completely set aside. . .

International industrial interests could pave the way for the economic unification of Europe more effectively than the multilateral, staged reduction of customs tariffs. Syndicates and distribution agencies of individual branches of the economy, cartellization or the horizontal development in large-scale industries, could be a surrogate for customs tariffs. They could also be more effective than customs tariffs as equalisation mechanisms, in the sense of protecting weaker groups against stronger ones and may even promote the general equalisation of production costs more quickly than the dismantling of customs barriers. One can see that a harmonisation of the conflicts in the creation of an inter-state economic union may occur not only from state to state. The planned cooperation of private economic interests in international production, distribution, transport and consumer organisations would vigorously promote the European division of labour without doing deep damage to individual economies, without shaking productive life. . .

For the near future, therefore, a regime of free trade in Europe is not to be expected. One needs only to recall how slowly and under what difficult circumstances the German customs union came about. . . In that case the presuppositions were incomparably more favourable. It was a question of an understanding between peoples of the same origin and the same political aspirations. It would already signify great progress if areas that were previously economically united would return to mutual free trade. For the present it is not a question of final goals but of tendencies and movements. The realisation of a European customs union will have to wait for a long time, but the idea itself must underlie all political and economic measures.

DOCUMENT 1.5

Aristide Briand, 'Memorandum on the Organisation of a Regime of European Federal Union', 17 May 1930

Aristide Briand held ministerial office in several French cabinets, including that of Premier. Together with the long-serving German Foreign Minister, Gustav Stresemann, he was regarded as the most pro-European of statesmen. His proposal for a European Federal Union, first made in 1929, was the first formal proposal for European union made by a government in this century. The proposal was consigned to further study and effectively buried later in 1930.

The proposal taken under consideration by twenty-seven European Governments found its justification in the very definite sentiment of a collective responsibility in face of the danger which threatens European peace, from the political as well as the economic and social point of view, because of the lack of coordination which still prevails in the general economy of Europe. The necessity of establishing a permanent regime of conventional solidarity for the rational organisation of Europe arises, in fact, from the very conditions of the security and well-being of the peoples which their geographical situation compels, in this part of the world to participate in a *de facto* solidarity.

No one doubts today that the lack of cohesion in the grouping of the material and moral forces of Europe constitutes, practically, the most serious obstacle to the development and efficiency of all political and juridical institutions on which it is the tendency to base the first attempts for a universal organisation of peace. . . The very action of the League of Nations, the responsibilities of which are the greater because it is universal, . . . might be exposed in Europe to serious obstacles if such breaking-up of territory were not offset, as soon as possible, by a bond of solidarity permitting European nations to at last become conscious of European geographical unity and to effect, within the framework of the League, one of those regional understandings which the covenant formally recommended.

This means that the search for a formula of European cooperation in connection with the League of Nations, far from weakening the authority of this latter must and can only tend to strengthen it, for it is closely connected with its aims. . .

The European organisation contemplated could not oppose any ethnic group, on other continents or in Europe itself, outside of the League of Nations, any more than it could oppose the League of Nations. . .

The policy of European union to which the search for a first bond of solidarity between European Governments ought to tend, implies in fact, a conception absolutely contrary to that which may have determined formerly, in Europe, the formation of customs unions tending to abolish internal customs houses in order to erect on the boundaries of the community a more rigorous barrier against States situated outside of those unions. . .

It is important, finally to place the proposed inquiry under the general conception that in no case and in no degree can the institution of the federal bond sought for between European Governments affect in any manner the sovereign rights of the States, members of such a *de facto* association . . . It is under the reservation of these observations and in the light of the general preoccupation recalled at the beginning of this memorandum that the Government of the Republic, in accordance with the procedure decided upon at the first European meeting of September 9, 1929, has the honour to submit to the consideration of the Government concerned a summary of the different points on which they are invited to formulate their opinions.

I

NECESSITY FOR A PACT OF A GENERAL NATURE, HOWEVER ELEMENTARY, TO AFFIRM THE PRINCIPLE OF THE MORAL UNION OF EUROPE AND SOLEMNLY TO SANCTION THE FACT OF THE SOLIDARITY ESTABLISHED AMONG EUROPEAN STATES

In a formula as liberal as possible, but clearly indicating the essential objective of this association in the service of the collective work of pacific organisation of Europe, the signatory Governments would engage to make regular contacts, in periodical or extraordinary meetings, for the examination in common of all questions which might concern primarily the community of European peoples. . .

NECESSITY OF A MECHANISM ADAPTED TO ASSURING TO THE EUROPEAN UNION THE ORGANS INDISPENSABLE TO THE ACCOMPLISHMENT OF ITS TASK

A. Necessity of a representative and responsible organ in the form of regularly establishing the 'European Conference', composed of all the European Governments which are members of the League of Nations and which would be the essential directing organ of the European Union, in liaison with the League of Nations.

The powers of the Conference, the organisation of its presidency and of its regular or extraordinary sessions, should be determined at the next meeting of the European States. . .

B. Necessity of an executive organ, in the form of a Permanent Political Committee, composed only of a certain number of Members of the European Conference and assuring, in practice, to the European Union its organisation for study at the same time as its instrument of action.

The composition and powers of the European Committee, the manner of designation of its members, the organization of its presidency and of its regular or extraordinary sessions should be determined at the next meeting of the European States. . .

C. Necessity of a secretariat service, however restricted at the beginning to assure the administrative execution of the instructions of the President of the Conference or of the European Committee, communications between Governments signatory to the European Pact convocations of the Conference or of the Committee, preparation of their discussions, recording and notification of their resolutions, etc. . .

III

NECESSITY OF DECIDING IN ADVANCE THE ESSENTIAL DIRECTIVES WHICH MUST DETERMINE THE GENERAL CONCEPTIONS OF THE EUROPEAN COMMITTEE AND GUIDE IT IN ITS STUDIES FOR THE ELABORATION OF THE PROBLEM OF EUROPEAN ORGANISATION

(This third point could be reserved for the consideration of the next European meeting.)

A.   General subordination of the Economic Problem to the Political.

All possibility of progress towards economic union being strictly determined by the question of security, and this question being intimately bound up with that of realisable progress toward political union, it is on the political plane that constructive effort looking to giving Europe its organic structure should first of all be made. It is also on this plane that the economic policy of Europe should afterwards be drawn up, in its broad outlines, as well as the special customs policy of each European State.

The contrary order would not only be useless, it would appear to the weaker nations to be likely to expose them, without guarantees or compensation, to the risks of political domination which might result from an industrial domination of the more strongly organised States.

It is therefore logical and normal that the justification of the economic sacrifices to be made to the whole should be found only in the development of a political situation warranting confidence between peoples and true pacification of minds. . .

B.   Conception of European political cooperation as one which ought to tend toward this essential end: a federation built not upon the idea of unity but of union; that is to say, sufficiently flexible to respect the independence and national sovereignty of each of the States, while assuring them all the benefit of collective solidarity for the settlement of political questions involving the fate of the European community or that of one of its Members.

(Such a conception might imply, as a consequence, the general development for Europe of a system of arbitration and security, and the progressive extension to the whole European community of the policy of international guarantees inaugurated at Locarno, until such time as special agreements are merged into a more general system.)

C.   Conception of the economic organisation of Europe as one which ought to tend to this essential end: a *rapprochement* of the European economic systems effected under the political responsibility of the Governments working in unison.

With this purpose in mind, the Governments might definitively associate themselves in an act of a general nature and of principle which would constitute a simple pact of economic solidarity, the purpose which they intend to set as the ideal end to their tariff policy (establishment of a common market to raise to the maximum the level of human well-being over all the territories of the European community). With the help of such a general orientation, immediate efforts could be undertaken practically for the rational organisation of European production and exchanges, by means of the progressive liberation and the methodical simplification of the circulation of goods, capital, and persons, with the single reservation of the needs of national defence in each State. . .

The time has never been more propitious or more pressing for the inauguration of constructive work in Europe. The settlement of the main problems, material and moral, incident to the late war, will soon have liberated New Europe from a burden which bore most heavily upon its psychology, as well as on its economic system. It appears henceforward to be ready for a positive effort and one which will fit in with the new order.

DOCUMENT 1.6

Edouard Herriot, 'The United States of Europe', 1930

Edouard Herriot was a former Premier of France. He had espoused the idea of European union while Premier in speeches in October 1924 and January 1925 and subsequently supported the efforts of Briand. The extract below reflects a widespread belief in the 1920s that European integration was being driven forward by businessmen's search for the rationalisation of production. The formation of the German chemical combine, I.G. Farben, in 1925 and the International Steel Cartel in 1926, are cited as models of this trend.

We believe we have already proved the three following truths:

1. Whereas attempts at a customs union have failed because they were premature, all the industries are being led by an irresistible movement toward a system of agreements.
2. Concluded in the first place for Europe, these agreements, when they are well established, extend to the other countries of the world, especially the USA and Japan. (For this latter country see the agreement with I.G. Farben Industrie.)
3. It is idle to ask whether Governments can be theoretically disinterested in these agreements. In fact, as the case of the Steel Trust shows, they are constantly concerned with them.

The whole problem to be decided is whether public men will have as much initiative and intelligence as private individuals, or whether in politics, we are going to be content to walk in the old ways, ignoring the great transformation, which is silently creating a new world. . .

The argument advanced in the preceding chapters would alone suffice to prove the urgency of establishing order in Europe. M. Aristide Briand, however, in his memorandum, goes further. Having indicated the necessity of studying the general economy of Europe, he shows that it is necessary to rationalise its economic machinery, to co-ordinate the public works carried out by the states of the Old World (automobile main roads, canals, rivers, railways, posts, telegraphs and telephone broadcasting). Nothing could be less disputable. . .

In the interests of clarity, however, at the end of a study which does not pretend to be more than preliminary, we feel it our duty to summarise the principles which, in our view, must guide the work undertaken.

1. A European understanding can be achieved only within the framework of the League of Nations, as a part of the League, and marking a stage in its development.

2. Since the League Covenant permits regional agreements within a continent it follows 'a fortiori' that it cannot oppose the agreement of a whole continent.

3. A European understanding must take account both of international and of national alignments.

4. It must be open to all the nations of Europe which are willing to enter.

5. It is rendered necessary by the laws of economic evolution, by industrial amalgamations, and by the necessity of defending the European market.

6. It must be sufficiently comprehensive to admit nations like Great Britain, which have both European and world-wide interests.

7. The nations must be represented on absolutely equal terms.

8. It might very well seek inspiration from the form taken by the Pan-American Union, its method of procedure would be the holding of periodical conferences with a permanent secretariat.

9. It must be flexible, prudent and patient.

10. It must regard the suppression of tariff barriers as the end, not the beginning, of an economic organisation of Europe.

11. It can achieve stability only by a European organisation of credit.

12. Its durability will depend upon a fixed system of arbitration, disarmament, and security.

DOCUMENT 1.7

Hans-Helmut Dietze, 'The Problem of Europe's Legal Unity', 1938

Dietze was one of several German legal theorists who sought to reconcile the expansionist nationalism of the Third Reich with a European mission. His invocation of an anti-Bolshevik crusade prefigures the response among sectors of the European population to the Nazi attack upon the Soviet Union in 1941 (see also Document 2.4).

If Europe is thereby understood as a community, its boundaries in the South, West and North are formed by the sea. Only the Eastern border is questionable. Here it is only certain that the Soviet Union stands beyond the European community of law. She embodies in herself the system of arbitrariness, lawlessness, a naked lust for conquest and anarchism. The destructive forces of the eternal nomad, which had already taken shape in Genghis Khan and Ivan the Terrible, find their modern representative in Stalin. If everything depends upon preventing the breakthrough of the destructive Asiatic conception of the world, then this task entails a gathering together of the occident around the values of law and peace. It is here that there is a legal basis for the formation of European unity: the political obligation of the great occidental states to protect their culture and civilisation from the Bolshevik chaos. This world – historical mission is also rooted in a second unifying force: in the consciousness of a great and common history and fate. . .

The relation of European peoples to one another cannot be shaped according to the mechanistic principles of an obsolete concept of law, but must rather be dominated by an organic incorporation of all the individual (peoples) into the community of peoples which will do justice to the peculiar national essence of each. This is the basis of a correctly understood Four Power Pact. A historyless 'Pan-Europe' is not going to be created. The goal is, rather, to find the unity amongst the multiplicity of European nations and to allow each, according to its position and gifts, to work on the collective European task. Thereby, Germany, especially today, is again fulfilling its eternal European duty of reinforcing the West against the East. The creation of a Great German Reich signifies a strengthening of this front, of the true Europe, against the East and a further step towards gathering together all constructive forces which are now dispersed in the turbulent zones of the European East.

DOCUMENT 1.8

R.W.G. MacKay, 'Federal Europe', 1940

An Australian by birth, MacKay was to become a Labour Party Member of Parliament. His book, Federal Europe, *was an example of the revival of interest in European union at the end of the 1930s and in the early 1940s. The extract exhibits his radical federalism and counters Marxist objections that political federation would not put an end to war.*

The primary problem at the end of this war, will be to reconcile the conflicting ambitions, demands and fears of the three Great Powers, Great Britain, France and Germany. No scheme of Federation is of practical value if it does not satisfy the reasonable claims of all three Powers. The following proposals are put forward as embodying the minimum requirements of any scheme:

1. A Federation of some, if not all, of the European States, must be established. The minimum number of States to join the Federation is three, namely Great Britain, France and Germany. It is to be hoped that the other belligerent countries in Europe, and the neutrals in Europe, will also join the Federation. The minimum, however, is a union of Great Britain, France and Germany. With that union, war amongst the European States is ended for all time. Without it, war in Europe will continue.
2. The form of government of the Federation should be democratic. The Parliament of the Federation should be elected by the peoples of the countries which join it, and the Government of the Federation should be at all times responsible to Parliament.
3. Each of the States joining the Federation should transfer to it a minimum number of powers, which shall give to the Federation exclusive power to legislate in four matters, namely external affairs, defence, customs and currency. . .

In the political field, national sovereignty leads to insecurity, to fear and to war . . . The desire to be secure leads to a determination to be strong. The strength of one nation leads others to build up their armaments. In this way, a race begins between the different Powers, which gains momentum and finally becomes uncontrollable. . .

In a similar way, the division of the world into independent national States exercising economic sovereignty and developing along the lines of economic nationalism has added to international instability. It has created a state of anarchy and unrest which, if not an immediate and direct cause of war, is an indirect cause, by the friction which it engenders among the nations. . .

It will be argued by some that this diagnosis is fallacious, and that national sovereignty is not the fundamental cause of war. It will be argued that the cause of war is not to be found primarily in the political organisation in the world, but in the economic system – capitalism – which the different States have adopted . . . Thus it is the economic system in each country, and not the political organisation of the nations that must be changed. . .

However cogently the Marxist may argue, it is difficult to accept the proposition that a change in the economic system must come before a change in the political system. . .

If, at the end of this war, it is possible to create a Federation in Europe, then, even if it is a capitalist Federation, or a Federation of capitalist States, it will provide an organisation which will remove war from Europe. Whatever the economic factors operating in the States of Maine and Virginia and Massachusetts, the capitalists of Massachusetts do not go to war with the capitalists of Virginia or of Maine. The capitalists of Manchester do not fight the capitalists of the South of England, in the same way that the Marxists would say the capitalists of Great Britain fight the capitalists of Germany.

DOCUMENT 1.9

Richard N. Coudenhove-Kalergi, 'Pan-Europa', 1923

This table from Coudenhove-Kalergi's manifesto reflects a geo-political approach to European integration which was commonplace at the time.

Pan-Europe

	Population (m.)	Area (Km^2)
Homelands	300	5.0
Colonies	129	19.7
Total	429	24.7

Pan-America

	Population (m.)	Area (Km²)
USA (with colonies)	118	9.7
Latin-America	91	22.8
Total	209	32.5

East Asia

	Population (m.)	Area (Km²)
China	440	11.10
Japan (with colonies)	80	0.68
Total	520	11.78

Russian Federation

	Population (m.)	Area (Km²)
Soviet Russia	90	16.4
Federated states	60	7.0
Total	150	23.4

British Federation

	Population (m.)	Area (Km²)
Homeland and Dominions	70	20.0
Colonies and vassal states	394	19.3
Total	464	39.3

Suggested reading

The political background to events in this period can be found in S. Marks, *The Illusion of Peace* (London, 1976) and Jon Jacobson, *Locarno Diplomacy* (Princeton, 1972). There are few recent accounts of the theme of

European integration. R. Vaughan, *Twentieth Century Europe* (London, 1979) is a good brief introduction. The movements for European integration in the 1920s are surveyed in detail by C.H. Pegg, *Evolution of the European Idea* (Chapel Hill, 1983). A broader perspective, including articles on the usually neglected 1930s, is provided by P.M.R. Stirk (ed.), *European Unity in Context: The Interwar Period* (London, 1989). There are contributions on Coudenhove-Kalergi and the Briand Plan in Preston King and Andrea Bosco (eds), *A Constitution for Europe* (London, 1991). On the Briand Plan see also W.D. Boyce, 'Britain's First "no" to Europe: Britain and the Briand Plan, 1929–30', *European Studies Review*, **10** (1980), pp. 17–45 and F.T. Murphy, 'The Briand Memorandum and the Quest for European Unity 1929–1932', *Contemporary French Civilisation*, **4** (1980), pp. 319–30.

2 World War II and the European order

Introduction

A superficial view of the war years might lead one to suppose that with the triumph of totalitarian nationalism on the Continent there was no space for ideas of European integration. In fact the discussion and advocacy of integration was widespread in the Resistance Movement throughout Europe. At the same time both the Nazis and Italian Fascists can be found developing ideas of a 'New Order', though these ideas were not always officially sanctioned and were frequently mutually inconsistent.

The initial military successes in Europe led the Nazis to consider in detail their longer-term plans for the Continent. The immediate priority was to exploit the conquered territories in the interests of the German war economy. Beyond that opinions diverged as to whether they should form customs unions and/or currency unions; which countries or regions should be included; whether integration should be undertaken primarily by political bodies or at the level of business enterprises. These were all issues which were raised in debate (see Documents 2.1, 2.2 and 2.3).

Economic integration was, however, only one dimension of Nazi policy. Racial policy was a paramount element and for Adolf Hitler this was so paramount that he was unable properly to exploit the potential sympathy of elements of European society for an anti-Bolshevik crusade (see Document 2.4). Although the idea of a racial restructuring of Europe, including the mass murder of European Jews, affected all of occupied Europe, it was on the Eastern Front that Nazi ideas came closest to being realised. There the populations were exposed to the full brutality of the New Order. The scale of this is clear from the General Plan East which envisaged racial engineering extending far into the Soviet Union (see Document 2.5).

The impact of Nazi hegemony in Europe was immense. The holocaust, massive population movements in Eastern Europe and the dominance of the Superpowers after the war meant that prewar Europe could never be restored in its entirety. The attempt to impose a New Order also, therefore, prompted a wartime debate on European unity, especially in resistance circles. All of the issues discussed in the interwar years resurfaced. The conflicting claims of nation, Europe and global organisation were reassessed in the context of war. For some at least the cause of European unity was suspect precisely because of its adoption by Nazi propaganda. Defence of the nation against the oppressor seemed the proper cause. Again, when thoughts turned to the postwar order, was not the construction of a global organisation the desirable sequel to a war which, from the bombing of Pearl Harbour in December 1941 had been a global war?

The restoration of nation states and the creation of a new world organisation, the United Nations, were to be the Allied response to the question of what sort of postwar order. Unaware of the deliberations of Allied policy-makers, members of the Resistance, exiles and citizens of the Allied States advanced a different view. Patriotism and European unification, European federation and a global peace order were, it was argued, complementary and not mutually exclusive. Few were in doubt, though, about the extent of changes required to reconcile these commitments. European integration as conceived in the pamphlets and proposals of this period represented a direct challenge to the notion of national sovereignty.

Nowhere was this clearer than in the oppressor states themselves, where opponents of the Nazi and Fascist ideologies formulated plans for a new Europe whose radicalism went further than anything achieved by European integration to date (see Documents 2.8 and 2.9). The prospects for European unification were generally overestimated though Altiero Spinelli, the leading Italian federalist, was clear-sighted in his prediction of the forces which would line up behind a restoration of a Europe organised on the basis of nation states (see Document 2.8).

At the end of the war both Stalin, who was consistently hostile to such schemes, and the US Administration were at one in rejecting European federal integration. During the war policy-makers in the State Department of the United States had toyed with ideas of combinations of regional groupings (see Document 2.9). Churchill, too, speculated upon a Europe reconstructed from a mixture of existing states and regional blocs. Of the 'Big Three', Churchill was most interested in some kind of European unity, but he was not backed up by his own government and, more significantly, ran into conflict with the increasing commitment of the US administration to the idea of a universal peace-keeping institution. In 1943, as the ultimate defeat of Germany came in sight, it became apparent that at the end of the war the Allies would not help Europe to unity.

At the same time the evidence of the integration achieved in Europe under Axis coercion and the coordination of their economies and war machines by the Allied Powers suggested a different way to unification. Integration, both European and worldwide might best be achieved not by confronting the rights and privileges of the sovereign states head-on, but by pragmatic and selective integration. This 'functionalist' approach was also a legacy of the war years and was to be extremely influential in subsequent decades. (See Document 2.13.)

Documents

DOCUMENT 2.1

Meeting at the Reich Economic Ministry, 22 July 1940

Several meetings were held within agencies of the Third Reich to discuss the political and economic fate of the New Order in Europe. This one was held in response to Goering's order for preparations for the 'joint organisation of our economy after the conclusion of military conflict' on 22 June 1940. (See also Documents 2.2 and 2.3.)

The preparatory work to be undertaken under the Minister's overall direction was to include the following:

1. Coordination of the incorporated and occupied territories within the Great German economy.
2. Economic settlement with the enemy states.
3. Reorganisation of the continental economy directed by Germany, and its relations with the world economy. . .

1. Currency questions. . .
    It was fantasy to talk at this stage of a unified economy on a European scale, and in the same way it was harmful to use slogans like 'Currency and customs union' and to expect them to solve all difficulties. A currency or customs union could only be envisaged with a country having a similar standard of life to our own. This was not the case in South-Eastern Europe, for instance, and it was not at all in our interest to confer on that area a similar standard of life to ours. This could only impair the efficiency of the local economy. In discussing postwar organisation we must always be clear what immediate measures were necessary and what might be called for in the long run.

2. . . .
    Germany now had the political power to reorganise the European economy in accordance with her own needs. There was also the political intention to use that power, so that other countries would have to adapt themselves and their economies to our plans and needs. But all our needs could not be met in Europe. The needs of Europe

(apart from Russia and Italy) for raw materials were such that, even counting parts of Africa and Asia as colonies, there would still be a considerable import requirement. This requirement must be decreased by intensifying European production: only thus could we regain our economic freedom. But we wanted more than this, as it was the Führer's special aim to improve the living standards of German workers. In order to satisfy needs that went beyond the bare minimum, we would have to trade with overseas countries. . .

4. Foreign trade
German foreign trade was based on bilateral arrangements. This had worked well so far, but it had the disadvantage that one was tied to a particular partner and could not start importing at will from some other country that might for a time have more of the commodity in question. Hence the bilateral system must be enlarged into a multilateral one. . .

6. Questions of organisation
To enable the other countries in our sphere of interest to take similar measures, which must be agreed with us as a matter of principle, their respective economies must be reorganised. The Reich organisation for agriculture could set up corresponding bodies in other countries, so supervise the whole economic process including production, processing and distribution to consumers. Similar cooperation is envisaged in industry and trade.

7. Two groups of countries
The European countries within the German sphere of interest fall into two groups. The first comprises countries with a similar price, wage and salary, tax and income level to ours: e.g. Denmark, Holland and Switzerland. The South-Eastern countries form the second group. While the first are to be organised similarly to ourselves and treated more generously in the matter of payments, the others are too different from us for a payments and currency union to be considered.

DOCUMENT 2.2

Gustav Schlotterer and Wilhelm Zangen at the Grand Council of the Reich Group Industry, 3 October 1940

Gustav Schlotterer was Ministerial Director in the Economics Ministry. He had been present at the meeting on 22 July (see Document 2.1) which had established a European Working Group headed by Schlotterer. Wilhelm Zangen was Chairman of the Reich Group Industry.

It is quite obvious that we must avoid falling into either of two extremes: on the one hand, that we should swallow up everything and take everything away from the others and, on the other, that we say: we are not like that, we don't want anything. Of course we want something, of course we must want something, for, if in the final analysis, we are in control in Europe, then we must have influence, and the precondition for that is that we acquire those positions in Europe that we need in order to play our leading role. . .

Gentlemen! From the comments which I have made on this question you can see that we envisage the European *Grossraumwirtschaft* essentially as a product of the initiative of business itself. We as the state can of course reach economic agreements (with other States). We can set up a customs or currency union here or there or implement a transfer agreement. But that can only lead to a general form of regulation and will remain suspended in mid-air unless it is underpinned by business itself. It is obvious that we will support you and that we must give the lead. But I emphasise very strongly that this European *Grossraumwirtschaft* ought to be a matter for business itself and be something administered by business (*Selbstverwaltung der Wirtschaft*).

DOCUMENT 2.3

Record of Vollrath Frhr. von Maltzan, 7 May 1941

Von Maltzan was head of the desk for foreign trade policy in the Foreign Ministry. The document reflects the kind of collaboration indicated by Schlotterer above (Document 2.2).

Under the patronage of the Plenipotentiary for Motorisation, General von Schell, discussions have taken place between representatives of the German, Italian and French automobile industries in recent weeks, which have as their goal the cooperation of the European automobile industry in mutual technical complementarity and thereby preparation for thoroughgoing international cooperation in the European realm. The incentive for these discussions was the restarting of the French automobile factories, which lie predominantly in the occupied regions, with the extensive assistance of the German economic group, *Fahrzeugindustrie*. The previous discussions have resulted in the first common session, on 5 June in Berlin, of representatives of the three countries. The theme of the discussions is the prospective refinement of Italian and French types according to the German model, the approximation to German norms and the standardization of accessories.

DOCUMENT 2.4

Martin Bormann, record of meeting on Nazi aims in Eastern Europe, 16 July 1941

The Nazi attack on the Soviet Union in 1941 was greeted with enthusiasm by collaborators and fervent anti-communists. Although Nazi officials sought to exploit this, Hitler himself was predominantly hostile to any efforts to present it as a European crusade.

By way of introduction the Führer emphasised that he wished first of all to make some basic statements. Various measures were now necessary; this was confirmed, among other events, by the assertion in an impudent Vichy newspaper that the war against the Soviet Union was Europe's war and that therefore, it had to be conducted for Europe as a whole. Apparently the Vichy paper meant by these hints that it ought not to be the Germans alone who benefited from this war, but that all European states ought to benefit from it.

It was essential that we should not proclaim our aims before the whole world; this was in any case not necessary, but the chief thing was that we ourselves should know what we wanted. In no event should our own course be made more difficult by superfluous declarations. Such declarations were superfluous because we could do everything wherever we had the power, and what was beyond our power we would not be able to do anyway. . .

We shall therefore emphasise again that we were forced to occupy, administer, and secure a certain area; it was in the interests of the inhabitants that we provide order, food, traffic, etc., hence our measures. It should not be recognisable thereby that a final settlement is being initiated. We can nevertheless take all necessary measures – shooting, resettling, etc. – and we shall take them.

But we do not want to make any people into enemies prematurely and unnecessarily. Therefore we shall act as though we wanted to exercise a mandate only. It must be clear to us, however, that we shall never withdraw from these areas.

Accordingly we should:

(1) do nothing which might obstruct the final settlement, but prepare for it only in secret;
(2) emphasise that we are liberators.

DOCUMENT 2.5

Comments on the General Plan East by Dr Erhard Wetzel, Reich Ministry for the Eastern Territories, 27 April 1942

The General Plan East was formulated within the Sicherheitsdienst *of the SS. Its approach to the Polish nation has been described as preparation for a 'second holocaust'. The document is a commentary upon the original plan.*

Re: the solution of the Polish question.
(a) The Poles.
Their numbers must be estimated at between 20–24 million. They are the most anti-German, numerically the strongest and therefore the most dangerous of all the alien ethnic groups which the Plan envisages for resettlement. . .

The Plan envisages the deportation of 80–85 per cent of the Poles. 16–20.4 million Poles will be deported, while 3–4.8 million are to remain in the German area of settlement. . .

I can well believe that the large and spacious Siberian Steppes with their black earth districts could take far more than twenty million people in more or less concentrated settlements, provided that the resettlement is properly planned. . .

If one estimates a period of thirty years, as the Plan does, then there will be approximately 700,000–800,000 settlers (per annum) so that the transportation of these masses of people would require 700–800 trainloads per year and several hundred more for the transportation of equipment and possibly farm animals. That would mean that approximately 100–200 trains per year would be required solely for the Polish transports. However, in a reasonably peaceful period that ought to be technically feasible.

The overwhelming number of racially undesirable Poles will come into consideration for resettlement to the East. . . Members of the South European countries will be more suited for emigration to tropical or subtropical countries. But it is not impossible that emigrants even from these regions might go to Siberia when they hear of the possibilities of this great region, which is one of the richest in raw materials on the earth. . . Why shouldn't Wallonian engineers, Czech technicians, Hungarian industrialists and merchants and such like work in Siberia. Here one could rightfully talk of a European settlement and raw material reserve. Also, here the European idea in all its aspects would have meaning, while it would be dangerous for us in the settlement area of the German Volk, since it would mean, in its consequences, the acceptance of the idea of racial mixture even for us. . . The greatest misfortune which could threaten the German Volk would be the triumph of the pan-European racial idea, which could only have as a consequence a great European racial swamp.

DOCUMENT 2.6

Léon Blum, July 1941

Léon Blum was a leading French socialist and several times Prime Minister. His views played an important part in shaping the attitude of the socialist section of the Resistance in France and the French Socialist Party in the postwar period.

When Hitler and Goebbels talk of organising Europe, when the French 'collaborators' echo their words, we know what they mean and what they want. In present realities their European Order is nothing but the utilisation of all European resources, the extraction and extortion of all we have, for the benefit of the Axis, and their so-called organisation of Europe is no more than the future total enslavement of Europe by the Nazi regime. Thus the same words are used with diametrically opposed meanings. When we talk of a European Order, we are thinking not of war but of peace; when we talk of European organisation, we are thinking not of a common subjection to the domination of a tyrant, but of the federation of free and equal nations, of a League of Nations! Let us not be afraid to admit that the ideal of 1919 was a fine one. It is cheap and easy today to mock at the League, but if we have the courage to ignore the mockery, we must agree that we shall yet have to return to the same inspiration.

As it was conceived at the end of the last war by all the great democrats of both hemispheres, the League of Nations was a noble and magnificent creation. I believe this to be true despite its failure, which I do not seek in any way to minimise or excuse. I remain convinced, despite its failure, that it would still be sufficient and able to impose respect for international order among those political societies that gave it birth. Its failure, moreover, was something from which the world will have to learn its lesson. The League of Nations, created by the Treaties of Versailles, failed because great powers like Russia and the United States, whose support was essential, were outside it from the start. It failed because its founders, trying to disarm suspicions here and fears there, did not dare give it the instruments and the living strength that it needed to function properly. It failed because it was not itself a great sovereign power, distinct from national sovereign powers and greater than they; because it had neither the political authority nor the material force to enable it to carry out its decisions and impose its will on national states; because its powers were too restricted and too intermittent to allow it to cover the same fields of activity as national sovereign states.

It would be easy to quote arguments and facts in support of each of these reasons. If we take the antithesis of each of them, we shall have outlined the principles which must be applied this time in order to have a living and effective international organisation. All the powers, and particularly America and Russia, must be parties to the new covenant. The international body must have the institutions and powers it needs to do what it is created to do; in other words it must be boldly and openly set up as a super-state on a level above the national sovereignties, and that, in turn, means that the Member States must have accepted in advance as much limitation and subordination of their particular sovereignties as this superior sovereign power requires.

DOCUMENT 2.7

Helmuth Von Moltke, 'Initial situation, aims and tasks', 24 April 1941

Helmuth von Moltke was a member of the Resistance Kreisauer Kreis in the Third Reich which was involved in the July 1944 attempt to kill Hitler. Moltke was killed by the Nazis on 23 January 1945.

III. Expected political and military situation at the end of the war.

A) External Relations
1. Germany has been defeated . . . For our purposes, the possibility of a German victory is of little interest since it would defer the conditions on which the fulfillment of our objectives depends to a much later period. . .
B) Domestic Politics
1. The European demobilisation has led to the creation of a large economic organisation, directed by an inter-European economic bureaucracy and by economic self-governing bodies. Economic policy has been unequivocally subordinated to the rest of domestic policy.
2. Europe is divided into self-governing adminstrative units, formed in accordance with historical traditions. They are somewhat similar in size and have special relations with each other within groups. In this way the absolute domination of the former Great Powers, Germany and France, has been broken without creating resentment.
3. The administration of cultural affairs is decentralised, but the possibility for regular exchanges between the regions remains. The confessional communities are disestablished, but they still have strong claims to be supplied with resources.
4. The constitutions of the individual states are entirely different. They all agree, however, in fostering the growth of all small communities. These latter enjoy certain rights in public law and they have an acknowledged claim to a share of public resources.

5. The highest legislative body in the European state is responsible to the individual citizens and not to the self-governing bodies. As a matter of principle, eligibility for both active and passive electoral rights will not be attained on the basis of age, but rather on the basis of specific constructive activities for the community. Whether universal suffrage ought to follow from this or whether the highest legislative body ought to be formed otherwise are questions of technique rather than principle.
6. Life and limb are to be protected by a legal process that allows no opportunity for the employment of police methods. Economic activity is to be assured by conferring on certain occupations a status similar to that enjoyed by property. A private sector in housing and consumer goods is to be safeguarded.
7. Non-functional rights over the means of production are to be further restricted, without removing the pleasure that can be derived from responsibility and initiative.
8. The highest executive power is exercised by a cabinet consisting of five persons: the Prime Minister, Foreign Minister, Defense Minister, Minister of the Interior and Minister of Economics. In addition there will be a number of junior ministerial posts which will be represented at Cabinet level by one of the five senior ministers.

DOCUMENT 2.8

Altiero Spinelli and Ernesto Rossi, The Ventotene Manifesto, August 1941

This manifesto is named after an island on which opponents of the Italian Fascist regime were imprisoned. Spinelli was to play a long and important role in the postwar development of European integration, becoming, inter alia, a Commissioner of the European Community and a Member of the European Parliament.

Germany's defeat would not automatically lead to the reorientation of Europe in accordance with our ideal of civilisation.

In the brief, intense period of general crisis (when the States will lie broken, when the masses will be anxiously waiting for a new message, like molten matter, burning, and easily shaped into new moulds capable of accommodating the guidance of serious internationalist-minded men), the most privileged classes in the old national systems will attempt, by underhand or violent methods, to dampen the wave of internationalist feelings and passions and will ostentatiously begin to reconstruct the old State institutions. Most probably, the British leaders, perhaps in agreement with the Americans, will try to restore the balance-of-power politics, in the apparent immediate interests of their empires. . .

The question which must be resolved first, failing which progress is no more than mere appearance, is the definitive abolition of the division of Europe into national, sovereign States. The collapse of the majority of the States on the Continent under the German steamroller has given the people of Europe a common destiny: either they will all submit to Hitler's dominion or, after his fall they will all enter a revolutionary crisis and thus will not find themselves separated by, and entrenched in, solid State structures. Feelings today are already far more disposed than they were in the past to accept a federal reorganisation of Europe. The harsh experience of recent decades has opened the eyes even of those who refused to see, and has matured many circumstances favourable to our ideal.

DOCUMENT 2.9

Memorandum (by Hugh R. Wilson) arising from conversations in Mr. Welles' office, 19 and 26 April, 1 May 1940

Sumner Welles, Under-Secretary of State of the United States and Hugh Wilson, a former Ambassador to Germany, were involved in planning for the postwar world from early 1940 onwards. Welles was later dismissed by Roosevelt after persistent conflicts with Cordell Hull. (See also Document 2.11.)

It seems clear that there must be in Europe such derogation to the sovereignty of states as will make for quick and decisive action by the body. This involves the abolition of the rule of unanimity. But the practical power will reside, as always, in the hands of the Great Powers unless, which is unlikely, we can conceive of a Federated Union along the pattern of the United States. Hence in some form, perhaps in that of an Executive Committee, the Great States must be able to consult at once and decisively. There are obvious advantages to be gained by the establishment in Europe of various blocs or free trade groups of states. There are political advantages as well which might flow from such formations, and if we consider each bloc as a political unit for the purposes of European administration it is possible to see a type of Executive Committee or Political Body which might function provided sovereignty could be curtailed to a point of agreement by each bloc to abide by a majority of two-thirds decision of the members of the body.

The blocs might be distributed as follows:

(1) Great Britain
(2) France

(These two nations may or may not serve as separate blocs, in accordance with their postwar political development)

(3) Italy
(4) Germany
(5) Iberian Peninsula
(6) The Oslo group
(7) The Eastern Baltic States and Poland
(8) The Danubian States (Bohemia-Moravia, Slovakia, Hungary, Yugoslavia)
(9) The Balkan States (Rumania, Bulgaria, Greece)

DOCUMENT 2.10

Churchill to Roosevelt, 'Morning thoughts', note on postwar security, 2 February 1943

On several occasions in 1943 Churchill suggested some form of postwar European unity, to the irritation of the British Foreign Office. The suggestion in the document was sent to Roosevelt as a reflection of Churchill's personal views, not those of the British Cabinet.

It is the intention of the chiefs of the United Nations to create a world organisation for the preservation of peace based upon the conceptions of freedom and justice and the revival of prosperity. As part of this organisation an instrument of European government will be established which will embody the spirit but not be subject to the weakness of the former League of Nations. The units forming this body will not be the great nations of Europe and Asia Minor only. Need for a Scandinavian bloc, Danubian bloc, and a Balkan bloc appears to be obvious. A similar instrument will be formed in the Far East with different membership and the whole will be held together by the fact that victorious powers as yet continue fully armed, especially in the air, while imposing complete disarmament upon the guilty.

DOCUMENT 2.11

The Memoirs of Cordell Hull (1948)

The Secretary of State of the United States, Cordell Hull, was an ardent supporter of worldwide international organisation and saw European integration as a threat to this broader ambition.

President Roosevelt agreed in general with the Prime Minister's regional ideas. During the spring of 1943 I found there was a basic cleavage between him and me on the very nature of the postwar organisation. . .

At that time he did not want an over-all world organisation. He did favour the creation of regional organisations, but it was the four big powers that would handle all security questions. . .

The more advanced regional ideas of President Roosevelt and Prime Minister Churchill, however, might lead to questions of balance of power, and regional organisations of the type they envisaged might deal arbitrarily with one another and in the internal affairs of their members, whether by military force or economic pressure or their equivalent. This would open the door to abuses and the exercise of undue privileges by greedy, grasping nations possessing great military and economic strength.

In various meetings at the White House, my associates and I presented these arguments to the President with all the force we could. As summer arrived he began to turn toward our point of view.

DOCUMENT 2.12

Yalta Conference, Trilateral Documents, 11 February 1945

The Yalta Conference was the last meeting of the Allied leaders, Churchill, Roosevelt and Stalin before the end of the war in Europe.

Declaration on liberated Europe

We have drawn up and subscribed to a Declaration on liberated Europe. This Declaration provides for concerting the policies of the three Powers and for joint action by them in meeting the political and economic problems of liberated Europe in accordance with democratic principles. The text of the Declaration is as follows:

The Premier of the Union of Soviet Socialist Republics, the Prime Minister of the United Kingdom, and the President of the United States of America have consulted with each other in the common interests of the peoples of their countries and those of liberated Europe. They jointly declare their mutual agreement to concert during the period of temporary instability in liberated Europe the policies of their three governments in assisting the peoples liberated from the domination of Nazi Germany and the peoples of the former Axis satellite states of Europe to solve by democratic means their pressing political and economic problems.

The establishment of order in Europe and the rebuilding of national economic life must be achieved by processes which will enable the liberated peoples to destroy the last vestiges of Nazism and Fascism and to create democratic institutions of their own choice. This is a principle of the Atlantic Charter – the right of peoples to choose the form of government under which they will live – the restoration of sovereign rights and self-government to those peoples who have been forcibly deprived of them by the aggressor nations.

DOCUMENT 2.13

David Mitrany, 'A Working Peace System', June 1943

David Mitrany was the founding father of the functionalist approach to international organisation. This approach was to be of great influence in the postwar world, especially in connection with the European Coal and Steel Community (see Documents 4.3 and 4.4).

The problem of our generation, put very broadly, is how to weld together the common interests of all without interfering unduly with the particular interests of each.

It is a parallel problem to that which faces us in a national society, and which in both spheres challenges us to find an alternative to the totalitarian pattern. A measure of centralised planning and control, for both production and distribution, is no longer to be avoided, no matter what the form of the state or the doctrine of its constitution. Through all that variety of political forms there is a growing approximation in the working of governments, with differences merely of degree and of detail. Liberal democracy needs a redefinition of the public and private spheres of action. But as the line of separation is always shifting, under the pressure of fresh social needs and demands, it must be left free to move with those needs and demands and cannot be fixed through any constitutional restatement. The only, possible principle of democratic confirmation is that public action should be undertaken only where and when and in so far as the need for common action becomes evident and is accepted, for the sake of the common good. In that way controlled democracy could yet be made the golden means whereby social needs might be satisfied as largely and justly as possible, while still leaving as wide a residue as possible for the free choice of the individual.

That is fully as true for the international sphere. It is indeed the only way to combine as well as may be international organisation with national freedom. We have already suggested that not all interests are common to all, and that the common interests do not concern all countries in the same degree. A territorial union would bind together some interests which are not of common concern to the group, while it would inevitably cut asunder some interests of common concern to the group and those outside it. The only way to avoid that twice-arbitrary surgery is to proceed by means of natural selection, binding together interests which are common, where they are common, and to the extent to which they are common. The functional selection and organisation of international relations would extend, and in a way resume, an international development which has been gathering strength since the latter part of the nineteenth century. The work of organising international public services and activities was taken a step further by the League in its health and drug control work, in its work for refugees, in its experiments with the transfer of minorities and the important innovations of the League loan system, and still more through the whole activity of the ILO (International Labour Organisation).

What would be the broad lines of such a functional organisation of international activities? The essential principle is that activities would be selected specifically and organised separately, each according to its nature, to the conditions under which it has to operate, and to the needs of the moment. It would allow, therefore, for freedom of practical variation in the organisation of the several functions, as well as in the working of a particular function as needs and conditions alter. Let us take as an example the group of functions which fall under communications, on which the success of postwar reconstruction will depend greatly. What is the proper basis for the international organisation of the railway system? Clearly, it must be European, or rather, continental, North American and so on, as that gives the logical administrative limit of coordination. A division of the continent into separate democratic and totalitarian unions would not achieve the practical end, as political division would obstruct that necessary coordination; while British and American participation would make the organisation more cumbrous without any added profit to the function.

. . . Peace will not be secured if we organise the world by what divides it. But in the measure in which such peace-building activities develop and succeed one might hope that the mere prevention of conflict, crucial as that may be, would in time fall to a subordinate place in the scheme of international things, while we would turn to what are the real tasks of our common society – the conquest of poverty and disease and of ignorance. The stays of political federation were needed when life was more local and active ties still loose. But now our social interdependence is all-pervasive and all-embracing, and if it be so organised the political side will also grow as part of it. The elements of a functional system could begin to work without a general political authority, but a political authority without active social functions would remain an empty temple.

Suggested reading

There is a wealth of documentary material together with useful introductions in W. Lipgens (ed.), *Documents on the History of European Integration* (Berlin, 1985ff). The two volumes covering the war period deal with Axis policy, the views of the Resistance, both West and East, and exiles and others in the Allied countries. On Nazi visions see also Robert Edwin Herzstein, *When Nazi Dreams Come True* (London, 1982). The economic reality of the New Order is best approached through A.S. Milward, *The New Order and the French Economy* (Oxford, 1970) and *The Fascist Economy in Norway* (Oxford, 1972), and J. Gillingham, *Ideology and Politics in the Third Reich* (London, 1985). Diverse perspectives on the attempt to create a New Order in Europe and the challenges it brought forth are in M.L. Smith and P.M.R. Stirk (eds), *Making the New Europe. European Unity and the Second World War* (London, 1990). On Allied policy see W. Lipgens, *A History of European Integration*, Vol. 1 (Oxford, 1982) whose Introduction contains a critical survey of Allied policy. There are limited, but incisive, comments in V. Rothwell, *Britain and the Cold War 1941–1947* (London, 1982) and G. Ross (ed.), *The Foreign Office and the Kremlin* (Cambridge, 1984). Also useful is J. Baylis, 'British Wartime Thinking About a Postwar European Security Group', *Review of International Studies*, **9** (1983), pp. 2265–81.

3 Europe between the Superpowers, 1945–50

Introduction

In the immediate aftermath of World War II the prospects for European integration were not encouraging. The Soviet Union rejected any ideas of federation in either Western or Eastern Europe. Any proposals for the former it regarded as proposals for a bloc hostile to its own interests. The United States on the other hand were initially keen to preserve as much of the Allied wartime cooperation as possible and were committed to the development of the United Nations as a global peace-keeping organisation.

Within two years expectations were transformed. The relations between the United States and the Union of Soviet Socialist Republics (USSR) had never been easy. There was a long tradition of mutual distrust which now became sharp confrontation in every way except direct military conflict between the Superpowers. According to George Kennan's 'Long Telegram' of February 1948, the wartime ally was inherently incapable of perpetuating the cooperation of the years 1941–5. At the time of this telegram the US President, Harry Truman, had not yet relinquished all hope of cooperation. With the promulgation of the 'Truman Doctrine' in March 1947, though, (a year after Churchill's 'Iron Curtain' speech) Truman promised aid to free countries threatened by 'outside pressures' and depicted the current international situation as a conflict between two ways of life, the democratic and totalitarian. The Cold War division which was to divide Europe, Germany and the world was staked out and Germany was to become the front line.

By then, however, the various groups of European federalists had begun to coordinate their activities. In December 1946 the European Union of Federalists (UEF) had been formed. The majority of the UEF were not only opposed to the division of Europe but also still hoped that it might be averted. Of more immediate importance was the economic plight of the countries of Western Europe with the 'dollar-gap' in 1947. Would they be able to sustain recovery from the devastation and losses of the war? In

Washington concern about their recovery escalated into alarm and fear that the populations of Western Europe would be driven by desperation to turn to Communism. American policy-makers were now, in the Spring of 1947, debating how much pressure they could or should apply to push the Western European states towards cooperation, and ultimately towards federation.

The idea that Europe might be reorganised along the lines of the United States was an old one (see Document 1.1). What was new was that this idea was now becoming commonplace in Washington. It was shortly to be enshrined in US legislation (see Document 3.5). The susceptibility of European states to American pressure was obvious. They were in chronic need of financial assistance if the economic recovery was to be maintained. The offer of coordinated aid was made by Secretary of State Marshall on 5 June 1947. After some hesitation the response of the Soviet Union became one of unrelenting hostility (see Document 3.4). European Communist Parties followed suit.

Among the Western nations differences and tensions arose as to the extent and pace of integration. The European states formed a Committee and then an Organisation for European Economic Cooperation (OEEC), but they resisted attempts to develop this beyond a temporary intergovernmental organisation. The role of the British Government was particularly important here. As the only major European power to escape defeat and occupation and as a member of the 'Big Three', Britain enjoyed a position of influence beyond that warranted by her underlying economic strength. The British approach to European integration was ambiguous: though often supportive, a line was quickly drawn at any measure or proposal which impinged upon British sovereignty or which might be prejudicial to the Commonwealth. Both the major political parties, Labour and Conservative, still saw the United Kingdom as primarily a global, rather than a regional power. The Foreign Minister Ernest Bevin's suspicion of 'rigid theses and directives' in his 'Western Union' speech of 1948 reflected the prevailing British view (see Document 3.6). Yet Britain needed the cooperation of Western European states and of the United States, economically and militarily. Despite his disparagement of 'rigid theses and directives', Bevin's speech formed a logical link in the chain which led from the defensive alliance with France, the Dunkirk Treaty of 1947, through to the North Atlantic Treaty of 1949. (See Document 5.1.)

Uncertainty about Britain's role was less of a problem compared with the fear about Germany's future role. Soviet apprehensions about Germany and especially the revival of her heavy industry were clear enough in the USSR's response to the Marshall Plan. France was scarcely less distrustful. This distrust was accepted as very understandable by many Germans. From the German perspective the need was to reassure Germany's neighbours that an independent, revived, and possibly united

Germany need not again be a threat to their interests and territories.

On the non-Communist Left, in Germany and elsewhere, a solution was sought in the idea that a united Europe, preferably a united Pan-Europe, might constitute a 'Third Force' between the Superpowers. Independent of each Superpower, Europe might also be able to mediate between the United States and the USSR. These hopes were quite unrealistic, given the Cold War division. At the same time, European economic integration without Germany, or at least without the most economically significant part of Germany, was not viable. The failure of many of the schemes for integration, especially for customs unions, which emerged in the 1940s (see Document 3.10) can be traced back directly to the lack of a solution for the 'German problem'.

It did prove possible to make progress on other fronts without Germany. Military cooperation in Western Europe was promoted by the conclusion of the Brussels Treaty of 1948 and was given the all-important backing of the United States through the North Atlantic Treaty of 1949. It was in the interest of the consolidation of the Western Alliance that Britain was induced to agree to negotiations which led to the creation of the Council of Europe in 1949. The pressure for negotiations came initially from the International Committee of the Movements for European Unity which organised a Congress of Europe at the Hague in May 1948. Although the Council of Europe was to fall far short of the ambitions embodied in the Resolutions of the Hague Congress it did provide a basis for the promotion of human rights in subsequent decades and, more immediately, it provided a platform from which the Federalists could harry reluctant governments (see Document 3.13).

Documents

DOCUMENT 3.1

Winston Churchill's speech at Zürich, 19 September 1946

Although several statesmen, including the French Socialist, Leon Blum, and the Italian Christian Democrat and Foreign Minister, Alcide de Gasperi, had spoken in favour of European union, Churchill's endorsement, coming from one of the wartime 'Big Three', had special significance. His speech, whose limits were well recognised by convinced Federalists, nonetheless helped revive the cause of European union in the autumn of 1946.

We must build a kind of United States of Europe. In this way only will hundreds of millions of toilers be able to regain the simple joys and hopes which make life worth living. The process is simple. All that is needed is the resolve of hundreds of millions of men and women to do right instead of wrong and gain as their reward blessing instead of cursing. . .

There is no reason why a regional organisation of Europe should in any way conflict with the world organisation of the United Nations. On the contrary, I believe that the larger synthesis will only survive if it is built upon coherent natural groupings. There is already a natural grouping in the Western Hemisphere. We British have our own Commonwealth of Nations. These do not weaken, on the contrary they strengthen the world organisation. They are in fact its main support. And why should there not be a European group which could give a sense of enlarged patriotism and common citizenship to the distracted peoples of this turbulent and mighty continent; and why should it not take its rightful place in shaping the destinies of men?. . .

I am now going to say something that will astonish you. The first step in the re-creation of the European family must be a partnership between France and Germany. In this way only can France recover the usual leadership of Europe. There can be no revival of Europe without a spiritually great France and a spiritually great Germany. The structure of the United States of Europe, if well and truly built, will be such as to make the material strength of a single state less important. . .

I must now sum up the propositions which are before you. Our constant aim must be to build and fortify the strength of the United Nations. Under and within that world concept we must re-create the European family in a regional structure called, it may be, the United States of Europe. The first step is to form a Council of Europe . . . In all this urgent work, France and Germany must take the lead together. Great Britain, the British Commonwealth of Nations, mighty America, and I trust Soviet Russia . . . must be the friends and sponsors of the new Europe and must champion its right to live and shine.

DOCUMENT 3.2

European Union of Federalists: resolutions of the Montreux Conference, August 1947

The European Union of Federalists was established in Paris in December 1946. The Montreux Conference was its first full conference.

Having in mind the anxieties and hopes of our time, this Conference of the European Union of Federalists affirms that no national government is any longer capable of assuring to its people liberty, prosperity and peace. . .

For the first time in history, all the European federalist movements have come together in a single association to make their voice heard – the voice of Europe itself. . .

European federalism, which alone can provide our peoples with the prospect of salvation, is based on the following foundations:

(1) The federal idea constitutes a dynamic principle which transforms all human activities. It brings with it not only a new political framework, but also new social, economic and cultural structures. Federalism is a synthesis, and it is made up of two elements indissolubly linked: of organic solidarity and of liberty, or, put differently, the expansion of the human personality in every sphere of daily life. . .

(2) Federalism can be born only from renunciation of all idea of a dictatorial 'New Order' imposed by one of its constituent elements, and of any ideological system . . . Each of the nations, each of the elements of which Europe is composed, has its own proper function, its own irreplaceable quality. It follows that, regarded from that angle, a minority has the same human value as a majority. That is why federalism is based on respect for qualities. For example, it is concerned not only with the method of election to a Council of States, but also and above all, with the value of customs, traditions, and the way in which people order their lives . . . even if a European Federation can at the beginning unite only some of the States of Europe, the European Union of Federalists will never accept as a *fait accompli* the division of Europe into two hostile blocs.

To start our efforts at unification in the West of Europe means for the West escaping the risk of becoming the victim of power politics, restoring to Europe, at any rate partially, her pride in her legitimate independence, and holding out a hand to the peoples of the East to help them to rejoin the other peoples in a free and peaceful community.

Federalists must declare firmly and without compromise that it is absolute national sovereignty that must be abated, that a part of that sovereignty must be entrusted to a federal authority assisted by all the functional bodies necessary to the accomplishment, on the federal plane, of its economic and cultural tasks, whether in whole or in part. In particular this authority must possess:

(a) a government responsible to the peoples and groups and not to the federated states;

(b) a Supreme Court capable of resolving possible disputes between state members of the Federation;

(c) an armed police force under its own control. . .

DOCUMENT 3.3

Summary of the discussion on problems of relief, rehabilitation and reconstruction of Europe, US Department of State, 29 May 1947

These discussions form part of the background to the Marshall Plan. Will Clayton was Under Secretary of State for Economic Affairs.

4. Some system for closer European economic cooperation must be devised to break down existing economic barriers.

The last point which parallels the recommendation in the Policy Planning Staff paper was elaborated in the ensuing discussion. Three major problems presented themselves:

1. The inclusion or exclusion of Soviet-dominated Eastern Europe.
2. US *vs.* European responsibility and initiative.
3. The timing and machinery to be utilized in developing the plan.

As to point 1, Mr. Clayton expressed the strong view that, while Western Europe is essential to Eastern Europe, the reverse is not true. Coal and grains from Eastern Europe are important to Western Europe, but these products will be exported westward in any event because the necessity of obtaining vital foreign exchange for necessary products from the West creates a suction which the USSR is incapable of counteracting, and there can only be absolute and final domination of Eastern Europe by force of arms. It was concluded, therefore, that a European economic federation is feasible even without the participation of Eastern European countries. . .

Regarding the problem of European *vs.* US initiative in the plan . . . Messrs. Cohen and Thorp emphasised the importance of substantial US responsibility and initiative because (a) experience has demonstrated the lack of ability of European nations to agree on such matters, (b) if agreement is reached, the scheme may not be a sound one and (c) the problem is so complex that no one can plot a definite, final plan now. It should, therefore, be approached functionally rather than by country, concentrating on the essentials, and this is an approach which the US is in a better position than Europe to take.

Balancing the dangers of appearing to force 'the American way' on Europe and the danger of failure if the major responsibility is left to Europe, Mr. Bohlen suggested that an alternative is to place strong pressure on the European nations to plan by underscoring their situation and making clear that the only politically feasible basis on which the US would be willing to make the aid available is substantial evidence of a

developing overall plan for economic cooperation by the Europeans themselves, perhaps an economic federation to be worked out over 3 or 4 years.

DOCUMENT 3.4

**Andrei Vyshinsky, A criticism of the Truman Doctrine and the
Marshall Plan, 18 September 1947**

*The Soviet Union, represented by Molotov had initially joined in the discussions in
Paris about the Marshall Plan. On 2 July 1947, after receiving instructions from
Moscow, Molotov rejected Anglo–French proposals for participation in the plan.
Vyshinsky was chief Soviet delegate to the United Nations.*

The so-called Truman Doctrine and the Marshall Plan are particularly
glaring examples of the way in which the principles of the United Nations
are violated, of the way in which the Organisation is ignored. . .

As is now clear, the Marshall Plan constitutes in essence merely a
variant of the Truman Doctrine adapted to the conditions of postwar
Europe. In bringing forward this plan, the United States Government
apparently counted on the cooperation of the Governments of the United
Kingdom and France to confront the European countries in need of relief
with the necessity of renouncing their inalienable right to dispose of their
economic resources and to plan their national economy in their own way.
The United States also counted on making all these countries directly
dependent on the interests of American monopolies, which are striving to
avert the approaching depression by an accelerated export of commodities
and capital to Europe. . .

It is becoming more and more evident to everyone that the implementation of the Marshall Plan will mean placing European countries under the
economic and political control of the United States and direct interference
by the latter in the internal affairs of those countries. Moreover, this plan
is an attempt to split Europe into two camps and, with the help of the
United Kingdom and France, to complete the formation of a bloc of
several European countries hostile to the interests of the democratic countries of Eastern Europe and most particularly to the interests of the Soviet
Union. An important feature of this Plan is the attempt to confront the
countries of Eastern Europe with a bloc of Western European States
including Western Germany. The intention is to make use of Western
Germany and German heavy industry (the Ruhr) as one of the most
important economic bases for American expansion in Europe, in disregard
of the national interests of the countries which suffered from German
aggression. . .

DOCUMENT 3.5

US Economic Cooperation Act, 1948

The European Cooperation Act implemented the Marshall Plan. The document reflects an emerging American consensus on Europe's road to recovery and the relevance of the United States as a model for Europe.

The restoration or maintenance in European countries of principles of individual liberty, free institutions, and genuine independence rests largely upon the establishment of sound economic conditions, stable international economic relationships, and the achievement by the countries of Europe of a healthy economy independent of extraordinary outside assistance. The accomplishment of these objectives calls for a plan of European recovery . . . based upon a strong production effort, the expansion of foreign trade, the creation and maintenance of financial stability, and the development of economic co-operation . . . Mindful of the advantages which the United States has enjoyed through the existence of a large domestic market with no internal trade barriers, and believing that similar advantages can accrue to the countries of Europe, it is declared to be the policy of the United States to encourage these countries through a joint organisation to exert substantial common efforts . . . which will speedily achieve that economic cooperation in Europe which is essential for lasting peace and prosperity.

DOCUMENT 3.6

Ernest Bevin, speech on Western Union, 22 January 1948

This speech was an important stage in Bevin's campaign for a Western defensive alliance. Negotiations began on 4 March and on 17 March Britain, France, the Netherlands, Belgium and Luxembourg signed a mutual defence treaty, the Brussels Treaty.

The conception of the unity of Europe and the preservation of Europe as the heart of Western civilisation is accepted by most people. . .

We did not press the Western Union – and I know that some of our neighbours were not desirous of pressing it – in the hope that when we got the German and Austrian peace settlements, agreement between the Four Powers would close the breach between East and West, and thus avoid the necessity of crystallising Europe into separate blocs. We have always wanted the widest conception of Europe, including, of course, Russia. It is not a new idea. The idea of a close relationship between the countries of Western Europe first arose during the war, and in the days of the Coalition it was discussed. Already in 1944 there was talk between my predecessor and the Russian Government about a Western association . . . the free nations of Western Europe must now draw closely together. . .

First in this context we think of the people of France. Like all old friends, we have our differences from time to time, but I doubt whether ever before in our history there has been so much underlying goodwill and respect between the two peoples as now. We have a firm basis of co-operation in the Treaty of Dunkirk, we are partners in the European Recovery Programme. . .

The time has come to find ways and means of developing our relations with the Benelux countries. I mean to begin talks with those countries in close accord with our French Allies. . .

Perhaps I may return to the subject of the organisation in respect of a Western Union. That is its right description. I would emphasise that I am not concerned only with Europe as a geographical conception. Europe has extended its influence throughout the world, and we have to look further afield . . . The organisation of Western Europe must be economically supported. That involves the closest possible collaboration with the Commonwealth and with overseas territories, not only British, but French, Dutch, Belgian and Portuguese. . .

To conclude, His Majesty's Government have striven for the closer consolidation and economic development, and eventually for the spiritual unity, of Europe as a whole; but, as I have said, in Eastern Europe we are presented with a *fait accompli*. No one there is free to speak or think or to enter into trade or other arrangements of his own free will . . . Neither we, the United States nor France is going to approach Western Europe on that basis. It is not in keeping with the spirit of Western civilisation, and if we are to have an organism in the West it must be a spiritual union. While no doubt there must be treaties or, at least, understandings, the union must primarily be a fusion derived from the basic freedoms and ethical principles for which we all stand. That is the goal we are trying to reach. It cannot be written down in a rigid thesis or in a directive. It is more a brotherhood and less of a rigid system.

DOCUMENT 3.7

The US Secretary of State to the US political adviser for Germany, 6 March 1948

The European Recovery Programme was the official designation of the Marshall Plan.

Purpose and scope of ERP (European Recovery Programme) and CEEC (Committee for European Economic Cooperation) are far beyond trade relations. Economic cooperation sought under ERP, and of which CEEC is a vehicle, has as ultimate objective closer integration of Western Europe. In this way it is a correlative of and parallel to the political and security arrangements sought under Bevin's proposals for Western Union. Full cooperation of the British is necessary if larger objectives are to be achieved.

DOCUMENT 3.8

The US Ambassador in France, Jefferson Caffery, to the Secretary of State, 23 March 1948.

The role of the CEEC and its successor, the Organisation for European Economic Cooperation (OEEC), continued to be a source of tension between the United States and the United Kingdom.

In summary, the first week of the CEEC meeting has been characterised by a rapid organisation of the working party and by adoption of a tight time schedule . . . While this activity is encouraging, there is little evidence that a majority of the delegates have instructions from their home governments which will permit them to come up with the type of continuing organisation we have in mind. The closest approach to the US concept has been the original French proposals which are also receiving support from the Italian delegation. . .

British approach . . . appears to us to lead to creation of weak organisation with primary responsibility for programming the other principal decisions centred in Washington. British have never stated this to be their objective but, on the contrary, state that the only way to get strong organisation in Europe is to have national representatives of high rank assigned full time at seat of organisation. They argue that their proposal for placing principal emphasis on role of national representatives ensures governmental support. British also argue that given uncertainties as to form of act and wishes of administrator, there must be great flexibility, and that consequent statement of functions of organisation should be limited to broad generalities. Although we recognise value of flexibility, we are concerned at vagueness of generalities and are not persuaded that British argument in favour of vagueness is genuine desire to create organisation which can adjust itself to meet responsibilities placed upon it, but may be desire to create organisation too weak to assume responsibility.

DOCUMENT 3.9

Carlo Schmid, 'Franco–German Relations and the Third Partner', 1947

The Social Democrat Carlo Schmid played a leading role in drafting the Basic Law of the Federal Republic of Germany although he had initially opposed the creation of a separate Western State.

On the basis of this experience confirmed by history, Franco–German rela-tions will necessarily appear as part of the European problem or rather perhaps a problem of the political world situated between the two fields of force based on the United States and the Soviet Union. But, given the interdependence of all questions that depend on the gravitational force of political bodies of supercontinental size, we are obliged to see the problem of the intermediate area as itself part of the problem of the political struc-ture of our present-day world.

A third power is necessary to prevent the world from being torn apart, but Europe can only become that power if it puts its house in order: in other words, its component states must abandon the principle of sovereignty, on which politics have essentially been based in modern times, in favour of a supranational community. All forms of activity involved in the external relations of a state must be transferred to that community, including foreign relations, defence, major communications, the supply of energy, economic planning and the management of key industries. Only thus will the individuality of individual states cease to be a disturbing and disruptive factor. . . In all other spheres, countries may remain as autonomous as they will: the vitality of the union can only be increased by the diversity of its members. . .

The following stages might be envisaged, bearing in mind that a scheme of this kind is not a blueprint but merely serves to illustrate the complexity of relationships and the processes that may be required.

(1)   . . . As the pressure on the 'middle zone' of Europe becomes stronger, so the centripetal forces within the British family of nations will inten-sify and extend by way of Britain herself, to Europe . . . We should not be deceived by certain superficial phenomena which in Germany, to our misfortune, we have so often interpreted as proofs to the contrary: the behaviour of the Dominions in the United Nations tells its own story.

These tendencies should be coordinated, given institutional effect and constitutional order, perhaps by transforming the British Commonwealth into a confederation or union with the same kind of powers as those proposed above for the United States of Europe.

(2) Concurrently one might envisage a federal union of the Scandinavian countries, and an extension of the Benelux system to France and Italy. In a short time this latter would necessarily evolve into a system of unified economic policy, which – given the dynamics inherent in all major economic conceptions, especially nowadays – would soon have political and no doubt constitutional consequences. . .

(3) When the two systems have achieved inner equilibrium and have proved to be valuable instruments for increasing the potential of all their members it will be possible for them, with the necessary modifications, to form a union, the attractive power of which will certainly be sufficient to attract other countries of the 'middle zone'. . .

(4) What should happen to Germany in the meantime? . . . It seems to me preferable for Germany to remain in its present interim state from the foreign policy point of view until some progress has been made towards creating the unions described above. The latter will then have provided Europe, apart from Germany, with a secure economic and political superiority such as to dispel much of the fear that at present acts as a bad counsellor, suggesting to foreign statesmen the discriminatory plans of which we hear from time to time. It will then be easy for the rulers of European states to convince their peoples that a Germany enjoying equal rights need not necessarily be presumed to be an aggressor, and that a United States of Europe can only fulfil its purpose if Germany is granted such equality.

DOCUMENT 3.10

Committee of European Economic Cooperation, General Report, July–September, 1947

The Report was produced at the insistence of the United States as a precondition for the receipt of Marshall Aid. It was intended by the Americans to provide the basis for the coordinated use of aid across Europe. The Study Group and the Franco–Italian negotiations on a customs union did not lead to concrete results.

90. The Committee has considered the question of Customs Unions as a means of achieving the speedier reduction and eventual elimination of tariffs between a group of countries. The advantages which the United States has enjoyed through the existence of a large domestic market with no internal trade barriers are manifest. . .

92. No Customs Union can be brought into full and effective operation by a stroke of the pen. A Customs Union, particularly between

several large and highly industrialised countries, involves complex technical negotiations and adjustments which can only be achieved by progressive stages over a period of years. Special problems also arise for countries with a high proportion of their trade outside any proposed Customs Union, or as between countries at widely differing states of economic development.

93. Nevertheless, the idea of a Customs Union including as many European countries as possible is one which contains important possibilities for the economic future of Europe, and it is in the general interest that the problems involved should receive careful and detailed study by governments. Several steps have been taken in this connection.

94. The Governments of Belgium, Luxembourg and the Netherlands signed a Customs Convention in London on 5th September, 1944 . . . The convention has been approved by the Parliaments of the three countries and will enter into force by 1st January, 1948. The three countries propose thereafter to conclude an economic union. . .

95. The four Scandinavian countries, namely Denmark, Iceland, Norway and Sweden, have announced after a meeting of their Foreign Ministers which took place in Copenhagen on 27th and 28th August, 1947, that they were taking steps to examine immediately the possibility of an extension of the economic cooperation between their countries, including the question of the elimination, wholly or partly, of the customs frontier between the four countries.

96. . . .The Governments of Austria, Belgium, Denmark, France, Greece, Ireland, Iceland, Italy, Luxembourg, the Netherlands, Portugal and the United Kingdom and Turkey have . . . decided to create a Study Group for the purpose of examining the problems involved and the steps to be taken, in the formation of Customs Union. . .

98. In this connection the French Government has made the following declaration:

> 'The French Government being of the opinion that the barriers which now exist in the way of a freer exchange of goods and capital, and of a freer movement of persons between the various European countries, constitute one of the most important obstacles to the economic recovery of these countries;
>
> that in the present state of the world only economic units sufficiently large to have at their disposal an important home market are able to lower the price of industrial and agricultural production sufficiently to ensure, thanks to better technique, an improved standard of living for their people and to allow the countries concerned to withstand world-wide competition;
>
> that the present division of Europe into small economic units does

not correspond to the needs of modern competition and that it will be possible with the help of a Customs Union to construct larger units on the strictly economic plane;

that these units must not be in any way "autarchic" in character but on the contrary should increase their trade to the utmost with all other countries or economic groups of countries to the maximum degree;

that the formation of such Customs Unions is foreseen in the Draft Charter for an International Trade Organisation;

declares that it is ready to enter into negotiations with all European Governments sharing these views who wish to enter a Customs Union with France and whose national economies are capable of being combined with the French economy in such a way as to make a viable unit;. . .'

99.   The Italian Government . . . wishes to associate itself with the above declaration by the French Government. . .

DOCUMENT 3.11

Foreign Economic Assistance Programme, 19 April 1949

This document is representative of the explicit use of the United States as a model for Europe.

Mindful of the advantages which the United States has enjoyed through the existence of a large domestic market with no internal trade barriers and believing that similar advantages can accrue to the countries of Europe, it is declared to be the policy of the people of the United States to encourage these countries through their joint organisation to exert sustained common efforts to achieve speedily that economic cooperation in Europe which is essential for lasting peace and prosperity. It is further declared to be the policy of the people of the United States to encourage the unification of Europe. . .

DOCUMENT 3.12

Statute of the Council of Europe

The Treaty establishing the Council of Europe was signed on 5 May 1949. The caution expressed in the Statute, and especially the restrictions placed upon the

Consultative Assembly disappointed the Federalists. (Cf. Documents 2.7 and 3.2.)

Article 1

(a) The aim of the Council of Europe is to achieve a greater unity between its Members for the purpose of safeguarding and realising the ideals and principles which are their common heritage and facilitating their economic and social progress.

(b) This aim shall be pursued through the organs of the Council by discussions of questions of common concern and by agreements and common action in economic, social, cultural, scientific, legal and administrative matters and in the maintenance and further realisation of human rights and fundamental freedoms.

(c) Participation in the Council of Europe shall not affect the collaboration of its Members in the work of the United Nations and of other international organisations or unions to which they are parties.

(d) Matters relating to National Defence do not fall within the scope of the Council of Europe.

Article 3

Every Member of the Council of Europe must accept the principles of the rule of law and of the enjoyment by all persons within its jurisdiction of human rights and fundamental freedoms. . .

Article 13

The Committee of Ministers is the organ which acts on behalf of the Council of Europe in accordance with Articles 15 and 16.

Article 15

(a) On the recommendation of the Consultative Assembly or on its own initiative, the Committee of Ministers shall consider the action required to further the aim of the Council of Europe, including the conclusion of conventions or agreements and the adoption by Governments of a common policy with regard to particular matters. Its conclusion shall be communicated to Members by the Secretary-General.

(b) In appropriate cases, the conclusions of the Committee may take the form of recommendations to the Governments of Members, and the Council may request the Governments of Members to inform it of the action taken by them with regard to such recommendations.

Article 22

The Consultative Assembly is the deliberative organ of the Council of Europe. It shall debate matters within its competence under this Statute and present its conclusions, in the form of recommendations, to the Committee of Ministers.

DOCUMENT 3.13

Memorandum by the Secretary of State for Foreign Affairs, Ernest Bevin, 19 October, 1950

The memorandum for Ernest Bevin was drafted in the context of pressure from the Assembly of the Council of Europe for reform of the Statute in a federalist direction. The memorandum was discussed by the Cabinet on 23 and 24 October where its suspicion of the Assembly was shared.

There have always been two conflicting views of the nature and purposes of the Council of Europe. To the majority of the Governments which set it up the Council of Europe was not an instrument for the immediate political unification of Europe, but part of the general material and moral build up of which other parts are represented by the OEEC, the Brussels Treaty and the North Atlantic Pact. . .

From the outset this conception has broken down. The idea of a European Assembly had been launched by the European Movement and the Assembly has from the first been dominated by that organisation . . . the Consultative Assembly has tended naturally to consist largely of enthusiasts for European federation. It is therefore biased in favour of federal solutions to an extent which wholly invalidates its claim to represent European opinion as a whole. . .

The line which I will have to take in Rome must clearly conform to the basic policy which His Majesty's Government have accepted hitherto and to which we must stick, of avoiding commitments in Europe which would affect our position as the leading member of the Commonwealth, our special relationship with the United States and our responsibilities as the centre of the Sterling Area. . ,

On the other hand, it would be very wrong, in the present state of morale in Europe, for His Majesty's Government to take up a position which obstructs the endeavours of other European Powers to achieve closer unity. There has always been a certain danger that a refusal by Great Britain to take full part in the movement towards European unity might lead to the creation of a bloc of European Powers inimical to our interests, especially if Germany were to get control of such a bloc. Traditionally, British policy has always been to prevent the formation of any such grouping in the Continent, but the emergence of the Soviet Union as an overriding threat to Europe has altered the basis on which this policy was founded. Subject to careful watch on the revival of German influence and power, I do not think it need any longer be regarded as necessary for His Majesty's Government to work against the creation of close groupings, even of a federal character, between Western European countries.

Furthermore, such is the present material and moral weakness of countries such as France and Italy that they are in danger of losing the will to survive as separate independent nations; and it might be fatal to the preservation of democracy in Western Europe if we were openly to discourage the conception of European unity which is reflected in the Council of Europe.

Suggested reading

A good survey of this period is to be found in W. Loth, *The Division of the World 1941–1955* (London, 1988). Two indispensable, detailed and contrasting studies are W. Lipgens, *A History of European Integration*, 1 (Oxford, 1982) and A.S. Milward, *The Reconstruction of Western Europe 1945–1951* (London, 1984). Assessment of recent debates can be found in R. Poidevin (ed.), *Histoire des débuts de la construction européene* (Baden-Baden, 1986) and P.M.R. Stirk and D. Willis (eds), *Shaping Postwar Europe* (London, 1991). There is an enormous specialist literature on the Marshall Plan. Among the most important contributions are I. Wexler, *The Marshall Plan Revisited* (Westport, 1983), M. Hogan, *The Marshall Plan* (Cambridge, 1987) and Charles S. Maier (ed.), *The Marshall Plan and Germany* (New York, 1991). French and British socialist perspectives are well covered by M. Newman, *Socialism and European Unity* (London, 1983). There has been an extensive reassessment of Britain's policy. See, for example, A. Bullock, *Ernest Bevin Foreign Secretary* (Oxford, 1983), J. Baylis, 'Britain, the Brussels Pact and the Continental Commitment', *International Affairs*, **60** (1984), pp. 615–29 and S. Croft, 'British Policy Towards Western Europe 1947-9', *International Affairs*, **65** (1988), pp. 617–29. For the Council of Europe see A.H. Robertson, *The Council of Europe* (London, 1956).

4 The Schuman Plan and the European Coal and Steel Community

Introduction

The European Coal and Steel Community (ECSC) does not now enjoy a high profile or feature significantly in the projected developments of the European Community. Indeed, in 1990, Sir Leon Brittan, EC Commissioner for Competition, argued unsuccessfully for the abolition of the ECSC on the grounds that it was obsolete and incompatible with the European Community's commitment to competition. Historically, though, the ECSC marked a decisive breakthrough in European integration, which led to the Rome Treaties of 1957. Although the road from the Treaty of Paris establishing the ECSC to the Rome Treaties may not have been as direct or the outcome as inevitable as has sometimes been suggested, the ECSC did reflect or embody decisions which were to shape the future of Western Europe.

Above all else it marked a step towards Franco–German reconciliation, without which little progress could be made. Secondly, Britain decided not to participate in it. Thirdly, the institutional model of Commission, Council of Ministers and Parliament, or in the language of the Paris Treaty, High Authority, Council of Ministers and Assembly, was established. Fourth, the United States, in spite of its traditional concerns about potentially protectionist policies and institutions, reaffirmed its commitment to European integration by supporting the ECSC.

A key figure in the creation of the ECSC was Jean Monnet, French Planning Commissioner and advocate of international organisation along functional lines (see Document 4.3). Monnet's role and motivation are subjects of fascination. Although he was genuinely committed to international cooperation, he was also concerned to guarantee France's future in the face of a resurgent Germany. French attempts to secure Allied control and supervision of German industrial development were faltering. The

United States was pressing for German recovery as part of the strengthening of the Western Alliance and was supported in this by the United Kingdom. Monnet knew that France could not withstand American pressure in the long run. His solution was to gain German acquiescence in the control of the basic industries of the Ruhr in return for the subjection of French coal and steel to the same regime. The idea itself, of course, was hardly new. When it was put to Konrad Adenauer, the West German Chancellor on 7 May 1950 he commented that he had been familiar with such ideas since the 1920s.

As the response of American statesmen to the French Foreign Minister, Schuman's Declaration of 9 May 1950 makes clear, France was taking the lead in moves towards European integration (see Documents 4.7 and 4.8). Britain was thrown on the defensive, her response was, as the United States' Secretary of State predicted, 'apt to be cautious'. The French insisted that negotiations be conducted on the basis of a prior commitment in principle to pooling resources under the control of a High Authority. As the subsequent negotiations demonstrated the meaning of this 'commitment' was highly elastic. But Britain refused to accept it and declined to enter the negotiations on these terms. British policy was guided both by a political opposition to any infringement of British sovereignty and by misjudgement of the likely progress and consequences of the negotiations (see Document 4.5).

The negotiations themselves were to lead to a treaty within the year. While the signature of the treaty represented an achievement for Monnet and his supporters, his success was, in other respects, limited. He had initially envisaged a short treaty establishing a High Authority which would then work out the details of the Community with the governments. Everything was geared to maximising the power and status of a supranational body free from the nationalistic constraints of the governments of the Member States. In this he was frustrated by the representatives of the smaller states. The Ministers for the Netherlands and Belgium, Spierenberg and Suetens, insisted upon the establishment of a Council of Ministers which would represent and guarantee national interests at the heart of the Community. Other institutional innovations included the Assembly, albeit one of limited powers, and a Court of Justice.

Beyond the immediate details of the negotiations for the ECSC, other broader concerns and prejudices surfaced. The link between the Community and the direction of national policies was evident in Monnet's original memorandum to Schuman. The Community was bound up with his strategy for the economic modernisation of France. In Britain, too, the Labour Government also saw a connection between key domestic policies and the Community. Their conclusion, though, was that the Community was incompatible with the aims of British Socialism. The manner in which this view was expressed caused great irritation to continental Socialists who favoured integration. The Labour Party's views seemed to them to be dubiously socialistic and to be tainted with an arrogant superiority more characteristic of imperialism (see Document 4.6). Yet it was not only British Socialists who were critical. The German Socialists, not to be outflanked on the national question, or to be regarded as lesser advocates of German interests and the German claim to equality with other nation states, denounced the Community with as much vigour as their British colleagues (see Document 4.11). Their arguments, though, did nothing to deflect the Christian Democrat Chancellor, Konrad Adenauer, from his commitment to European integration.

The ECSC was one of a number of developments in this period. The OEEC, NATO and the Council of Europe had already recently come into existence. In October 1950 M. René Pleven, the French Prime Minister responded to US pressure for German rearmament by proposing a European Army (see Chapter 5). The relationship between these institutions was far from clearly defined. The Dutch Foreign Minister Stikker was but one of many who were concerned to strengthen the OEEC as a more inclusive body committed to free trade. In Britain an attempt was made to recover lost ground and to subordinate the ECSC and the proposed European Defence Community, with their supranational elements, to the Council of Europe which remained more firmly answerable to national governments (see Document 4.14). Western Europe was undergoing a process of partial integration, partial both in its geographical and economic extent.

Documents

Document 4.1

Jean Monnet, Memorandum to Robert Schuman and Georges Bidault, 4 May 1950

Jean Monnet was Planning Commissioner, responsible for plans for the modernisation of France. Monnet himself traced his suggestions in the memorandum back to discussions in 1943.

Wherever we look in the present world situation we see nothing but deadlock – whether it be the increasing acceptance of a war that is thought to be inevitable, the problem of Germany, the continuation of French recovery, the organisation of Europe, the very place of France in Europe and in the world.

From such a situation there is only one way of escape: concrete action on a limited but decisive point, bringing about on this point a fundamental change and gradually modifying the very terms of all the problems. . .

The continuation of France's recovery will be halted if the question of German industrial production and its competitive capacity is not rapidly solved. . .

Already Germany is asking to increase her production from 11 to 14 million tons. We shall refuse, but the Americans will insist. Finally, we shall state our reservations but we shall give in. At the same time, French production is levelling off or even falling.

Merely to state these facts makes it unnecessary to describe in great detail what the consequences will be: Germany expanding, German dumping on export markets; a call for the protection of French industries; the halting or camouflage of trade liberalisation; the reestablishment of prewar cartels; perhaps an orientation of German expansion towards the East, a prelude to political agreements; France fallen back into the rut of limited, protected production. . .

The USA do not want things to take this course. They will accept an alternative solution if it is dynamic and constructive, especially if it is proposed by France. . .

At the present moment, Europe can be brought to birth only by France. Only France can speak and act.

But if France does not speak and act now, what will happen? A group will form around the United States, but in order to wage the Cold War with greater force. The obvious reason is that the countries of Europe are afraid and are seeking help. Britain will draw closer and closer to the United States; Germany will develop rapidly, and we shall not be able to prevent her being rearmed. France will be trapped again in her former Malthusianism, and this will lead inevitably to her being effaced.

DOCUMENT 4.2

Robert Schuman, Declaration of 9 May 1950

This declaration by the French Foreign Minister led directly to the negotiations for a European Coal and Steel Community.

World peace cannot be safeguarded without the making of creative efforts proportionate to the dangers which threaten it.

The contribution which an organised and living Europe can bring to civilisation is indispensable to the maintenance of peaceful relations. In taking upon herself for more than 20 years the role of champion of a united Europe, France has always had as her essential aim the service of peace. A united Europe was not achieved and we had war.

Europe will not be made all at once or according to a single plan. It will be built through concrete achievements which first create a *de facto* solidarity. The coming together of the nations of Europe requires the elimination of the age-old opposition of France and Germany. Any action which must be taken in the first place must concern these two countries. With this aim in view, the French Government proposes that action be taken immediately on one limited but decisive point. It proposes that Franco–German production of coal and steel as a whole be placed under a common High Authority, within the framework of an organisation open to the participation of the other countries of Europe.

The pooling of coal and steel production should immediately provide for the setting up of common foundations for economic development as a first step in the federation of Europe, and will change the destinies of those regions which have long been devoted to the manufacture of munitions of war, of which they have been the most constant victims.

The solidarity in production thus established will make it plain that any war between France and Germany becomes not merely unthinkable, but materially impossible. The setting up of this powerful productive unit, open to all countries willing to take part and bound ultimately to provide all the member countries with the basic elements of industrial production on the same terms, will lay a true foundation for their economic unification.

DOCUMENT 4.3

Letter from Jean Monnet to E. Plowden, 25 May 1950

This letter to Plowden, Chief Planning Officer at the Treasury, reveals Monnet's approach to integration (See also Document 2.13.)

The independence of the Authority *vis-à-vis* Governments and the sectional interests concerned is the precondition for the emergence of a common point of view which could be taken neither by Governments nor by private interests. It is clear that to entrust the Authority to a Committee of Governmental Delegates or to a Council made up of representatives of Governments employers and workers, would amount to returning to our present methods, those very methods which do not enable us to settle our problems. It should be possible to find quite a small number of men of real stature able without necessarily being technicians, and capable of rising above particular or national interests in order to work for the accomplishment of common objectives. . .

Furthermore the general objective assigned to the High Authority can be summarised by the formula of raising the standard of life by increasing productivity. All tasks entrusted to it derive from this principle, which would justify the establishment of identical price conditions no less than the effort to modernise production and assistance for rationalising enterprises which would in turn facilitate the maintenance of full employment by redistributing labour in more productive occupations. To accomplish this objective, it seems to us that the Authority will usually be able to confine itself to indirect and general means of action without interfering in the management of the enterprises concerned nor directly determining which of them should be eliminated.

DOCUMENT 4.4

Extract from Dirk Stikker's 'Men of Responsibility', 1963

Dirk Stikker was Foreign Minister of the Netherlands between 1948 and 1952. Stikker put forward a plan to the OEEC for sectoral integration in June 1950.

In the years 1950 to 1952 it became clear that little progress could be made in altering the United Kingdom's stand on European integration. The British could not agree to any purely European discussion of tariffs. When we tried during the functionalist, or sector by sector, approach to discuss the whole field of tariffs and preferential agreements, the United Kingdom was only willing to study a particular sector, but never the whole field. When we had to find solutions for agricultural problems by the introduction of long-term contracts, no satisfactory results could be reached. Gradually, the conviction grew that the United Kingdom would not only not agree to European tariff discussions, or to a concept like the agricultural Green Pool for Europe, but would also abstain from any 'community system' such as was embodied in Schuman's Coal and Steel proposal as well as even less ambitious projects. . .

But as British hesitation and reluctance about joining Europe grew, so did continental enthusiasm for unity. France and Italy had tried unsuccessfully in 1949 to create a customs union such as Benelux had concluded in 1947. This was followed by French and Italian suggestions to get together, even without Germany, with the successful Benelux – presumably in a 'Fritalux' or 'Finebel'. These plans I always rejected, for I was afraid of diminishing the importance of the wider European concept embodied in the OEEC.

Nevertheless, the trend towards supranational groups was growing apace; soon after the British refusal to join the European Coal and Steel Community, negotiations between the Six on the European Defence Community started. Meanwhile, throughout Western Europe the influence of the European Movement and simultaneously that of Jean Monnet, also in Europe, but particularly in Washington, were growing. In May 1949 the Council of Europe at Strasbourg, with its Ministerial Committee and Consultative Assembly – originally conceived by their ardent champions as an embryonic European Cabinet and legislature, respectively, had come into existence. This was the period of fervent intense debates between the 'intergovernmentalists' – those who favoured European cooperation between governments and no establishment of supranational institutions and 'federalists', who aimed at the political integration of Western Europe in general supranational institutions. Somewhere between the two lay the 'functionalists' who emphasised the idea of international, intergovernmental, specialised authorities which although containing some supranational elements fell short of the full political integration desired by the federalists. As a practical matter, the distinction between functionalists and a federalist was often only a matter of championing a slower or quicker pace of integration. . .

DOCUMENT 4.5

Minutes of a meeting of the British Cabinet, 22 June 1950

The meeting was held after the decision by the Cabinet, on 2 June 1950, not to take part in the negotiations on the terms set by the French government. The report was subsequently considered by a Committee of Ministers and the issue raised again in Cabinet.

The Cabinet had before them a note by the Secretary of the Cabinet . . . covering a report by a Committee of officials appointed to advise on the French Foreign Minister's proposal for integrating the coal and steel industries of Western Europe.

In a preliminary discussion of the report the following points were raised:

(a)   Some concern was expressed about the attitudes which trade unions might take towards this proposal. . .

(b)   The Government had already given ample proof that they were prepared in principle to support all reasonable plans for promoting closer economic co-ordination in Europe. They were not therefore opposed in principle to some integration of the coal and steel industries of Western Europe. They must, however, reject any proposal for placing these industries under the control of a supranational authority whose decisions would be binding on Governments. Equally they could not accept proposals for placing these industries under the control of an industrial cartel on the prewar restrictionist model. . .

(e)   The issues raised by this proposal were complex and far-reaching and it was essential that Ministers should have full opportunity to consider them in detail. There was no reason to suppose that this opportunity would be lacking; for it was likely to be some time before any detailed scheme emerged from the international discussions now proceeding in Paris. The greatest risk was perhaps that a deadlock would be reached in those discussions and the United Kingdom Government would be asked to assist in resolving it.

DOCUMENT 4.6

André Philip, 'Socialism and European Unity', 1950

André Philip was one of the most enthusiastically pro-European members of the SFIO (French Socialist Party). His reaction to the Labour Party statement was shared by many socialists on the continent, especially in Italy and France.

On page seven (of 'European Unity. A Statement by the National Executive Committee of the British Labour Party') we read 'The Labour Party would welcome with pleasure an economic union which was based upon international planning for full employment, social justice and stability'. After, however, this agreeable reassurance has been given, they go on to prove that it is unattainable. This is done by imposing three preconditions:

1.   'The achievement of this goal assumes a degree of uniformity in the internal policies of the member states which does not now exist and is unlikely to exist in the near future.'
2.   'Only public ownership can make such planning possible, control without ownership can be effective only for negative purposes.'
3.   'All industries concerned in European planning should first be subject to government direction in their own country.'. . .

These three statements by our Labour friends do not appear immediately persuasive.

1.   Can one really say that international planning is impossible because of currently existing divergencies which will, supposedly, exist in the future politics of Member States? . . . One may not forget that the nationalised sector in France is no smaller than in Great Britain . . . Although our government has a preference for liberal economic

reforms, the pressure of events has proven so strong that industrial development in the last few years has taken place under the guidance of the state and with public investment. . .

2. Can one say without further ado that planning would be unrealisable and would lead to purely negative consequences if it was not preceded by nationalisation? . . . It appears (rather) that we have now reached a point in economic development where power and ownership more and more fall away from each other. No one claims any more that shareholders in a limited company exercise any kind of power.

3. A more serious question, the decisive one is: is international planning possible only on the basis of national planning. . .? Does one begin in a single country by first establishing regional planning before one creates a national plan? To the contrary, if we want European planning would it not be unavoidable to establish planning offices directly superordinate to the enterprises, and if gradations appear necessary, to place European regional institutions over more national associations?. . .

How can a party which disposes of a majority of a mere five votes look down so arrogantly upon the socialist parties of the continent and declare that a European legislative body would 'exhibit a permanent anti-socialist majority' and that, furthermore, 'the civic and administrative traditions would prevent some countries from applying socialist methods even if they had a socialist majority.' With what original sin are the socialist parties of the continent afflicted, from which solely and only the Labour Party is exempted?. . .

How can the Labour Party reject with horror cooperation with a non-socialist Europe and then affirm its unshakeable ties, its community of world views, its untainted solidarity – on the one hand with a Commonwealth whose governments are all currently conservative and on the other hand with an America which, despite its progressive policies, can certainly not be considered as a representative of socialist ideas?

DOCUMENT 4.7

Telegram from US Secretary of State, Dean Acheson, 10 May 1950

Dean Acheson had been convinced of the need for European integration for several years. His hesitation reflected traditional American fears about European cartels. (See also Documents 4.8 and 4.9.)

In commenting on proposal believe it is important that French be given credit for making a conscious and far-reaching effort to advance Franco–German rapproachment and European integration generally. On the other hand, it is too early for us to give proposal our approval because of the possible cartel aspect and known previous French efforts to secure detailed control over investment policies and management of Rühr coal and steel industry, and certainly until we know about the character and the details of the scheme. British reaction has not yet developed but believe it is apt to be somewhat cautious.

DOCUMENT 4.8

The Acting Secretary of State to the US Secretary of State, 10 May 1950

The Acting Secretary, John Foster Dulles, was to become Secretary of State in the new Eisenhower administration.

While obviously many details are lacking necessary for final judgement, it is my initial impression that the conception is brilliantly creative and could go far to solve the most dangerous problem of our time, namely the relationship of Germany's industrial power to France and the West. The proposal is along lines which Secretary Marshall and I thought about in Moscow in 1947 but which we did not believe the French would ever accept.

DOCUMENT 4.9

The US ambassador in the United Kingdom, Douglas, to the Secretary of State, 6 June 1950

Ambassador Douglas reflected a changed emphasis in US hopes for European integration, relying upon France instead of the United Kingdom. (See also Document 3.5.)

The political advantages of the plan. . .

(a) The plan is the result of French creative leadership . . . it should facilitate France's resumption of continental leadership, which hitherto the United States has had to look to a latterly somewhat reluctant Britain to carry.

(b) It should abate, if not dispel, fears of recurrent Franco–German war, and thereby encourage France to acquiesce in increased economic strength of Germany and, possibly at a later date, even in German military participation in Western defense. . .

(e) It should constitute an important first stage for a possible future European federation. . .

   As far as political disadvantages are concerned, it is important that the plan not be used as a vehicle:

   (a) To underwrite the economic base of a 'third force'. . .

   (b) To permit the resurgence of Germany as the dominant element in Western continental Europe. . .

Economic merits, difficulties and potential abuses: . . . If plan, in operation conforms to general principles of an expanding economy, which the French Government has declared to be its purpose, and does not degenerate into a super-cartel with price fixing, licensing, division of markets, restriction or artificial allocation of funds for investment, and suppression of competition and technical improvements, then the positive economic potentialities of scheme should predominate.

DOCUMENT 4.10

Report by the US Department of State to the Council on Foreign Economic Policy, 16 March 1955

The Council on Foreign Economic Policy considered issues which cut across Departmental boundaries. At its meeting on 20 December the Council agreed with a subsequent State Department text, the conclusions of which are similar to those given below.

(a) The European Coal and Steel Community represents a dramatic development in the direction of European unity, the promotion of which has been established by Congress and the Executive Branch as a basic objective of US policy. . . The President has on frequent occasions expressed his support for this objective, and has described the CSC as 'the most hopeful and constructive development so far toward the economic and political integration of Europe.'. . .

(c) While the Community's progress in combating restrictive practices has been slow, it has been substantially more active in this sphere than most individual European governments or other international bodies. Further, it should be realised that the CSC cartel problem cannot be considered entirely apart from the same basic cartel problem in other segments of the European economy. Some progress on this problem has been made by Western European governments since the war. Much remains to be done. . .

DOCUMENT 4.11

Fritz Baade, 'Problems of the Schuman Plan', 1951

Fritz Baade was a member of the SPD, the German Social Democratic Party. His hostility to the Schuman Plan and strident tone reflect the desire of the SPD to demonstrate its nationalist credentials.

The London Economist writes quite briefly of the Schuman Plan on 10 March: 'The Americans can and should use the Germans' dependence on the grain and raw materials to press for signature: . . .' Ladies and Gentlemen, for a German who has experienced the times after the First World War and who knows what it means when one is forced to sign a Treaty under the threat that otherwise one will not receive grain, these are scarcely friendly tones. The Economist continues: 'And the western governments should now explain firmly to the Germans that acceptance or rejection of international control of heavy industry will be treated as evidence of their reliability as equal partners in Europe.'

Ladies and Gentlemen, this is the theory of prepayment, the theory that the Germans have to sign whatever is presented to them time and again before they can be trusted and treated as equal partners.

The Economist continues: 'On the other hand let it be recognised that the Germans are being asked to give up a great deal: the fruits of their natural advantage in raw materials, a form of industrial organisation whose efficacy has been proved, and a monopoly selling agency which, they claim, enabled uneconomic mines to be worked and employment to be maintained. These are advantages that no German politician can surrender without misgivings.'

Ladies and Gentlemen, what the Economist writes here appears to me to be the basic truth about the Schuman Plan. We are expressly asked to sign something which the others are convinced we would not sign without duress. And we are asked to give up things which no responsible German politician may give up without very serious misgivings and without very pressing reasons.

DOCUMENT 4.12

Konrad Adenauer, Chancellor of the Federal Republic of Germany, in the *Bundestag*, 12 July 1952

Konrad Adenauer, Chancellor of the Federal Republic of Germany, had been familiar with ideas on the integration of the European coal and steel industries since the 1920s. His prime concern, however, was with the political rehabilitation of Germany and reconciliation with France.

It is my opinion and belief that the parliaments of the six European countries which will have to deal with this European Coal and Steel Community realise exactly what it is all about and that in particular they realise that the political goal, the political meaning of the European Coal and Steel Community, is infinitely larger than its economic purpose. . .

Something further has resulted during the negotiations, I believe that for the first time in history, certainly in the history of the last centuries, countries want to renounce part of their sovereignty, voluntarily and without compulsion, in order to transfer the sovereignty to a supranational structure.

DOCUMENT 4.13

The Treaty of Paris establishing the European Coal and Steel Community

The Treaty was signed on 18 April 1951.

Article 1
By this Treaty, the High Contracting Parties establish among themselves a European Coal and Steel Community, founded upon a common market, common objectives and common institutions.

Article 2
The European Coal and Steel Community shall have as its task to contribute, in harmony with the general economy of Member States and through the establishment of a common market as provided in Article 4, to economic expansion, growth of employment and a rising standard of living in the Member States. . .

Article 4
The following are recognised as incompatible with the common market for coal and steel and shall accordingly be abolished and prohibited within the Community, as provided in this Treaty:

(a) import and export duties, or charges having equivalent effect, and quantitative restrictions on the movement of products;
(b) measures or practices which discriminate between producers, between purchasers or between consumers, especially in prices and delivery terms or transport or transport rates and conditions, and measures or practices which interfere with the purchaser's free choice of supplier;
(c) subsidies or aids granted by States, or special charges imposed by States, in any form whatever;

(d)   restrictive practices which tend towards the sharing or exploiting of markets.

Article 7

The institutions of the community shall be: a High Authority, assisted by a Consultative Committee; a Common Assembly (hereinafter called the 'Assembly'); a Special Council of Ministers (hereinafter called the 'Council'); a Court of Justice (hereinafter called the 'Court').

Article 9

The High Authority shall consist of nine members appointed for a year and chosen on the grounds of their general competence . . . The members of the High Authority shall, in the general interest of the Community, be completely independent in the performance of their duties. In the performance of these duties, they shall neither seek nor take instructions from any Government or from any other body. They shall refrain from any action incompatible with the supranational character of their duties.

Article 24

The Assembly shall discuss in open session the general report submitted to it by the High Authority.

If a motion of censure is . . . carried by a two-thirds majority of the votes cast, representing a majority of the Members of the Assembly, the Members of the High Authority shall resign as a body. . .

Article 26

The Council shall exercise its powers in the cases provided for and in the manner set out in this Treaty, in particular in order to harmonise the action of the High Authority and that of the Governments, which are responsible for the general economic policies of their countries. . .

Article 57

In the sphere of production, the High Authority shall give preference to the indirect means of action at its disposal, such as:

–   cooperation with Governments to regularise or influence general consumption, particularly that of public services;
–   intervention in regard to prices and commercial policy as provided for in this Treaty.

Article 65

1.   All agreements between undertakings, decisions by associations of undertakings and concerted practices tending directly or indirectly to prevent, restrict or distort normal competition within the common

market shall be prohibited, and in particular those tending:
(a) to fix or determine prices;
(b) to restrict or control production, technical development or investment;
(c) to share markets, products, customers or sources of supply.
2. However, the High Authority shall authorise specialisation agreements or joint-buying or joint-selling agreements in respect of particular products if it finds that:
(a) such specialisation or such joint-buying or -selling will make for a substantial improvement in the production or distribution of those products;
(b) the agreement in question is essential in order to achieve these results and is not more restrictive than is necessary for that purpose; and
(c) the agreement is not liable to give the undertakings concerned the power to determine the prices, or to control or restrict the production or marketing of a substantial part of the products in question within the common market, or to shield them against effective competition from other undertakings within the common market.

DOCUMENT 4.14

Anthony Eden, British Foreign Minister, 20 March 1952

The 'Eden Proposals' were approved by the British Cabinet on 13 March 1952 as part of an extensive review of British policy towards European integration. They were not successful. Dirk Stikker was Foreign Minister of the Netherlands.

Following is a summary of my statement at this afternoon's meeting of the Committee of Ministers putting forward our proposals on the future of the Council of Europe:

The Council of Europe can best fulfil the important role which it is to play in promoting European unity by developing along lines complementary to the European Defence Community, the Schuman Plan and future European bodies of the same kind. Its organs should serve as institutions of these organisations. The Council of Europe would also continue to serve as an organisation for intergovernmental cooperation in Western Europe and would, in particular, continue to discuss periodic reports from the OEEC. . .

This statement provoked an immediate and favourable reaction from my colleagues. M. Schuman welcomed our initiative and stated that the French Government had for some time been seeking a method of linking the Schuman Plan with the Council of Europe. He stated that he would give our proposals his wholehearted support. M. Stikker endorsed these remarks . . . M. Taviani (Italy) considered our declaration of the utmost importance and interest.

Suggested reading

The extent to which the ECSC marked a breakthrough in terms of European integration and the role of Jean Monnet are both hotly disputed. Two publications of the European Commission have indicative titles: *Jean Monnet. A Grand Design for Europe*, European Documentation 5/1988 (Luxembourg, 1988) and *Europe – A Fresh Start*, European Documentation 3/1990 (Luxembourg, 1990). Monnet's own account is in his *Memoirs* (London, 1978). Among the older scholarly accounts W. Diebold, *The Schuman Plan* (New York, 1959) and E. Haas, *The Uniting of Europe* (Stanford, 1968) are still essential. A more recent, and critical, survey is given by K. Schwabe (ed.), *The Beginnings of the Schuman Plan* (Baden-Baden, 1988). See also A.S. Milward, *The Reconstruction of Western Europe* (London, 1984). In addition to Schwabe (ed.), for British policy see John Young (ed.), *The Foreign Policy of Churchill's Peacetime Administration 1951–1955* (Leicester, 1988), John Young, 'Churchill's No to Europe', *Historical Journal*, **28** (1985), pp. 923–37, and Roger Bullen 'An Idea Enters Diplomacy: The Schuman Plan, May 1950', in R.J. Bullen, H. Pogge von Strandmann and A.B. Polonsky (eds), *Ideas into Politics* (London, 1984) pp. 193–204. For the Paris Treaty in full, see B. Rudden and D. Wyatt (eds), *Basic Community Laws* (2nd edn) (Oxford, 1986).

5 From NATO to the Western European Union: The debate over the European Defence Community

Introduction

The invasion of South Korea in June 1950 sharply intensified the Cold War. Following on the Berlin Blockade and the testing of the atom bomb by the Soviet Union, it raised acute fears in the West of further Soviet pressure on Europe. In April 1949 the formal US commitment to Europe in the North Atlantic Treaty had added military reassurance to the economic support of Marshall Aid (see Document 5.1). But a divided Germany looked vulnerable and of particular concern to the West was the disparity in conventional armed strength between East and West in Europe.

By August 1950 the United States had come to the view that credible conventional defence necessitated the rearmament of Western Germany. Already Jean Monnet had suggested a common NATO defence budget to provide for a German contribution to the Western defence effort without a German Army. But Dean Acheson, the US Secretary of State, instructed the American ambassador to France to press on his government the idea of a European defence force which would include ten divisions of German troops under a NATO Commander-in-Chief. This idea was quickly accepted by all members of NATO except France.

The French Foreign Ministry, the *Quai D'Orsay*, took the view that, although the idea of German rearmament would be exceedingly unpopular among the French so soon after the atrocities of war, France should not challenge the principle of German rearmament as such. Instead she should prepare 'means permitting the retention of sufficient control on the part of the French Government'. This could only be accomplished 'in the framework of a collective organisation in which France would participate and play, by the nature of things a determining role'.

The outcome was the Pleven Plan (see Document 5.2). This, in

Monnet's words, 'by the same spirit as the ECSC. . . proposes the creation, for common defence, of a European Army under the authority of the political institutions of a united Europe'. The French Government intended, at all costs, that it should be impossible for German forces to be an instrument of German policy. There was another important consideration: during the long debate over the European Army (European Defence Community (EDC)) proposal a large part of the French Army and much expenditure were tied up in a losing war in Indochina. In these circumstances it was probable that any German contingent would outweigh any possible French contribution. This would be even more risky if Britain failed to participate in the proposed Army. (For the initial British response to this proposal see Document 5.3.)

The US Administration was initially unenthusiastic about this plan. It seemed cumbersome and they wondered whether the French were simply advancing it as a delaying ploy. Delay German rearmament it certainly did. An impassioned debate which has been compared for its intensity with the Dreyfus Affair, which had divided the French Third Republic at the turn of the century, continued until the final non-ratification of the EDC Treaty in the French National Assembly on 30 August 1954 (see Document 5.9). From the end of 1951 the United States accepted the view that German rearmament could only be palatable to the French if it meant rearming Germans without rearming Germany. This is reflected in the speech by General Eisenhower (see Document 5.4), as is the linking of rearmament with the idea of further progress towards Western European integration. Eisenhower had recently been appointed Supreme Allied Commander in Europe and he was soon to become US President.

Ironically, if predictably, the more attractive the EDC plan became to the United States the less it appealed to the French. In Germany, too, there was vocal opposition to the European policy of Chancellor Adenauer (see Document 5.8). This was both because to many the military consolidation of Western Europe, with the emergence of the Federal Republic as an equal sovereign state seemed to be (whatever Adenauer might claim) a renunciation of the possibility of German reunification, and because of the hostile mood of German youth towards any prospect of revived militarism.

While coming to support the idea, the British Government refused to participate. The very significant accompanying proposals for a European Political Community were especially unacceptable to her. These would have gone further in the establishment of European federal institutions (see Document 5.7). These proposals were embodied in the Draft Treaty of March 1953. They provided, among other things, for the establishment of a European Parliament elected by universal suffrage.

Impatience mounted in the United States with the repeated delays over ratification. John Foster Dulles, the new US Secretary of State abandoned the restraint of his predecessors. In December 1953 he issued the following warning: 'If the EDC should not become effective, if France and Germany should remain apart, so that they would again be potential enemies, then indeed there would be grave doubts whether Continental Europe could be made a place of safety, that would compel an agonising reappraisal of basic US policy'. For his response to the rejection of the Treaty see Document 5.10.

Stalin had died in March 1953. With the 'peace initiative' of his successors the Soviet threat appeared to be receding. The *coup de grâce* to the EDC Treaty came with a Gaullist motion in the French National Assembly to move to other business. It has sometimes been argued that this outcome might have been averted if the British Government under Sir Winston Churchill (see Document 5.5) had been willing to offer guarantees against any prospect of a revived German threat. In the end, though, opposition came not simply from Gaullists and Communists, but from others who strongly supported Western European integration (see Document 5.9).

The Pleven Plan had attempted to defend French security interests while responding to US pressure. Apart from the issue of German rearmament, however, there was the broader question of European defence integration as such. Many deduced from the failure of the EDC that defence integration was only feasible if it followed from economic and political integration. Was defence, being either transatlantic with NATO, or national, as with the later French nuclear 'force de Frappe', a suitable case for specifically European integration?

In any case, with the collapse of the EDC France was faced with the solution to the rearmament question which the Pleven Plan had been contrived to avoid. Following the initiative of Sir Anthony Eden, Germany was admitted to NATO. The Brussels Treaty was transformed into a Western European Union including Germany and Italy. Britain made an unprecedented long-term commitment to European defence with the British Army on the Rhine and Germany promised not to manufacture atomic, chemical or biological weapons. The settlement of this defence question made it possible to proceed with an agreement between Britain, France, the United States and Germany for the establishment of the Federal Republic as a fully sovereign power.

After this, for many years the Western European Union (WEU), including Britain and the ECSC Six, was of little practical significance, although it was a useful forum for Britain for contact with the Six in the years before her accession to the Community. In the 1980s, though, the idea of a distinct 'European defence identity' has undergone a marked revival, particularly encouraged by the French and German governments. Even more recently, the transformation of Eastern Europe since 1989 and the reappraisal of European security needs has prompted new interest in the WEU.

Documents

DOCUMENT 5.1

The North Atlantic Treaty, 4 April 1949

The following articles were included in this Treaty which was initially signed by the Foreign Ministers of Belgium, Canada, Denmark, France, Iceland, Italy, the Netherlands, Norway, Portugal, the United Kingdom and the United States. It was an important step in the evolution of the policy of Western containment of the Soviet Union.

The Parties to this Treaty reaffirm their faith in the purposes and principles of the Charter of the United Nations and their desire to live in peace with all peoples and all governments. They are determined to safeguard the freedom, common heritage and civilisation of their peoples, founded on the principles of democracy, individual liberty and the rule of law.

They seek to promote stability and well-being in the North Atlantic area.

They are resolved to unite their efforts for collective defence and for the preservation of peace and security.

They therefore agree to this North Atlantic Treaty:

Article 1

The Parties undertake, as set forth in the Charter of the United Nations, to settle any international dispute in which they may be involved by peaceful means in such a manner that international peace and security and justice are not endangered, and to refrain in their international relations from the threat or use of force in any manner inconsistent with the purposes of the United Nations.

Article 2

The Parties will contribute towards the further development of peaceful and friendly international relations by strengthening their free institutions, by bringing about a better understanding of the principles upon which these institutions are founded, and by promoting conditions of stability and well-being. They will seek to eliminate conflict in their international economic policies and will encourage economic collaboration between any or all of them.

Article 3

In order more effectively to achieve the objectives of this Treaty, the Parties, separately and jointly, by means of continuous and effective self-help and mutual aid, will maintain and develop their individual and collective capacity to resist armed attack.

Article 4
The Parties will consult together whenever, in the opinion of any one of them, the territorial integrity, political independence or security of any of the Parties is threatened.

Article 5
The Parties agree that an armed attack against one or more of them in Europe or North America shall be considered an attack against them all and consequently they agree that, if such an armed attack occurs, each of them, in exercise of the right of individual or collective self-defence recognised by Article 51 of the Charter of the United Nations, will assist the Party or Parties so attacked by taking forthwith, individually and in concert with the other Parties, such action as it deems necessary, including the use of armed force, to restore and maintain the security of the North Atlantic area. Any such armed attack and all measures taken as a result thereof shall immediately be reported to the Security Council. Such measures shall be terminated when the Security Council has taken the measures necessary to restore and maintain international peace and security.

Article 6
For the purpose of Article 5 an armed attack on one or more of the Parties is deemed to include an armed attack on the territory of any of the Parties in Europe or North America . . . on the occupation forces of any Party in Europe, on the islands under the jurisdiction of any Party in the North Atlantic area north of the Tropic of Cancer or on the vessels or aircraft in this area of any of the Parties.

DOCUMENT 5.2

The Pleven Plan for a European Defence Community (EDC)

The following announcement of the plan was made to the French National Assembly by the French Prime Minister, René Pleven on 24 October 1950.

Ladies and Gentlemen, the ideal of collective security has just achieved a victory in Korea which marks an historic advance in the efforts of the free nations to create in the world conditions of security such as to discourage any aggressive designs.

The nations which concluded the Atlantic Treaty wished to forge the instrument for that security for the region covered by the Treaty. They have in the last few months achieved unprecedented progress in defining their views on a common defence programme and embarking on the implementation of those views. . .

The associated nations have recognised the need to defend the Atlantic community against any possible aggression, on a line situated as far to the East as possible. They have decided to increase the forces stationed in Europe for this purpose. They have agreed that all those forces irrespective of their nationality, should be placed under the command of a single commander-in-chief. . .

Germany, which is not a party to the Atlantic Treaty, is nevertheless also destined to enjoy the benefits of the security system resulting therefrom. It is consequently right that it should make its contribution towards setting up a system of defence for Western Europe. Consequently, before opening discussions on this important problem in the Assembly, the (French) Government have decided to take the initiative of making the following declaration. . .

It proposes the creation, for our common defence, of a European Army tied to political institutions of a united Europe. This suggestion is directly inspired by the recommendations adopted on 11 August 1950 by the Assembly of the Council of Europe, demanding the immediate creation of a unified European Army destined to cooperate with the American and Canadian forces in the defence of peace.

The setting up of a European Army cannot result from a mere grouping together of national military units, which would in reality only mask a coalition of the old sort. For tasks which are inevitably common ones, only common institutions will do. The army of a united Europe, composed of men coming from different European countries, must, so far as is possible, achieve a complete fusion of the human and material elements which make it up under a single European political and military authority.

A Minister of Defence would be appointed by the participating governments and would be responsible, under conditions to be determined, to those appointing him and to a European Assembly. That assembly might be the Assembly in Strasbourg, or an offshoot thereof, or an assembly composed of specially elected delegates. His powers with respect to the European Army would be those of a national Minister of Defence with respect to the national forces of his own country. He would, in particular, be responsible for implementing such general directives as he might receive from a Council composed of Ministers of the participating countries. He would serve as the normal channel between the European community and outside countries of international organs for everything relating to the carrying out of his task.

The contingents furnished by the participating States would be incorporated in the European Army at the level of the smallest possible unit.

The money for the European Army would be provided by a common budget. The European Minister of Defence would be responsible for the implementation of existing international obligations and for the negotiation and implementation of new international engagements on the basis of directives received from the Council of Ministers. The European armament and equipment programme would be decided and carried out under his authority. The participating States which currently have national forces at their disposal would retain their own authority so far as concerned that part of their existing forces which was not integrated by them into the European Army.

Conversely, the European Minister of Defence might, with the authorisation of the Council of Ministers, place at the disposal of a participating government a part of its national forces comprised in the European force, for the purpose of meeting requirements other than those of common defence. The European force placed at the disposal of the unified Atlantic command would operate in accordance with the obligations assumed in the Atlantic Treaty, both so far as concerns general strategy and so far as concerns organisation and equipment.

The European Minister of Defence would be responsible for obtaining from member countries of the European community the contingents, the equipment, the armaments, and the supplies due from each State to the common army.

During the establishment of this European Army a transitional phase will be necessary. During this period, a part of the existing national armies, although placed under the unified Atlantic Command, will probably not be capable of immediate incorporation into the European Army. The latter would have to develop progressively, each country furnishing its contribution of men, in proportions decided by the Council of Ministers and taking into account the general plan of defence drawn up by the Atlantic Council.

Finally, the creation of a European Army cannot, either in the initial phase or in its ultimate realisation, in any way constitute a cause for delay in the implementation of programmes envisaged or under way within the Atlantic organisation for the establishment of national forces under a unified command. On the contrary, the projected creation of the European Army should facilitate the implementation of the Atlantic programmes.

It is on the basis I have just sketched out that the French Government proposes to invite Great Britain and the free countries of continental Europe, should they agree to participate with it in the creation of a European Army, to work together on ways of realising the principles just stated. Those studies would begin in Paris as soon as the coal and steel treaty is signed. . .

DOCUMENT 5.3

Ernest Bevin, Labour Foreign Secretary of the United Kingdom, to the House of Commons, 29 November 1950

This speech expressed the British government's initial reaction to the proposal for the EDC.

The French Government have now produced a proposal for a European Army with a European Minister of Defence, subject to a European Council of Ministers and a European Assembly. This European Army would contain German units as well as units from the other European countries. His Majesty's Government do not favour this proposal. To begin with, we fear that it will only delay the building up of Europe's defences. Our first and most urgent need is to set up the integrated Force under the Supreme Commander. The next step is to provide for a German contribution to that force. These are immediate matters of great urgency. We take the view that the proposal for a European Army is also too limited in scope. We cherish our special ties with our old European friends but, in our view, Europe is not enough; it is not big enough, it is not strong enough and it is not able to stand by itself.

I understand the urge towards European unity and sympathise with it and, indeed, I did much to help bring the Council of Europe into being. But I also understand the new paradox that European unity is no longer possible within Europe alone but only within the broader Atlantic community. It is this great conception of an Atlantic community that we want to build up. This union of twelve free, equal and independent nations, organised for the defence of peace and for the growth of prosperity, comprising most of the free nations of Europe and working in harmony with the aims and purposes of the United Nations, is a great new force in the world. It includes two Commonwealth countries, Canada and ourselves, who will always work in the closest association with the other 53 members of the Commonwealth.

We have set our hopes on this conception. We want it to develop far beyond its immediate purpose of defence into a lasting association of like-minded nations. That is why, I am sorry to say, we cannot accept the French proposal. That is why His Majesty's Government, looking at the problem of the future security of the West, are in favour of the Atlantic conception. Nevertheless, if it is the wish of the French Government and of other Governments in Europe to proceed to examine the possibilities of forming a European Army as a part of the integrated force for the defence of Europe, His Majesty's Government would not stand in their way.

We are trying to reconcile the different approach caused by our geographical   position,   our   international   responsibilities,   our

Commonwealth connection and every other factor concerned, and we are not at loggerheads with the French. If the French, with their long tradition and their European view, take one line regarding Europe and if they will not try to force us into an awkward position, we certainly will put no pressure on them with regard to their desire for a European Army. But I repeat what I said, and I appeal to them to let us get on. We are anxious to avoid delay. The situation in the world is very dangerous. All peoples can combine on this problem of security and peace. It is in the interests of all of us in Western Europe that the solution should be found promptly, and security assured. . .

DOCUMENT 5.4

US General Eisenhower's address to the North Atlantic Council on the defence of Western Europe, Rome, 26 November 1951

At the time, Eisenhower was Supreme Allied Commander in Europe. In 1953 he was to become President. The following extracts indicate his enthusiasm for European integration and the EDC proposal.

I do not need to recite to such a body as this the great advantages that would come to us through unification of Western Europe, unification in its economy, its military systems, finally its political organisms. Under such conditions we would no longer have the job of trying to determine what each nation would have; we would have Mr. Monnet's true concept of a single balanced force for the whole. No nation would have to keep, for prestige purposes alone, particular units, officers, organisations, or services. All this you can easily comprehend. But even as we long for such a great advance, I assure you that under the programs now in hand we can, in Western Europe, erect a defense that can at least, although expensively and uneasily, produce a stalemate. But that is not good enough. As my chief of staff pointed out to you, we need depth to our defensive position; we need German assistance, both in geography and in military strength, if these can be obtained with justice and respect to them and to ourselves.

It is because of these reasons, of which the ones I have given you are only a few, that I have come to believe that we should have a European Defense Force. But merely because I believe we must have a European Defense Force does not mean that I am stopping for one instant my efforts to co-operate with every one of the chiefs of staff in all our countries to produce, now, what they can as effective national forces.

But if we can go ahead with the European Defense Force, gaining

German strength without creating a menace to any others and in such a way that the Germans could co-operate with self-respect, our goals will become much more readily obtainable. Here I must say one word about the German position. We cannot have mere hirelings and expect them to operate efficiently. NATO has no use for soldiers representing second-rate morale or a second-rate country. German help will be tremendously important as it is freely given; and it can be so given, I believe, through a European Defense Force.

This European Force would serve another great purpose – it would stand alongside the Schuman plan – which must be successful – and the two would constitute great steps toward the goal of complete European unity.

Just as European unity is important to all of us, there is nothing more important to the entire NATO organisation than an underlying unity among all of us based upon a clear comprehension of the facts at issue. It is not enough that all of our governments agree. The important thing is that the populations standing behind those governments must agree. Our peoples must understand that, for each nation, the concept of collective security by co-operation must be successful or there is no acceptable alternative for any of us. All of us must understand that the task we have set for ourselves can be done because of our great resources and our determination and skill. All of us must understand that this task must take first priority over and above all else except only that of assuring acceptable levels of living in our own countries. Unless this kind of information is gotten out and understood, we are victims first of our own laziness, our own failures as leaders, and secondly, we are victims of Soviet propaganda, because they will, in all cases, assert the contrary. They will assert that we are trying to get together to launch a great invasion, when they well know that the entire aggregate of the forces we are talking about have no power to launch any attack across Europe. All soldiers know that it is an entirely different thing to establish a military stalemate in Western Europe on the one hand, and, on the other, to conduct an offensive. The Soviet general staff is completely capable of understanding this. . .

DOCUMENT 5.5

The Conservative Prime Minister, Sir Winston Churchill, to the House of Commons, 6 December 1951

The following extract from this speech stresses the British position of support for, but refusal to merge with, the proposed EDC.

At Strasbourg in 1950 the Germans did not press for a national army. On the contrary, they declared themselves ready to join a European Army without having a national army. Dr. Adenauer has renewed to us this assurance, and that is still the German position and their preference – no national army. This is a very great and helpful fact which we must all take into consideration. The size and strength of any German army, whether contingent or otherwise, and its manufacture of weapons, would in any case have to be agreed between the Allied Powers concerned. There, in short, is the policy which I have always advocated and which I am very glad to find is steadily going forward.

Difficulties have, however, arisen about the texture of the European Army. Should it be an amalgam of the European nations divested of all national characteristics and traditions, or should it be composed of elements essentially national but woven together by alliance, common organisation and unified command? On this point the discussions have at times assumed an almost metaphysical character, and the logic of continental minds has produced a scheme for what is called the European Defence Community. That is, at least, an enlightened if not an inspiring title.

The European Defence Force, which is to be a vital element in the defence of Western Europe, will be closely and effectively associated with the British Forces which constitute another element in the same defence system through their common allegiance to NATO.

The European Defence Community has not yet taken its final shape. The Paris Conference has been sitting for nine months, and it is now on the point of producing its Report. I am sorry the late Government did not send a delegation to this Conference instead of only an observer. The technical discussions have proceeded smoothly and in great detail, and at last the far-reaching political issues which have been raised and which surround the military questions have been reached. We do not know how these will be settled, and we have had no voice or share in the long argument. As soon as the Conference reaches its final conclusions we shall consider the way to establish the most effective form of association with the resultant organisations. In this way a European Army, containing a German contribution of agreed size and strength, will stand alongside the British and United States Armies in a common defensive front. That, after all, is what really matters to the life or death of the free world.

As far as Britain is concerned, we do not propose to merge in the European Army but we are already joined to it. Our troops are on the spot, and we all do our utmost to make a worthy and effective contribution to the deterrents against aggression and to the causes of freedom and democracy which we seek to serve. These matters will, of course, require to be further discussed as the weeks pass by, and we shall probably know much more about what is the decision taken on the Continent than we can attempt to anticipate and imagine at this moment.

DOCUMENT 5.6

Communiqué issued after the Six-Power Conference on a European Army, Paris, 30 December 1951

The six participant states were France, Western Germany, Italy, Belgium, Holland and Luxembourg. Negotiations on the establishment of a EDC had begun in February 1951.

The Foreign Ministers of the six countries represented at the conference for the organisation of a European Defence Community met in Paris from December 27 to 30 to pursue the discussion which began at Strasbourg on November 11. The Finance and Defence Ministers took part in these conversations. The problems reserved for the decision of the Ministers by the conference of experts have been examined and, particularly, the institutional, military, and financial questions. The Ministers agreed that the setting up of a European Defence Community constituted a step towards the unification of Europe, such unification remaining one of the essential objectives of their Governments.

In accordance with the suggestion made during their last meeting at Strasbourg by Signor De Gasperi, they decided to entrust to the Assembly envisaged in the European Defence Community the task of studying the creation of a European organisation of a federal or confederal character which would take the place, when the time came, of the organisation embodied in this treaty. For this purpose the Assembly of the European Defence Community will, within six months of the treaty coming into force, make proposals to the six Governments, which, three months later, will call an international conference to examine them.

In accordance with the proposal of Dr. Stikker, the Governments, on their side, as soon as the treaty has come into force, will take joint measures to facilitate the realisation of these aims. The Ministers have agreed that the institution of the European Defence Community would include an executive authority on a collegiate basis, an Assembly, a Council of Ministers, and a Court of Justice.

The conference agreed on the principle of a common budget for the Community but left over for further examination the details and method of the transformation of national budgets into a common defence budget.

Finally, agreement was reached on most of the problems concerning the integration and composition of the defence forces. Thus, the Ministers have noted that on the fundamental points referred to them by the experts an agreement was reached which will make possible the continuation of the work of the experts' conference.

Another meeting of the Ministers was decided. It will take place in January.

DOCUMENT 5.7

Article 38 from the Treaty establishing the European Defence Community, 27 May 1952

Following this article it was proposed that the ECSC Assembly be turned into an ad hoc *EDC Assembly to consider a more wide-ranging political integration. Early in 1953 it reported in favour of a European Political Community (EPC) which would go beyond the sector-by-sector approach to integration. This would be the beginning of a comprehensive political federation to which the ECSC and EDC would be subordinated. The EPC was abandoned with the collapse of the EDC.*

Article 38

1. Within the period laid down in the second paragraph of this Article, the Assembly shall study:

(a) the constitution of an Assembly of the European Defence Community, elected on a democratic basis;
(b) the powers which would devolve on such an Assembly;
(c) any changes which might have eventually to be made to the provisions of the present Treaty concerning the other institutions of the Community, particularly with a view to safeguarding an appropriate representation of States.

The Assembly will be particularly guided in its study by the following principles:
The final organisation which will replace the present provisional organisation should be so conceived as to be able to constitute one of the elements in a subsequent federal or confederal structure, based on the principle of the separation of powers and having, in particular, a two-chamber system of representation.
The Assembly shall also examine problems arising from the co-existence of different agencies for European co-operation already established or which might be established, with a view to ensuring co-ordination within the framework of the federal or confederal structure.

2. The proposals of the Assembly shall be submitted to the Council within six months from the assumption of duties by the Assembly. On the advice of the Council, these proposals will thereafter be transmitted by the Chairman of the Assembly to the Governments of the Member States who will, within three months from the date on which the matter has been brought to their notice, convene a conference to consider the proposals.

DOCUMENT 5.8

Extract from Konrad Adenauer's 'Memoirs 1945–53', 1966

Adenauer was the first Chancellor of the German Federal Republic. He regarded integration with the West as essential for his country's security, prosperity and political rehabilitation. In 1952 he had rejected Stalin's suggestion of a neutral reunited Germany.

In my opinion the European nation states had a past but no future. This applied in the political and economic as well as in the social sphere. No single European country could guarantee a secure future to its people by its own strength. I regarded the Schuman Plan and the European Defence Community as preliminary steps to a political unification of Europe. In the EDC Treaty there was a specific provision for a controlling body, the so-called Parliamentary Assembly – incidentally the same assembly that exercised the parliamentary controlling function in the Coal and Steel Community – to examine the questions arising from the parallelism of diverse existing or future organisations for European cooperation, with a view to securing their coordination in the framework of a federal or confederate structure.

The military aspect was only one dimension of a nascent Europe, or, more rightly at first, Western Europe. If a perfect partnership was to be achieved within Western Europe, one could not stop with defence. . .

After twelve years of National Socialism there simply were no perfect solutions for Germany and certainly none for a divided Germany. There was very often only the policy of the lesser evil.

We were a small and very exposed country. By our own strength we could achieve nothing. We must not be a no-man's-land between East and West for then we would have friends nowhere and a dangerous neighbour in the East. Any refusal by the Federal Republic to make common cause with Europe would have been German isolationism, a dangerous escape into inactivity. There was a cherished political illusion in the Federal Republic in those years: many people believed that America was in any case tied to Europe or even to the Elbe. American patience, however, had its limits. My motto was 'Help yourself and the United States will help you'. . .

There were those in Germany who thought that for us the choice was either a policy for Europe or a policy for German unity. I considered this 'either/or' a fatal error. Nobody could explain how German unity in freedom was to be achieved without a strong and united Europe. When I say 'in freedom' I mean freedom before, during and above all after all-German elections. No policy is made with wishes alone and even less from weakness. Only when the West was strong might there be a genuine point of departure for peace negotiations to free not only the Soviet zone but all of enslaved Europe east of the iron curtain, and free it peacefully. To take the road that led into the European Community appeared to me the best service we could render the Germans in the Soviet zone. . .

DOCUMENT 5.9

Extracts from the debate in the French National Assembly on 29–30 August 1954

The EDC plan was voted down by 319 to 264 votes.

M. Mendès-France (Prime Minister):

'I wish to speak of the situation that will arise if you accept or if you reject the Treaty. If you ratify the Treaty, the proposals made by our five colleagues at Brussels will be maintained . . . The most important advantage, in my opinion, is that the EDC links the German Federal Republic politically to the Western World . . . The entry of the Treaty into force will mark an important step on the road to Franco–German reconciliation, which is one of the conditions of peace. . . Should you decide to refuse ratification, the problem of Western Europe, and of Germany and her rearmament will still arise in one form or another and will again come before you. . .

'Our British and American Allies have already made it known that, in the event of the French Parliament rejecting the Treaty, they would be ready to take important international decisions – notably to restore full sovereignty to the Federal Republic. That country (Western Germany) would receive all the attributes of sovereignty except in the military field. The decision of our allies seems to me inevitable, whether the Treaty is ratified or not . . . If we do not ratify the Treaty our allies will not renounce their attempt to obtain a German contribution to Western defence. That means that we would soon be faced with proposals for the rearming of Germany, on which you would be called upon to pronounce. . .

'We have been speaking about tomorrow and we must look facts in the face. What is the basis on which the Government's foreign policy rests? It is the Atlantic Alliance. To avoid any misunderstanding, I solemnly affirm that my Government will accept no measure, proposal or suggestion contrary to that alliance. Voices have been heard in our country which speak of the isolation of France, of the reversal of alliances, of French neutralism, of German neutralisation. The Government's views have not changed; our foreign policy remains one of faithfulness to the alliance which gives us our security, an alliance based on the friendly cooperation of associates enjoying equal rights, debating their common problems, and remaining judge of their own vital interests.

'As regards our relations with Great Britain it is an axiom of French policy that nothing should ever separate us. Whether or not we are members of the same grouping, our two peoples are united by an alliance which does not need to be defined in writing because it is vital. There remains the last problem – Germany's place in Europe. Our constant aim is to bring about a definite reconciliation between the two countries within a European framework . . . and I have already indicated our intention of giving back to Germany her full sovereignty in agreement with our allies.'

General Aumeran (Independent Republican):

'Ratification [of the EDC Treaty] will put us in the same ranks as two vanquished peoples and three small nations (the other members of the Six) . . . We should have no illusions about the fact that Germany has been chosen as the pivot of European defence. As the Atlantic Pact can be revised in 1959, a good opportunity will arise to substitute Germany for France, who in the meantime would have been deprived of her army and perhaps of her empire . . . The EDC with its forty divisions will never frighten the Soviet Union. What is frightening is the prospect of a sovereign Germany entering this organisation, a Germany admitted to atomic secrets and bent on revenge . . . A catastrophe would rapidly result. It is the task of France to create a climate of peace and prevent the rearming of Germany . . . The rejection of the Treaty will not only permit the reconciliation of Frenchmen, but will bring about conditions in which we can seek a defensive system that will take into account the great changes that have come about in recent years.'

M. Herriot (Radical, Président d'Honneur of the Assembly):
'I say with my fullest conviction that no international negotiations aimed at securing liberty and peace can be carried out without the mutual support of France and Britain . . . I have read the [EDC] texts with anguish. There is nothing in them to show that Britain would be at our side to resist the strength and any eventual manoeuvres of Germany. Britain must be at the side of France in this matter to act with equal responsibility in the face of a new German threat, should it arise. The absence of solidarity between Britain and France is, in itself, sufficient to make me reject EDC.

'But we have other reasons for opposing the Treaty, the chief of which is the loss of our country's sovereignty and independence. The EDC Treaty aims at restoring Germany's sovereignty but represents a backward step for France with regard to her sovereignty. . .

'I say that the EDC means the end of France . . . I shall be told: "If you do not believe in the EDC you do not believe in Europe". I protest against such a conclusion . . . We do not want a solution through rearmament . . . We want a solution for Europe as a whole, for United Europe, not for the "Europe of the Five or Six". We want peace for its own sake, not the rearmament of certain countries. I do not want the EDC – I want a *rapprochement* with Germany and with all the countries of Europe based on other principles.'

DOCUMENT 5.10

Statement by the US Secretary of State, John Foster Dulles, to the press on 31 August 1954

This reflects the anger and disappointment of the US Administration at the failure of the French National Assembly to ratify the EDC.

The French rejection of the European Defense Community is a saddening event. France thus turns away from her own historic proposal made nearly four years ago. That proposal sought a unification of the military strength of continental Europe into a single European Army so as to end the era of recurrent European wars, the last two of which became world wars.

The French action does not change certain basic and stubborn facts:

(a)   The effective defense of continental Europe calls for a substantial military contribution from the Germans; yet all, including the Germans themselves, would avoid national rearmament in a form which could be misused by resurgent militarism.

(b)   Germany cannot be subjected indefinitely to neutrality or otherwise be discriminated against in terms of her sovereignty, including the inherent right of individual and collective self-defense. Limitations on German sovereignty to be permanently acceptable must be shared by others as part of a collective international order.

(c)   The prevention of war between neighbouring nations which have a long record of fighting cannot be dependably achieved merely by national promises or threats but only by merging certain functions of their government into supranational institutions.

To deal with these facts was the lofty purpose of EDC. Four of the six prospective members of EDC had ratified that treaty – Belgium, Germany, Luxembourg, and the Netherlands. A fifth, Italy, was on the point of ratifying it. The United Kingdom and the United States had made far-reaching commitments of association with EDC. France thus disassociates herself not only from her own proposal but from her prospective partners who had stood united at the recent Brussels conference.

The US postwar policies beginning in 1946 were framed on the assumption that Western Europe would at long last develop a unity which would make it immune from war between its members and defensible against aggression from without. The imperative need for the unity was recognised by the leading statesmen of all the free nations of Europe. The United States joined the North Atlantic Treaty defensive alliance with the Western European countries. We assisted these countries to recover from the weakening of World War II. Both on the economic and military side we made massive contributions. We stationed the equivalent of six divisions in Europe. We furthermore made our leading military figures available to assume high positions in the military organisation designed to defend Western Europe.

The French negative action, without the provision of any alternative, obviously imposes on the United States the obligation to reappraise its foreign policies, particularly those in relation to Europe. The need for such a review can scarcely be questioned since the North Atlantic Council of Ministers has itself twice declared with unanimity that the EDC was of paramount importance to the European defense it planned. Furthermore, such review is required by conditions which the Congress attached this year and last year to authorisations for military contributions to Europe.

The Western nations now owe it to the Federal Republic of Germany to do quickly all that lies in their power to restore sovereignty to that Republic and to enable it to contribute to international peace and security. The existing treaty to restore sovereignty is by its terms contingent upon the coming into force of EDC. It would be unconscionable if the failure to realise EDC, through no fault of Germany's, should now be used as an excuse for penalising Germany. The Federal German Republic should take its place as a free and equal member of the society of nations. That was the purport of the resolution which the US Senate adopted unanimously last July, and the United States will act accordingly.

The United States stands ready to support the many in Western Europe who despite their valiant efforts are left in grave anxiety. We need not feel that the European idea is dead merely because, in one of the six countries, a present majority seems against one of its manifestations. There is still much on which to build, and those foundations should not be shaken by any abrupt or any ill-considered action of our own.

It is a tragedy that in one country nationalism, abetted by communism, has asserted itself so as to endanger the whole of Europe.

Suggested reading

A comprehensive account is E. Fursdon, *The European Defence Community* (London, 1980). There are useful chapters in F.R. Willis, *France, Germany and the New Europe* (London, 1968). Chapters 9 and 10 in P.M.R. Stirk and D. Willis (eds), *Shaping Postwar Europe* (London, 1991) consider the British and Italian views of the EDC. E. van der Beugel, *From Marshall Aid to Atlantic Partnership* (Amsterdam, 1966) traces the evolution of US policy towards European integration. For the British role there are also J.W. Young, *Foreign Policy of Churchill's Peacetime Administration 1951–55* (Leicester, 1988) and S. Dockrill, *Britain's Policy for West German Rearmament 1950–55* (Cambridge, 1991). For context, see J. Baylis, *Anglo–American Defence Relations 1939–84* (London, 1984); A. Grosser, *The Western Alliance* (London, 1980); and O. Riste (ed.), *Western Security: The Formative Years, European and Atlantic Defence 1947–53* (Oslo, 1985). For the subsequent evolution of the idea of a European defence identity see T. Taylor, *European Defence Cooperation* (London, 1982) and A. Cahen, *The Western European Union and NATO: Building a European Defence Identity in the Context of Atlantic Solidarity* (London, 1989).

6 From Messina to the Treaty of Rome

Introduction

The defeat of the EDC proposals by the French National Assembly came as a disappointment to many supporters of Western European integration, not least since it also involved the rejection of the ambitious draft statute for the European Political Community (EPC). Others, though, had been unhappy about the association of such integration, which they conceived as a guarantee of peace among the nations of Western Europe, with rearmament. While the protracted EDC debate had been in progress, it was hardly practicable to pursue other plans for integration. Now the question of German rearmament was resolved by NATO membership with guarantees, a block to further integration was removed.

What subsequently happened has often been presented as the great 'rélance', a revival of European initiative spurred by the challenge of earlier defeat. Seen from another perspective, the meeting at Messina (see Document 6.1) was a further stage in efforts towards integration that had never really stopped. The subsequent founding of the European Economic Community (EEC) and Euratom (for the peaceful uses of nuclear power) in 1957 was the result of detailed negotiations and the combination of and coincidence of different national interests, at the same time as the recognition of common interests. The hope of many of those involved, however, was that political unity would ultimately evolve out of economic integration.

The EDC had not been favoured by international circumstances. The French Army was tied up in Indochina. The Korean War was brought to an end and the new Soviet leaders seemed to hold out some prospect of *détente*. The need for German rearmament no longer appeared so pressing. The formulation of the Rome Treaties, though, was arguably aided by international circumstances.

The Soviet suppression of the Hungarian uprising in 1956 coincided with the Suez Crisis, in which the British and French were forced by international, particularly US pressure, to call off their invasion of Egypt before they had repossessed the Canal. These events were reminders of the vulnerability of Western Europe and of the decline of French and British power. Both France and Britain were forced to reappraise their role in the world. M. Guy Mollet, the French Prime Minister, humiliated by his involvement in Suez, was the more determined to push through the EEC and Euratom. Suez increased French distrust of the United States and of Britain who had led the retreat. The advantages of further cohesion with the other Five seemed very evident. At the same time, the question of the rich mining region of the Saar, which had been separated from Germany in 1946 at French insistence, and had been a very contentious issue in Franco–German relations, was resolved when the Saar was integrated with the Federal Republic on 1 January 1957. These facts help to explain why a France which rejected the EDC in 1954 was willing to sign the Treaties of Rome in 1957.

A committee was appointed at Messina under the chairmanship of Paul-Henri Spaak, the Belgian Foreign Minister. It went to work with great speed, meeting for long sessions at the Château de Val Duchesne outside Brussels. After eight months this committee produced the Spaak Report which led to the EEC and Euratom. 'The object of a European common market', it stated, 'should be to create a vast area with a common political economy which will form a powerful productive unit and permit a steady expansion, an increase in stability, a more rapid rise in the standard of living, and the development of harmonious relations between the member states'. This report was accepted by the Foreign Ministers of the Six in May 1956 and the committee were asked to draw up formal treaties. The Rome Treaties were signed on 27 March 1957 by the Six.

At the time the idea of Euratom was a very major preoccupation, particularly of Jean Monnet. He and his staff had worked out a plan for extending integration to atomic energy and placing it under the High Authority of the ECSC. There were widespread fears of the depletion of traditional sources of energy. It was hoped that Euratom would coordinate nuclear research and development and establish a common market for fissionable materials.

After resigning from the Presidency of the ECSC, Monnet had founded his own pressure group, the Action Committee for the United States of Europe. This body came into existence in October 1955, bringing together representatives of the Socialist, Christian Democratic and Liberal Parties and the non-Communist trade unions of the Six. To achieve their objective, it was necessary, the first annual memorandum of the movement stated, 'to put aside all specious solutions. Mere cooperation between governments will not suffice. It is indispensable for states to delegate certain of their powers to European federal institutions, mandated by all the participating countries taken as a whole'. (For the significance attached to Euratom see Documents 6.2 and 6.3.) In fact Euratom failed to develop as anticipated. In spite of substantial funding for research in the late 1950s and 1960s national nuclear policies predominated over cooperative joint efforts. To start with, though, it was regarded as very significant. One of the early associates of Monnet, Pierre Uri, even went so far as to describe the Common Market as 'a kind of by-product of Euratom'.

While the nuclear aspect was of particular interest to the French, the Germans and Benelux were mainly interested in the creation of a customs union. The Germans, too, were particularly concerned with trade liberalisation and the removal of all barriers to trade among the Six. Spaak, an astute and dynamic chairman and his committee brought these aims together. The European Economic Community came into existence on 1 January 1958, pledged to 'establish the foundation of an ever-closer union among the European peoples'. Its purpose was not simply to promote the economic self-interest of the participating states via an associa-tion, but to commit them to a community of interest. Under Article 237 it was possible for any other democratic European state to accede if it was ready to identify with all the Community goals, though any enlargement required a unanimous vote in favour by the Six. The Community was based on the belief in the benefits of free trade in a large market, which would encourage both prosperity and political stability.

The Treaty of Rome prescribed a customs union, the free movement of capital and labour, fair competition and common policies in transport. It also gave powers to the institutions to achieve balance in the development of the Community, to prohibit monopolies and assist the less well-off regions through a Social Fund and Investment Bank. In agriculture it called for 'reasonable prices' and a stable market in food. The economic benefits of an enlarged and unified market, it was hoped, would increase the standard of living in the countries of the Six and enable Western Europe to compete more effectively in world markets. The further consolidation of West Germany with the other Five would also reduce even more the possibility of her orien-tating herself towards Eastern Europe or adopting a neutral role.

The EEC created a 'new legal order' independent of the Member States whose acts, however, had direct legal effect in those states. The broad aims of the Treaty are listed in Article 2 (see Document 6.5). The Treaty also set down timetables for the reduction of external tariffs, for the removal of quotas internally and for the creation of the external common tariff. These objectives were to be achieved a year-and-a-half before schedule (see Docu-ment 8.1). Behind the arrangements on trade there was an implicit political agenda. With the customs union and, more far-reaching, the crea-tion of common policies or the progressive coordination of national policies, the Community would produce 'closer relations between the Member States'. The removal of barriers to trade in agricultural produce, a sector where all Member States had managed and protected markets was to become possible only with the formulation of the Common Agricultural Policy, something which was to present more difficulties than any other in the history of the Community (see Documents 7.9 and 9.6).

The main decision-making body was the Council of Ministers, drawn from the governments of the individual Member States. The European Commission, on the other hand was to represent the common European interest. This reflected the mixture of the intergovernmental and the supranational in the Community. On the one hand the Member States wanted to retain ultimate powers of decision and legislation. On the other, the Treaty, to be workable, had to be applied at the supranational level. Further progress towards integration was constrained by the Member States. On the other hand if the governments of the Six had the political will to advance further the Community would be able to do so. This explains the uncertain pace of future integration. The Assembly, later to be re-named the European Parliament, was not comparable, for instance, with the British Houses of Parliament. Its powers are described in the Treaty of Rome as being 'advisory and supervisory'. To begin with it was given the power only to debate the work of the Commission and to adopt, if there were very good reason, a motion of censure by a two-thirds majority which would force the Commissioners to resign. The Treaties also provided for the European Parliament to be consulted on certain categories of draft legislation. From the 1970s onwards, though, its role has increased. (See Appendix A for more detail on the Community Institutions.)

Document 6.6, an extract from the 'Seventeen Theses', offers an interesting example of the invective which the Soviet Union directed against the emerging Community. (For a defence of the Community against this sort of attack see Document 7.5.) The British position at this time is criticised by a recent member of the Conservative Government, Anthony Nutting, in Document 6.7.

Britain, using the OEEC, introduced the proposal for a European Free Trade Area. She significantly underestimated the interest of the Six in the construction of a customs union and believed that the negotiations after Messina would collapse just as the EDC had. She was aware that France was apprehensive about ending protectionism and she believed that an industrial free trade area which excluded agriculture, a very major concern of French governments, would, economically and politically, be a sufficiently attractive alternative.

The Germans had certain sympathy for continuing free trade negotiations and Ludwig Erhard, the Minister of Economic Affairs, was known to be apprehensive of Western Europe evolving into a protectionist bloc, and of too many 'dirigiste' controls in the Community. But Germany was to be persuaded by President de Gaulle, in return for strong support for the Federal Republic over Berlin, which was a focus of acute East–West tension in the years 1958–62, to suspend the free trade negotiations. Anthony Nutting's comments reflect the disappointment felt by those in the United Kingdom who considered she was missing a major opportunity, and by others in the Six who wanted her accession to the Community.

Following the collapse of their plans for a free trade area encompassing all of Western Europe, Britain narrowed its objectives. In November 1959 the European Free Trade Association was set up. It included Austria, Iceland, Denmark, Norway, Portugal, Sweden, and the United Kingdom, and had Finland as an associate member. Within two years Britain was to perform a volte-face and apply for membership of the Community (see Document 7.7).

Documents

DOCUMENT 6.1

Resolution adopted by the Foreign Ministers of the Member States of the European Coal and Steel Community at the Messina Conference, 1–2 June 1955

The Messina negotiations resulted from a Benelux proposal that the ECSC be extended to a general Common Market and a French proposal for a European atomic energy committee. This resolution incorporates both proposals.

The Governments of the Federal German Republic, Belgium, France, Italy, Luxembourg and the Netherlands believe that the time has come to make a fresh advance towards the building of Europe. They are of the opinion that this must be achieved, first of all, in the economic field.

They consider that it is necessary to work for the establishment of a united Europe by the development of common institutions, the progressive fusion of national economies, the creation of a common market and the progressive harmonisation of their social policies.

Such a policy seems to them indispensable if Europe is to maintain her position in the world, regain her influence and prestige and achieve a continuing increase in the standard of living of her population.

I

To these ends, the six Ministers have agreed on the following objectives:

A.

1. The expansion of trade and the freedom of movement call for the joint development of the major channels of communication.

    A joint study will accordingly be undertaken of development plans based on the establishment of a European network of canals, motor highways, electrified railways and on a standardisation of equipment, as well as a study of possible means of achieving a better co-ordination of air transport.

2. A fundamental condition of economic progress is that the European economies should have at their disposal cheaper and more plentiful supplies of power.

   For this reason, all possible steps will have to be taken to develop exchanges of gas and electricity as necessary to increase the profitability of investment and to reduce the cost of supplies.

   Study will be given to methods for co-ordinating a joint approach to questions affecting the future production and consumption of power, and for drawing up the general lines of an overall policy.

3. The development of atomic energy for peaceful purposes will in the near future open up the prospect of a new industrial revolution out of all proportion to that which has taken place over the last hundred years. The six signatory States consider that it is necessary to study the creation of a common organisation to be entrusted with the responsibility and the means for ensuring the peaceful development of atomic energy, while taking into account the special arrangements made by certain Governments with third countries.

   These means should comprise:

   (a) The establishment of a common fund derived from contributions from each of the participating countries, from which provision could be made for financing the installations and research work already in progress or planned.

   (b) Free and sufficient access to the raw materials, and the free exchange of expertise and technicians, by-products and specialised equipment.

   (c) The pooling of the results obtained and the grant of financial assistance for their exploitation.

   (d) Co-operation with non-member countries.

B.

The six Governments recognise that the establishment of a European market, free from all customs duties and all quantitative restrictions, is the objective of their action in the field of economic policy. They consider that this market must be achieved by stages and that its entry into force requires a study of the following questions:

(a) The appropriate procedure and pace for the progressive suppression of the obstacles to trade in the relations between the participating countries, as well as the appropriate measures for moving towards a progressive unification of their tariffs against third countries.

(b) The measures to be taken for harmonising the general policy of the participating countries in the financial, economic and social fields.

(c) The adoption of methods designed to make possible an adequate coordination of the monetary policies of the member countries so as to permit the creation and development of a common market.

(d) A system of escape clauses.

(e) The creation and operation of a readaptation fund.

(f) The gradual introduction of the free movement of manpower.

(g) The elaboration of rules which would ensure the play of competition within the common market so as to exclude, in particular, all discrimination on a national basis.

(h) The institutional arrangements appropriate for introducing and operating the common market.

C.

The creation of a European Investment Fund will be studied. The object of this fund would be the joint development of European economic potentialities and in particular the development of the less developed regions of the participating states.

D.

As regards the social field, the six Governments consider it essential to study the progressive harmonisation of the regulations in force in the different countries, notably those which concern working hours, overtime rates (night work, Sunday work and public holidays) and the length and rates of pay for holidays.

The six Governments have decided to adopt the following procedure:

1. Conferences will be called to work out treaties or other arrangements concerning the questions under consideration.

2. The preparatory work will be the responsibility of a Committee of Governmental representatives, assisted by experts, under the chairmanship of a political personality responsible for co-ordinating the work in the different fields.

3. The Committee will invite the High Authority of the ECSC and the Secretariats of OEEC, the Council of Europe and the European Conference of Ministers of Transport, to give the necessary assistance.

4. The report of the Committee, covering the whole field, will be submitted to the Ministers of Foreign Affairs by not later than the 1 October 1955.

5. The Ministers for Foreign Affairs will meet before that date to take note of the interim reports prepared by the Committee and to give it the necessary directives.

6. The Government of the United Kingdom, as a power which is a member of WEU and is also associated with the ECSC, will be

invited to take part in this work.

7. The Ministers of Foreign Affairs will decide in due course whether
    other States should subsequently be invited to take part in the
    conference or conferences referred to in paragraph (1) above.

DOCUMENT 6.2

Resolution and Joint Declaration of the Action Committee for the United States of Europe, 18 January 1956

The Action Committee, founded by Jean Monnet in October 1955, issued the follow-
ing as their first major declaration. Note the emphasis on the extension of European
integration to atomic energy.

1. Our organisations, political parties and trade unions, joining together
    for the first time over and above the national issues that may divide
    them, are unanimous in the belief that the hopes of our peoples for
    improvements in living conditions, for justice, freedom, and peace will
    not be fulfilled if each nation tries to work alone. Our countries must
    pool their energies and resources. That is why we have taken the
    initiative in forming the Action Committee for the United States in
    Europe.

    The Committee stresses that it remains open to all similar organisa-
    tions in other European countries which declare themselves to be in
    agreement with the avowed principles and the objectives pursued by
    it. It refuses to consider as final the present situation in which the
    organisations of only six European countries have been able to give
    their agreement, and unanimously renews its hope of seeing other
    European countries taking without reservations the place that is theirs
    in the building of Europe, or at the very least associating themselves
    closely in that effort.

2. The action of the Committee and of the participating organisations will
    consist first of all in making clear to Governments, Parliaments, and
    public opinion that the Committee and its constituent organisations are
    determined that the Resolution agreed on at Messina on 2 June last
    by the Foreign Ministers of Belgium, France, Germany, Italy, Luxem-
    bourg, and the Netherlands, becomes a real step towards the United
    States of Europe.

Just as the six Foreign Ministers declared in their Resolution at Messina

on 1–2 June 1955, so too do our organisations believe that the establishment of a united Europe must be pursued by the development of common
institutions, the progressive merger of national economies, the creation of
a common market, and the progressive harmonisation of social policies.

In Brussels, experts of the 'Intergovernmental Committee created by the
Messina Conference' have studied the technical problems posed by that
Resolution. They have submitted their reports. In the near future the
Governments will have to make the necessary decisions to translate the
experts' conclusions into actual achievements.

Among these achievements that our Committee wants to be realised, the
one that could and should be most rapidly carried out concerns atomic
energy.

3.   The development of atomic energy for peaceful uses opens the prospect
     of a new industrial revolution and the possibility of a profound change
     in living and working conditions.

Together, our countries are capable of themselves developing a nuclear
industry. They form the only region in the world that can attain the same
level as the great world Powers. Yet separately they will not be able to
overcome their time-lag which is a consequence of European disunity.

Action is urgently needed if Europe is not to let her opportunity pass by.

An atomic industry producing atomic energy will inevitably be able to
produce bombs. For that reason the political aspects and the economic
aspects of atomic energy are inseparable. The European Community must
develop atomic energy exclusively for peaceful purposes. This choice
requires a water-tight system of control. It opens the way to general control
on a world-wide scale. It in no way affects the implementation of international agreements already in force.

Mere cooperation among Governments will not suffice to achieve these
objectives. It is indispensable that our States delegate the necessary powers
and give the necessary common mandate to European institutions.

4.   In order that the necessary measures may be taken rapidly, we have
     agreed to submit the attached declaration for Parliamentary approval
     in Belgium, France, Germany, Italy, Luxembourg, and the
     Netherlands, and to invite our Governments to conclude without delay
     a Treaty conforming to the rules set forth therein.

5.   Lastly, the Committee has decided to meet again on 5 April 1956 to
     examine the following points:
     Parliamentary approval of the attached joint declaration concerning
     atomic energy;
     decisions to be taken on the necessary measures for supporting the
     actions of the Governments for implementation of the Messina

Resolution, particularly as regards the progressive establishment of the Common Market.

Joint declaration to be submitted for Parliamentary approval in Belgium, France, Germany, Italy, Luxembourg, and the Netherlands, adopted unanimously on 18 January 1956.

1. In order to bring about an exclusively peaceful development of atomic energy, as well as to ensure the security of workers and populations and to improve the standard of living of the populations;
    In order to facilitate the work and progress of the industries concerned:

    by ensuring a sufficient supply of nuclear fuels;
    by financial and technical assistance;
    by the creation of essential common services and establishments;
    by the creation of a common market for special materials and equipment defined by the Commission; and
    by the pooling of knowledge;

    it is indispensable that our countries jointly delegate to a European Commission for Atomic Energy the necessary powers and the necessary common mandate.

2. In order to guarantee the exclusively peaceful character of nuclear activities as well as to guarantee the security of labour forces and populations, the Commission should establish a system of control. It is indispensable:

    (a) On the one hand, that exclusively for that purpose, all nuclear fuels produced in, or imported into, the territories coming under the jurisdiction of our countries be acquired by the European Commission for Atomic Energy. This rule shall not affect the carrying out of international agreements already in force. The Commission must retain exclusive ownership of nuclear fuels throughout their processing. The Commission will place such fuels at the disposal of users equitably and without discrimination, in periods of normal supply as well as in time of shortage.

    (b) On the other hand, that the construction and operation of nuclear installations be subject to prior authorisation by the Commission, to be issued when the conditions are fulfilled allowing the Commission to follow the processing and use of such fuels and to maintain the security of workers and populations.

    Security rules to be observed in the transportation and handling of nuclear materials, the construction and operation of installations, and the disposal of waste should be laid down by the Commission in cooperation with international organisations, particularly the UN. The Commission will ensure the application of these rules.

3. Parliamentary control over the Commission should be exercised by the Common Assembly and juridical control by the Court of Justice of the ECSC.

The number of members of the Common Assembly should be increased in view of its new tasks.

The Special Council of Ministers should harmonise the activities of the Commission with those of the national Governments responsible for the general economic policy of their countries.

A Consultative Committee composed of workers, employers, and consumers should be attached to the Commission.

4. Every opportunity for participation in the Community must be open to European countries other than our own.

(a) These European countries must be able to participate fully if they accept the above rules. The more numerous the participating countries, the more profitable the common effort will be to each.

(b) In particular, everything must be done to obtain the full participation of Great Britain. If Great Britain does not accept full participation, the necessary measures should in any case be taken to ensure her close association.

(c) Finally, possibilities should be open to European non-member countries for using the common services and establishments, or for participating in their setting-up, in accordance with special agreements to be concluded later.

The Commission alone should be empowered to negotiate and conclude all agreements with third countries necessary for the accomplishment of its mission, particularly in matters concerning the supply of nuclear materials.

The rights and obligations of the participating countries resulting from agreements in force relative to the peaceful uses of atomic energy should be transferred to the Commission, subject to the consent of the third countries with which these agreements have been concluded.

DOCUMENT 6.3

A telegram from the US Ambassador in France (Dillon) to the US Department of State, 19 November 1956

The following casts an interesting light on the United States' response to Jean

Monnet's enthusiasm for Euratom. At this time US relations with Britain and France were severely strained as a consequence of the Franco–British–Israeli invasion of Egypt after Nasser's nationalisation of the Suez Canal.

I had long and interesting conversation Saturday with Monnet. Theme of his thought was that unusual opportunity has been created for US to reap large dividends of good will from close and generous association with EURATOM. He believes that EURATOM treaty will probably be successfully completed and signed by end of year.

Monnet feels that Middle East events, i.e., closing of Suez Canal and sabotage of pipelines, have amply demonstrated unhealthy dependence of European economy on Middle East oil and necessity for development of alternate source of energy. The only substantial alternative seems to him to be atomic energy, and he feels time is ripe for very far-reaching development of atomic power in Europe, which, because of higher cost of fuel here, could develop much more rapidly than will be the case in continental US.

Monnet feels that public opinion throughout Europe would be captured by a broad scale and generous program of US support for EURATOM, both in the supply of materials and in technical cooperation. This would breathe substantial new life into President's program 'Atoms for Peace', which so far has been considered primarily as fine theory and as propaganda effort and so has failed to make any very solid impression on European public opinion.

Monnet recognises that Middle East crisis has caused strain on Atlantic solidarity and does not feel that this can be very satisfactorily patched up, except by diverting the attention of public opinion to some other field. He feels that concrete US support of EURATOM would capture European imagination in the same way as the Marshall Plan, and could not be objected to by the Arab states. He feels that such support by the US should meet the US objective of finding some way to tighten our relationships with Europe without at the same time doing damage to our position in the Middle East.

Monnet feels that to obtain maximum of good will for US, it is of great importance that US accept principle that control by EURATOM organisation will be adequate for US purposes, thus avoiding necessity for US inspectors in Europe. He realises that no firm decision by US can be taken prior to finalisation of EURATOM treaty, but emphasised importance of this aspect of matter both as means of gaining good will for US and as important element in promoting rapid ratification of treaty.

Monnet recognises that what he has in mind will probably require amendments to US legislation and will require relatively prompt and very high level support in the US Government if it is to be successful.

I think Monnet's idea is of real importance and I agree with his views. The US has always favored EURATOM as a means of strengthening European unity. Now, however, I think Monnet is right in feeling that EURATOM presents us with a remarkable new opportunity of improving America's position with European public opinion. I would recommend that Monnet's concept be given high level consideration in order that we can be prepared to give prompt and practical support to EURATOM as soon as it comes into being.

DOCUMENT 6.4

Resumé of debate in the French National Assembly on the ratification of the Rome Treaties for the EEC and Euratom, 2–9 July 1957

In contrast to the EDC, these treaties were passed by the Assembly, by 342 to 239 votes.

M. Pineau (Foreign Minister) refuted the argument that the creation of a 'Little Europe' would impede the creation of a 'Big Europe'. He declared that the interest of other countries (and more especially Great Britain) in Europe would be all the greater once 'solid and dynamic' European organisations were in existence. On the question of the participation of overseas territories in the Common Market M. Pineau maintained that the treaty, in fact, dealt more favourably with the 'territoires d'outre mer' than with metropolitan France, for the following reasons: a) the territories would receive an ever-increasing flow of cheaply-priced goods; b) they would have big new markets for their own products; c) they would be entitled to set up customs barriers to protect their own industries; d) the Community countries would provide them with funds for investment.

Turning to the situation which would arise if Germany were reunified, M. Pineau said that if a reunified Germany decided to withdraw from the European Communities, that, in the French Government's opinion, would entail their dissolution. On the other hand, if a reunified Germany were to take the Federal Republic's place as a Community member, any of the other member-countries would be entitled to withdraw on that account. However, it was impossible to say exactly what would happen in the event of German reunification, since no one knew what the terms of a reunification agreement would be, or, more specifically, whether a reunified Germany would assume the existing commitments of the Federal-Republic.

M. Mendès-France (formerly Prime Minister) attacked the Treaties on several grounds. He asserted, first, that the main beneficiary of the Common Market would be the Rhineland and that it would be the fate of

French underdeveloped regions, such as Brittany, to provide labour for Germany. Secondly . . . there were really seven members in the two communities, the seventh being East Germany, which would enjoy all the benefits of the system but would be under no obligation towards it. Moreover, the products of the Eastern European and Scandinavian countries would have unimpeded entry to the Common Market zone across the customs-free German zonal boundary. Thirdly, as regards the overseas territories, he criticised the fact that while France's five partners were committed for no more than five years to assist financially in their development, the overseas territories themselves would be open indefinitely to the products of other member-countries.

[He] . . . went on to declare that while European economic integration was greatly to be desired, France was not really ready to embark upon such an experiment at that particular moment. It was very doubtful whether the French economy would be out of difficulties within 18 months when the first tariff reductions were due to be made. Moreover, the Algerian campaign, with its attendant effects on the national economy, was likely to continue for another two or three years. . .

M. Maurice Faure (Secretary of State for Foreign Affairs and chief representative for France on the Inter-governmental Committee which worked out the two treaties) had previously emphasised that, far from impeding the recovery of the French economy, the Common Market would actually help to bring it about. Replying to those critics who had expressed concern lest France would be compelled to implement decisions of the Council of Ministers of the Community in the event of a balance-of-payments crisis, M. Faure declared that these decisions would certainly not be in the form of a 'Diktat' but would be the result of free deliberations. He asked in this connection what interest the five other member countries could have in ruining the sixth at the price of being unable to sell their own goods to it any longer.

Replying to critics who had expressed concern about the situation of French farmers, M. Faure declared that France 'with the richest and most varied land in the Community' would now get the 'industrial masses of the North of Europe' as buyers without any barriers or limitations – an opportunity which she should seize by conducting an 'active, and at the same time, reasonable agricultural policy, charging fair prices'. French farm production would be protected against non-Community countries by the common customs tariff, while, as regard cereals, farmers would be protected by the system of long-term contracts between member-countries.

M. Bourgès-Manoury (Prime Minister), speaking on the last day of the debate, emphasised that if France refused to ratify the treaties she would run the risk of 'political and economic isolation'. Moreover, the other five countries might go ahead to create the Community without French participation, in which case France would be without the guarantees now accorded to her. Referring particularly to French relations with Western Germany [he], declared 'Our wish has been always to set up a democratic and stable framework firm enough to guide the expansion of German industrial power in the direction of the common interests of the European countries, and sufficiently flexible to guarantee respect for our own fundamental interests. . . Those who fear the weight of Germany at our side should think about the weight of a Germany not linked with us, or even ranged against us.' In conclusion he emphasised that the Government would neglect no effort to bring about a wider trade association including, above all, Great Britain.

M. Robert Schuman (MRP), *M. Paul Reynaud* (Independent) and *M. René Pleven* – all former Prime Ministers and protagonists of European unification warmly supported the ratification. M. Duclos for the Communist denounced the treaties as 'an economic–military enterprise of a syndicate of capitalist exploiters serving German imperialism'.

DOCUMENT 6.5

The Treaty of Rome establishing the European Economic Community, 25 March 1957

The following are only a selection of the 248 articles which make up the Treaty. For the Treaty in full see references in bibliography.

Article 1
By the present Treaty, the High Contracting Parties (Belgium, West Germany, France, Italy, Luxembourg and The Netherlands) establish among themselves a EUROPEAN ECONOMIC COMMUNITY.

Article 2
It shall be the aim of the Community, by establishing a Common Market and progressively approximating the economic policies of Member States, to promote throughout the Community a harmonious development of economic activities, a continuous and balanced expansion, an increased stability, an accelerated raising of the standard of living and closer relations between its Member States.

Article 3
For the purposes set out in the preceding Article, the activities of the Community shall include, under the conditions and with the timing provided for in this Treaty:

(a) the elimination, as between Member States, of customs duties and of quantitative restrictions in regard to the importation and exportation of goods, as well as of all other measures with equivalent effect;

(b) the establishment of a common customs tariff and a common commercial policy towards third countries;

(c) the abolition, as between Member States, of the obstacles to the free movement of persons, services and capital;

(d) the inauguration of a common agricultural policy;

(e) the inauguration of a common transport policy;

(f) the establishment of a system ensuring that competition shall not be distorted in the Common Market;

(g) the application of procedures which shall make it possible to co-ordinate the economic policies of Member States and to remedy disequilibrium in their balances of payments;

(h) the approximation of their respective municipal law to the extent necessary for the functioning of the Common Market;

(i) the creation of a European Social Fund in order to improve the possibilities of employment for workers and to contribute to the raising of their standard of living;

(j) the establishment of European Investment Bank intended to facilitate the economic expansion of the Community through the creation of new resources; and

(k) the association of overseas countries and territories with the Community with a view to increasing trade and to pursuing jointly their effort towards economic and social development.

Article 4

1. The achievement of the tasks entrusted to the Community shall be ensured by: An Assembly, a Council, a Commission, a Court of Justice.

Each of these institutions shall act within the limits of the powers conferred upon it by this Treaty. . .

Article 6

1. Member States, acting in close collaboration with the institutions of the Community, shall co-ordinate their respective economic policies to the extent that is necessary to attain the objective of this Treaty.

2. The institutions of the Community shall take care not to prejudice the internal and external financial stability of Member States.

Article 8

1. The Common Market shall be progressively established in the course of a transitional period of twelve years.

The transitional period shall be divided into three stages of four years each; the length of each stage may be modified in accordance with the provisions set out below.

2. To each stage there shall be allotted a group of actions which shall be undertaken and pursued concurrently.

3. Transition from the first to the second stage shall be conditional upon a confirmatory statement to the effect that the essence of the objectives specifically laid down in this Treaty for the first stage has been in fact achieved and that, subject to the exception and procedures provided for in this Treaty, the obligations have been observed.

This statement shall be made at the end of the fourth year by the Council acting by means of a unanimous vote on a report of the Commission. The invocation by a Member State of the non-fulfilment of its own obligations shall not, however, be an obstacle to a unanimous vote. Failing a unanimous vote, the first stage shall automatically be extended for a period of one year.

At the end of the fifth year, the Council shall make such confirmatory statement under the same conditions. Failing a unanimous vote, the first stage shall automatically be extended for a further period of one year.

At the end of the sixth year, the Council shall make such a statement acting by means of a qualified majority vote on a report of the Commission. . .

Article 9

1. The Community shall be based upon a customs union covering the exchange of all goods and comprising both the prohibition, as between Member States, of customs duties on importation and exportation and all charges with equivalent effect and the adoption of a common customs tariff in their relations with third countries. . .

Article 12

Member States shall refrain from introducing, as between themselves, any new customs duties on importation or exportation or charges with equivalent effect and from increasing such duties or charges as they apply in their commercial relations with each other.

Article 38

The Common Market shall extend to agriculture and trade in agricultural products. Agricultural products shall mean the products of the soil, of stock-breeding and of fisheries as well as products after the first processing stage which are directly connected with such products. . .

4. The functioning and development of the Common Market in respect of agricultural products shall be accompanied by the establishment of

a common agricultural policy among the Member States. . .

1. The common agricultural policy shall have as its objectives:
   (a) to increase agricultural productivity by developing technical progress and by ensuring the rational development of agricultural production and the optimum utilisation of the factors of production, particularly labour;
   (b) to ensure thereby a fair standard of living for the agricultural population, particularly by the increasing of the individual earnings of persons engaged in agriculture;
   (c) to stabilise markets;
   (d) to guarantee regular supplies; and
   (e) to ensure reasonable prices in supplies to consumers.

2. In working out the common agricultural policy and the special methods which it may involve, due account shall be taken of:
   (a) the particular character of agricultural activities, arising from the social structure of agriculture and from structural and natural disparities between the various agricultural regions;
   (b) the need to make the appropriate adjustments gradually; and
   (c) the fact that in Member States agriculture constitutes a sector which is closely linked with the economy as a whole.

Article 85

1. The following shall be deemed to be incompatible with the Common Market and shall hereby be prohibited: any agreement between enterprises, any decisions by associations of enterprises and any concerted practices which are likely to affect trade between the Member States and which have as their object or result the prevention, restriction or distortion of competition within the Common Market, in particular those consisting in:

   (a) the direct or indirect fixing of purchase or selling prices or of any other trading conditions;
   (b) the limitation or control of production, markets, technical development or investment;
   (c) market-sharing or the sharing of sources of supply;
   (d) the application to parties to transactions of unequal terms in respect of equivalent supplies, thereby placing them at a competitive disadvantage; or
   (e) the subjecting of the conclusion of a contract to the acceptance by a party of additional supplies which, either by their nature or according to commercial usage, have no connection with the subject of such contract.

2.   Any agreements or decisions prohibited pursuant to this Article shall
     be null and void. . .

DOCUMENT 6.6

**The 'Seventeen Theses' on the Common Market, issued by the
Institute of World Economics and International Relations, Moscow,
1957**

*The following is an example of the line of argument directed against Western European
integration by the Soviet Union, something which dated back to the 1920s. These
comments are a response to the signature of the Rome Treaties by the Six. For a
Community reply to such criticism see Document 7.5.*

1.   . . . The agreements on the Common Market, Euratom and Eurafrica
     have a history. They form the continuation of a whole series of initiatives
     designed to promote the so-called 'integration' of Europe. The Western
     powers have pursued this integration in various directions throughout
     the entire postwar period: economic, political, ideological and above all
     military. In the economic sphere they have had recourse, for this
     purpose, to measures like the creation of Benelux the OEEC and the
     European Payments Union, and the ECSC. To promote political and
     ideological integration they have summoned European conferences, set
     up various organisations for the unification of Europe, created a Council
     of Europe composed of a Consultative Assembly and a Council of
     Ministers. With a view to achieving military integration they conceived
     the Brussels Pact which has given birth to a Western union subsequently
     transformed into the Western European Union thanks to the participa-
     tion of the German Federal Republic. [Furthermore], various European
     states have signed the North Atlantic Pact and joined NATO. Thus,
     under cover of the 'unification' of Europe, the imperialist promoters of
     integration have divided Europe into economic, political and military
     groups opposed to one another; they have created an aggressive military
     bloc of Western European powers aimed against the Soviet Union and
     the popular democracies. All these measures have been taken mostly on
     the initiative, and in every case with the active support, of the ruling
     circles of the United States who are the leaders of the imperialist
     camp. . .

3.   Who inspired these agreements on the economic 'union of Europe?
     Which classes and social groups will benefit from the realisation of the
     plans for a Common Market, Euratom and Eurafrica? Behind the six

governments which signed the Treaties of Rome are the monopolies in each of these countries. These six countries form a group of developed capitalist states with a high degree of industrial concentration and of capital centralisation, and a powerful financial oligarchy at their disposal. The process of fusion of monopolies with the state characterises all these states. This explains why the agreements on the Common Market, Euratom and Eurafrica represent in reality an alliance of the most powerful monopolies, cartels, and trusts of the industry and banks in these six countries. In no sense have the Six been persuaded to sign these agreements to further the interests of the broad mass of people, whose opinion they did not even consult. . .

4. What causes lie behind the agreements on the Common Market, Euratom and Eurafrica and to what end have they been concluded? The formation of international unions of monopolies is one of the characteristic traits of imperialism. These unions have precise economic and political aims: the universal struggle for markets, for the sources of raw materials, for possibilities of capital investment; the partition of the world; the safeguarding of the common interests of the class of exploiters; the defence of capital which knows no country . . . Behind the project for a Common Market and the other measures already taken by the monopolists of the Six lies the desire to unite the forces of imperialism with a view on the one hand to doing battle against socialism and against the movements of national liberation of the colonised peoples and in the lands under their thumb, and on the other hand to consolidate the power of capitalism by resorting to international unions of a governmental and monopolistic kind. . .

5. The Common Market and Euratom have been created in order to reinforce the economic and military foundations and to extend the activities of the aggressive blocs of imperialist powers. . .

6. It goes without saying that the promoters and signatories of the Treaties of Rome, instructed by the unhappy experience of the failure of the EDC, have to pretend that these Treaties do not have a supranational character and that they contain nothing which could threaten the sovereign rights of any state. But the language of facts tells otherwise. The Treaties establishing the EEC and Euratom provide for the setting up of various controlling organs (Council of Ministers, Commission, Assembly, etc.). The transference to these institutions of certain important competences in the economic, political and military fields will result in the curtailment of the sovereignty of the weaker states; it will inevitably limit the rights of the Parliaments of these countries to make important social and national decisions . . .

In transferring, to the detriment of the legislative powers of Member States, certain competences to the supranational organs of the 'Little Europe' and in reinforcing the supranational executive power closely linked to the monopolies, the reactionary circles of the different West European states hope to enfeeble the opposition of the broad mass of people to this aggressive 'Atlantic policy' and to undermine the peoples' struggle for their national sovereignty and the independence of their domestic and foreign policies. . .

10. The Common Market and Euratom may also have the most baneful consequences for the political rights and democratic liberties of the working class. . .

11. The Treaty of Rome is also aimed against the interests of the peasantry. Although because of bitter disputes among the imperialists the question of agriculture still remains open, the Treaty of Rome establishes nevertheless a 'special arrangement' for agriculture. In any event the fundamental differences in the agricultural economies of the Six, the wish to lower the costs of production where they are relatively high, the attempts of large-scale capital to make use of the slogan 'agricultural common market' to proceed to a further concentration of agricultural production – all these are prejudicial to the peasantry and the farm workers and threaten to aggravate their situation. . .

13. The problem of the tariff wall with which the Six plan to surround their Common Market is causing disquiet in the ruling circles of non-member states. Many of them have come out against the Common Market, estimating rightly that this institution will have unfavourable effects on their exports to the Six countries of the 'Little Europe' and will create new obstacles to the development of international economic relations. This position has been adopted by various West European countries, in particular Switzerland, Austria, and the Scandinavian countries. . .

DOCUMENT 6.7

Extract from 'Europe Will Not Wait' by Anthony Nutting, 1960

The author was Conservative Minister of State for Foreign Affairs from 1954–56 when he resigned over the Suez expedition. This book was critical of both Labour and Conservative governments for their failure to take a lead in the integration process.

In June 1955, on Spaak's initiative, the Foreign Ministers of the Six foregathered at Messina in Sicily. Great Britain, alas, was absent –not because she had not been invited but because the British Government did not want to be there and did not really believe that the ambitious schemes that were to be considered would ever see the light of day. How, asked the wiseacres of Whitehall, could the French, with 300 years of protectionism behind them and the highest tariff walls in Western Europe, ever agree to a free market, especially one which would throw France open to German competition? Besides, the supranational concept had, surely, been buried by Mendès-France and there was no one of sufficient stature to revive it. As to economic co-operation, British officialdom could never see any need to go outside the existing machinery of the OEEC. Admittedly with some justice, but with a fatal lack of insight into the postwar European mood and mentality, British officials commented somewhat acidly at the time that, if Europe wanted freer trade, the remedy lay in simply obeying some of the liberalisation procedures of the OEEC, which the highly protectionist countries such as France and Italy, for all their sudden enthusiasm for a common market, had flouted consistently from the start.

In the light of this logical reasoning Great Britain declined to send a Minister to Messina and the six Foreign Ministers met once again to launch a European project without any British representative present. From their meeting two plans emerged, one for a European Economic Community, or Common Market, and the other for a European atomic energy pool, or as it is now called, Euratom.

In the words of the preamble to the final resolution of the Conference, 'The governments of the German Federal Republic, Belgium, France, Italy, Luxembourg and the Netherlands consider that the moment has arrived to initiate a new phase on the path of constructing European unity. They believe that this has to be done principally in the economic sphere and regard it as necessary to continue the creation of a United Europe through an expansion of joint institutions, the gradual fusion of national economies, the creation of a common market and the gradual co-ordination of social policies. Such a policy seems to them indispensable to preserve for Europe its place in the world, to restore its influence and to improve steadily the living standards of its peoples.'

Having reached agreement in principle on these two bold new projects – a Common Market and an Atomic Energy Pool – the Foreign Ministers decided to appoint a committee of experts from each of the six governments to work out detailed plans of action. The Committee, which took its name from its place of meeting – Brussels – was presided over by the principal initiator of the Messina plans, Paul-Henri Spaak.

At this stage of the proceedings Great Britain did vouchsafe to be represented by an observer. But, as if to emphasise our deliberate coolness towards the whole business, we selected for the task a relatively junior official and gave him a set of completely negative instructions. As Spaak told me a while later, nothing could have demonstrated more clearly the attitude of total British indifference to Europe than the series of negative interventions made by this luckless representative in the debates of the Brussels Committee.

Maybe we were technically correct in insisting that most, if not all, of what the Messina Conference set out to do could be done within the existing framework of the OEEC and without creating new institutions. But to Europeans such as Spaak and Adenauer, Schuman and René Mayer (who had just taken Jean Monnet's place as Head of the Coal and Steel Authority) the idea of a United Europe could never be achieved, or certainly could not be achieved fast enough, through the OEEC. Only a closer-knit organisation with real powers to function as a unit could do the trick.

If the thinking in London which blurred our understanding of this European attitude was unimaginative, its repercussions were certainly tragic. Twice before – over the Coal and Steel Pool and the European Army – Great Britain had been offered the chance to come in on the ground floor. Both times we had turned it down. The Brussels talks offered us the third – and it could be the last – opportunity of leading Europe and of negotiating our way into the European Community on mutually acceptable terms. Yet instead we insisted that such a community would be superfluous to requirements. Small wonder that our negation served finally and conclusively to convince Spaak and his disciples that Great Britain wanted no part in Europe and that the Six must go ahead without us.

Suggested reading

For a sound introduction to the institutions and workings of the Community see N. Nugent, *The Government and Politics of the European Community* (London, 1989) and J. Harrop, *The Political Economy of Integration in the European Community* (Aldershot, 1989). For the legal aspect, T.C. Hartley, *The Foundation of Community Law* (Oxford, 1988). Accounts of the Community by key figures involved in its creation and early days include: J. Monnet, *Memoirs* (London, 1978), W. Hallstein, *Europe in the Making* (London, 1972), P-H. Spaak, *The Continuing Battle: Memoirs of a European 1933–66* (London, 1971), R. Marjolin, *Memoirs 1911–86* (London, 1989). For the long historical perspective, S. Pollard, *European Economic Integration 1815–1970* (London, 1974). A good, if dated, historical account of the development of the Community, which lays particular emphasis on the Franco–German *rapprochement* there is F.R. Willis, *France, Germany and the New Europe 1945–67* (New York, 1968). An admirable recent introduction to the history of European integration after 1945 is D.W. Urwin, *The*

Community of Europe (London, 1991). R. Pryce (ed.), *The Dynamics of European Union* (London, 1987) contains excellent chapters on the development of the Community, giving particular attention to historical circumstance. For an incisive overview from a federalist angle see J. Pinder, *European Community: The Building of a Union* (Oxford, 1991). For the entire EEC Treaty, arranged to incorporate later amendments, see B. Rudden and D. Wyatt (eds), *Basic Community Laws* (2nd edn) (Oxford, 1986).

7 The Common Market of the Six

Introduction

The new French President, General de Gaulle, who had come to office in France through the Algerian War in 1958 had strongly attacked the EDC. Many thought that we would take France out of the recently instituted Economic Community. He was quick to see, though, the potential economic benefits to France in membership provided her agricultural interests were protected and he further saw an opportunity for French political leadership in Europe through the Community. Indeed, though it came to nothing, he put forward the Fouchet Plan in 1961, an intergovernmental variant of the EPC idea. It foundered due to conflicting views among the Six as to the methods and extent of integration and whether it should be enlarged. As Pierre Gerbet the French historian has put it, 'was it to be a "European Europe" or an "Atlantic Europe", a "Europe of the States" or a "Community Europe", a Europe of the Six or a Europe enlarged to take in Great Britain?'

De Gaulle was to make his concept of the Community quite explicit: 'There is and can be no Europe other than a Europe of the States – except, of course, for myths, fictions and pageants' (see also Document 7.11). He was to fight two major battles in the Community, first against the inclusion of Britain, which he vetoed in 1963 and, again in 1967; and secondly against those who supported the strengthening of the institutional powers of the Commission and European Parliament. Central to his European strategy was the maintenance of a strong understanding with the Federal Republic. While Adenauer was in power this held.

The first step on the freeing of trade was taken on 1 January 1959 and on 12 May 1960 the decision was taken to speed up the application of the Treaty of Rome. By 1 July 1962 customs duties among the Six had been reduced by half and trade in industrial products between the Community States was to double in four years. The average growth rate among the economies of the Six in the 1960s reached nearly 6 per cent per annum. At the same time the foundations of the Common Agricultural Policy (CAP) were agreed after thorny negotiations, and the first regulations were adopted in January 1962. By the 1980s the CAP was taking up nearly 70 per cent of the EC budget. It had, as Peter Calvocoressi puts it, 'converted under-production into sufficiency and then, almost ruinously, into over-production'. For the question of agricultural reform see Document 7.9.

The EEC also began to play a role on the international stage. The establishment of a common external tariff confirmed the unity of the Community and enabled it to negotiate as a single voice in GATT for tariff reductions with the other industrialised countries. In 1967 the Treaty provisions entered into force establishing a single Council and a single Commission to administer the EEC, the ECSC and Euratom. The Community was set to become a very important force in the global economy, an economic giant. But this did not, at this stage, extend to foreign or defence policy. She was not a political giant.

The negotiations after the Messina Conference had concentrated on the economic sphere. Whereas the ECSC Treaty had explicitly laid down a federal aim, the Rome Treaties went no further than expressing the will to establish 'an ever closer union'. The authors of the Treaties of Rome were very clearly hoping that the establishment of the customs union would encourage political cooperation or even integration. The formation of the Community was to provoke numerous theoretical analyses of the process of regional integration (see Documents 7.1 and 7.2). The so-called 'functionalists' predicted a 'spill-over effect' of Community action from the economic into the political sphere. Federalists like Altiero Spinelli did not accept such an automatic transition and argued for the election of a European constituent assembly. Jean Monnet held there should be no headlong rush forward, saying 'political Europe will be created by men, when the moment comes, based on realities' (see his comments on the Community in 1959, Document 7.4). The European Assembly adopted in 1960 a proposal for its own election by universal suffrage (something which was not to take place, however, until 1979). It took the name of European Parliament in 1962. Some wanted to extend the authority of the Community into new political and foreign policy spheres. Others wished to give priority to 'consolidating economic integration' and to extend only with caution and as the need arose, the powers and influence of the Community.

The continuing enthusiasm and encouragement by the United States for Western European integration is well-illustrated by Document 7.3. The British Prime Minister, Harold Macmillan, was left in no doubt by President Kennedy that he was keen on British entry. His wish further to strengthen the Anglo–US relationship was one of the considerations which led the Prime Minister to open negotiations with the Six (see Document 7.7). Others were the success of the Common Market, the very evident decline of Commonwealth trade with Britain by contrast with the increase of European trade, the relative failure of the European Free Trade

Association (EFTA) to offer comparable advantages to those of the Community, fear of exclusion from the new trading bloc and the desire to reassert British influence in the world. With decolonization and the decline of empire, Britain at last started to reorientate her policy towards a more, though not exclusively, regional role. Document 7.8 gives another angle to US support for British entry.

De Gaulle's veto (see Document 7.9) came as a very considerable shock. The anger of the other Five is clearly expressed by Spaak in Document 7.10. De Gaulle's reason for the rejection was largely political, as Edward Heath, the chief British negotiator recognised in his statement. De Gaulle had one view of Europe; the British Government had another. The latter's dependence upon the United States, illustrated particularly by the Nassau Meeting of Macmillan and Kennedy in December 1962 which arranged for the British to receive the Polaris submarine-launched nuclear missiles, conflicted with De Gaulle's proclaimed mission to free Europe from the 'double hegemony' of the Superpowers. The rejection of Britain was part and parcel of the French President's campaign against 'Anglo-Saxon' influence and for a 'European Europe' – one in which French influence might be paramount.

The momentum of the Community derived from three main sources: the implementation of the Rome Treaties, the need for the Community to negotiate as an entity with other countries and blocs and thirdly, the development of the institutions. France had set the pace of European integration, with the Schuman and Pleven plans, but now her role was to obstruct further political development with her 'empty chair' boycott of the institutions in 1965 which was only brought to an end with the Luxembourg Agreement (see Document 7.12).

The 1965 crisis concerned several issues; agriculture, the method of financing the Community, the budgetary powers of the Parliament. The most important consequence of the Agreement – or 'Disagreement', as it was sometimes nicknamed – was that the Community did not pass, as the Rome Treaty provided, to majority voting. Since an important national interest could be advanced as a justification of veto by a Member State, what in fact happened was that the Council of Ministers negotiated on issues towards a common consensus. This left an accumulating backlog of proposals and led to slow progress. De Gaulle's stand had the effect of reducing the importance of the Commission. The widespread recognition that the Luxembourg Agreement was obstructing the development of the Community led the European Council to introduce qualified majority voting for a number of policy areas in the Single European Act of 1986 (see Appendix B).

Documents

DOCUMENT 7.1

Bela Balassa, 'The Theory of Economic Integration', 1962

The following is an extract from Balassa's theoretical exposition of the process of economic integration, based on his study of European organisations.

Economic integration can take several forms that represent varying degrees of integration. These are a free-trade area, a customs union, a common market, an economic union, and complete economic integration. In a free-trade area, tariffs (and quantitative restrictions) between the participating countries are abolished, but each country retains its own tariffs against non-members. Establishing a customs union involves, besides the suppression of discrimination in the field of commodity movements within the union, the equalisation of tariffs in trade with non-member countries. A higher form of economic integration is attained in a common market, where not only trade restrictions but also restrictions on factor movements are abolished. An economic union, as distinct from a common market, combines the suppression of restrictions on commodity and factor movements with some degree of harmonisation of national economic policies, in order to remove discrimination that was due to disparities in these policies. Finally, total economic integration presupposes the unification of monetary, fiscal, social, and countercyclical policies and requires the setting-up of a supranational authority whose decisions are binding for the Member States.

Adopting the definition given above, the theory of economic integration will be concerned with the economic effects of integration in its various forms and with problems that arise from divergences in national monetary, fiscal, and other policies. The theory of economic integration can be regarded as a part of international economics, but it also enlarges the field of international trade theory by exploring the impact of a fusion of national market on growth and examining the need for the coordination of economic policies in a union. Finally, the theory of economic integration should, incorporate elements of location theory, too. The integration of adjacent countries amounts to the removal of artificial barriers that obstruct continuous economic activity through national frontiers, and the ensuing relocation of production and regional agglomerative and deglomerative tendencies cannot be adequately discussed without making use of the tools of locational analysis.

DOCUMENT 7.2

Memorandum on 'Free Trade and its Conditions', 26 February 1959

The following is an extract from the first memorandum from Commission of the European Economic Community to the Council of Ministers, Brussels, 26 February 1959.

33. Free trade and its conditions

Free trade is an objective impossible of attainment unless certain conditions are fulfilled.

In the first place, it is difficult to conceive of a complete abolition of customs barriers and quotas as long as no sufficient guarantee exists that the free play of competition will not be hindered by understandings and monopolies, dumping practices, aids granted by States or specific distortions.

In the second place, the States will hardly be prepared to eliminate obstacles to trade in certain products if the volume of liberalisation is insufficient to ensure an adequate balance of advantages and burdens. This question concerns primarily the problems of freedom of movement for workers, of the liberalisation of services and of increased trade in agricultural products.

In the third place, it is unrealistic to contemplate total abolition of customs barriers and quotas if the maintenance of the liberalisation measures adopted is not guaranteed by adequate co-ordination of policy relating to economic trends.

In the fourth place, it would seem necessary that any large-scale elimination of customs barriers and quotas between highly developed countries on the one hand and developing countries on the other, should be accompanied by a concerted and active development policy. In point of fact, experience shows that free trade of itself does not lead to the elimination of disparities in levels of development.

Fifth, and lastly, it is only possible to conceive of large-scale elimination of obstacles to trade if there is no appreciable distortion of competition, either in respect of imports or of exports, as a result of diversities in the external tariffs and trade policies of the participating states. A special problem exists in relation to countries with low living and wages standards, which are in a position to offer their products at abnormally low prices, and in relation to those with a centralised, state-controlled economy whose prices do not result from free competition but are fixed arbitrarily by the monopoly of external trade.

DOCUMENT 7.3

'The Developing Atlantic Partnership', speech by US Undersecretary George W. Ball, 2 April 1962

This offers a clear illustration of the rationale behind the US support for Western European integration. See also Document 7.8.

. . . Through the whole of the postwar period we Americans have taken no comfort from the disparity between our own resources and those of any other nations of the free world. We have been proud that the United States is a world leader, but we have sometimes found it less than satisfactory to be a world leader isolated by the possession of an overwhelming proportion of the total wealth, power, and resources. In our minds – and I am sure to your minds as well – a strong partnership must almost mean a collaboration of equals. When one partner possesses over 50 per cent of the resources of so great an enterprise and the balance is distributed among 16 or 17 others, the relationship is unlikely to work with full effectiveness. And so long as Europe remained fragmented, so long as it consisted merely of nations small by modern standards, the potentials for true partnership were always limited.

But a Europe united and strong can be an equal partner in the achievement of our common endeavours – an equal partner committed to the same basic objectives as we ourselves. For, after all, you and we alike believe in the preservation and extension of freedom and in the values that distinguish free men from slaves.

I cannot overstate the enthusiasm with which Americans have welcomed the burgeoning strength and cohesion of Europe. But why is it that one sometimes hears in Europe – almost never in America – timid voices ominously complaining that a united Europe might become a neutralist 'third force'.

Let me say emphatically that we Americans have no fear that the new Europe will be neutralist any more than we fear that America will return to isolationism. The neutralism of which we heard a fair amount a decade ago was an expression of weakness, not strength. It sprang from a belief that Europe could no longer play a significant role in the power contest between the United States and the Communist bloc. Persuaded that they could not influence the outcome by taking sides, its advocates assumed a role of Olympian detachment from the battle, measuring out equal amounts of criticism for each side. As the nations of Western Europe have grown more united, the voices of neutralism that produced such a frightful cacophony 10 years ago have been largely stilled.

But there are a few who still profess fear of a strong, united Europe for yet a different reason. They see the spectre not of a neutralist third force but of a third force and an America following increasingly divergent paths. A powerful continental entity, they argue, could be tempted to try a new kind of balance-of-power politics, to ply the East against the West, to sell its weight and authority to the highest bidder to serve its own parochial and selfish objectives.

Such a prediction, I am persuaded, misconceives the nature of the forces at work on both sides of the Atlantic. It overlooks the vitality and solidity of our common heritage. It ignores the reality of our common objectives. It ignores the direction in which Europe is already moving. It rejects, in fact, the very interdependence of the members of the NATO alliance on which our national security is now based.

To my mind both you and we have everything to gain by the construction of a strong united Europe. Europe united will almost certainly display a deeper and stronger feeling of responsibility for the defence of western values than will the individual nation states in a Europe weak and fragmented. Unity builds strength. The experience and awareness of strength engender not only the ability but the will to influence events.

And for the Europeans, as for Americans, the will to influence events is merely another way of expressing a sense of responsibility.

We Americans are thoroughly convinced, therefore, that the further Europe proceeds down the road towards unity the more Europe can be expected to play an affirmative and responsible role in our common concerns. In expressing this belief we recognise, of course, that the Atlantic partnership can never be one-sided and that we ourselves must fulfil the obligations of a good partner.

United States support for European integration and for the European Economic Community has deep roots. It springs from a recollection of our own Federal experience and from a desire to end the sanguinary rivalry that once divided the great states of Western Europe.

But Americans have recognised that the commercial manifestation of the Community – the Common Market – implies a substantial degree of discrimination against American trade. Of necessity it will require adjustments for the industry, agriculture and labour of the United States and of non-member third countries. Yet this has never deflected us from the larger objectives of our policy. In spite of the problems for America implicit in the development of the Common Market, we have given consistent and active support to the growth of the European Community.

In providing this support we have acted on two convictions: first, that the Community would be conducted as an outward-looking society, liberal in its trading and economic policies; and second, that it would be increasingly prepared to bear responsibilities around the world as its strength and unity develop. . .

DOCUMENT 7.4

Jean Monnet, 'Prospect for a New Europe'

The following is an extract from an interview given by Monnet in 1959.

The Community and the Free Trade Area

M. Monnet, you have been pointing out that a big market is the essential basis for further economic expansion. Why does the six-nation Community oppose British proposals for an even bigger market in the form of a 17-nation European Free Trade Area or customs union?

The European Economic Community is much more than a customs union. The Free Trade Area proposed by Britain is much less than a customs union.

The Free Trade Area would exclude agriculture, from which 18 million persons and their children in the six-nation area earn their livelihood. It does not provide, as a customs union would, for a common external tariff. Each of the member nations would be free to maintain its own external tariffs. The Free Trade Area would be a market in which you exchange goods but do not build a common policy. Each nation would have its own economic policy.

The six-nation Common Market, on the other hand, is not just a customs union or a big market. It is a Community with common rules and common institutions which can gradually build a common policy to foster rapid economic growth.

Towards Majority Voting

How can the Community arrive at a common economic policy if each nation, in the Community's Council of Ministers, has a veto over the actions of the executive?

The unanimity rule only applies during a transition period. Subsequently, almost all decisions will be made by majority vote. In fact, some decisions are made by majority vote right from the start.

The Community's institutions consist of a Council of Ministers, a European Economic Commission, an Assembly, which is a kind of Parliament, and a Court of Justice, which is an embryo Supreme Court. What we have is a system of checks and balances similar to that in most constitutions.

The Council of Ministers is designed to bring together national views, the views of the six governments. It meets at intervals. Each government is represented in the Council by its Foreign Minister or by one or more other Ministers, such as the Finance, Transport or Agricultural Ministers, as the subject matter requires.

The continuing, day-to-day executive work of the Community is handled by the nine-member European Economic commission. The Commission is responsible to the Assembly of the Community. It defends the common interests of the Community and represents the Community viewpoint, rather than national views. It acts by majority vote in all things.

The Commission has numerous real powers, specified in the Treaty, which it exercises on its own authority. Where general rules have to be set, the Council of Ministers makes the decisions. But it must do so on the proposals of the Commission. It cannot amend the Commission's proposals except by unanimous vote.

The British have proposed a majority vote in the Council of Ministers of the proposed Free Trade Area. Why wouldn't this work as well?

There would be no independent Commission in the Free Trade Area representing the Community-wide viewpoint. Under such circumstances, a majority in this Council of Ministers may just represent a coalition of interests. In difficulties arising between one nation and another, there would be arbitration by coalition, instead of the creation of common policies to solve common problems.

In the Community, the Council will vote on positive programmes proposed by the Commission from a Community-wide point of view. And the Treaty gives these institutions many major tasks beyond the establishment of a customs union.

For example, a European Social Fund will be established to help finance the retraining and relocation of workers whose jobs are effected adversely by industrial changes. The Community as a whole will contribute to aid these workers wherever they live. A European Investment Bank will finance development of backward areas, such as those in southern Italy and some parts of France and Germany. An overseas investment fund will finance developmental projects in the overseas territories of the member nations. The institutions of the Community are empowered to break up cartels.

There is a provision for mutual aid when one country has balance of payments deficits. The institutions of the Community are instructed to build common policies in agriculture and transport, to achieve free movement of labour and capital across frontiers. There not only will be a common external tariff but a common commercial policy toward the rest of the world. The European Commission, after a transition period, will be the spokesman in negotiations for trade agreements with third countries on behalf of the whole Community.

Do you mean that member countries will no longer negotiate their own trade agreements with the United States, Russia or the Argentine, for example?

Exactly. The Community will negotiate its agreements as a Community.

DOCUMENT 7.5

'Russia – Hallstein Answers Soviet Attacks', 1962

This article was published in 1962. Walter Hallstein was President of the Commission for nine years from the institution of the EEC and a very major influence in the early years of the Community.

One of the major arguments of Soviet propaganda alleges that the Common Market is aggravating the contradictions of the capitalist world, and is precipitating a relentless struggle for position in the European market among rival monopolistic groups.

A strange argument indeed. What lies behind the growing interpenetration in the internal market of the Community, which has brought about an increase of 73 per cent in internal trade in four years, an increase of 19 per cent in the gross national product of the Community, and an increase of 29 per cent in industrial production? Does this look like a murderous struggle for position among monopolies? How can this argument be reconciled with the freely expressed aspirations of our European neighbours . . . to join the Common Market or to be associated with it in one form or another?

The basic meaning of the attacks made against us is that the Soviet leaders have clearly recognised, albeit very late in the day, that something has happened, with unexpected speed and surprising success, which is absolutely impossible according to Marxist–Leninist theory. According to this theory capitalist states cannot overcome their differences and unite; such a union cannot create conditions for long-term economic planning covering large areas and ensuring stability and security in face of crises; these phenomena cannot be the forerunners of an economic system that might one day include the whole free world.

All this is impossible, in the Communist mind, not only for theoretical reasons, but for practical ones as well. It is impossible because the Eastern bloc has now reached a state of crisis in its economic evolution which is causing increasing anxiety among Soviet leaders. They are not only concerned with a crisis in the Soviet economy itself . . . they are also concerned, ironically, with a crisis of integration, as shown by the tortured, strained and insipid text of the latest Comecon resolution.

Before I draw any conclusions, however, let me return to what seems to me to be the second basic argument of Soviet propaganda. It is aimed principally at countries in the process of development, and seeks to play on their many apprehensions and susceptibilities. It states, broadly, that the Community is a union of the rich for exploiting the poor; and that for the associated African countries in particular, the aim of these attachments is to keep them in a state of subjection or to prevent the development of their industries.

These arguments are fairly easy to refute in themselves, but they have also a deeper significance.

I believe that historians of the future will see our era as one of rapid and profound change for the free world. If yesterday we became aware of the strength of nations, today we are in the process of becoming aware of the strength of the family of peoples. What is more, this new prospect of affairs conducted in a spirit of goodwill, in our case initially by financial partnership as an aid to development and the establishment of a worldwide economic and social system will enable this strength to be used rationally.

Let us look at facts and figures for a moment. In the four years which have elapsed since the coming into force of the Rome Treaty, the member countries of the Community have devoted nearly 10 billion dollars to aiding development. In addition, the Community has also formed a Development Fund from which the associated African countries will have received 580 million dollars during the first five years of the Treaty.

But this is not all. More important is the fact that our association is a perfectly free one. The present arrangement expires at the end of this year, and we are currently negotiating a new agreement with the African states, and if negotiations take place, it is because they themselves wish it. These are free countries.

The allegation that the Common Market prevents these countries from developing their industry is particularly absurd – 65 per cent of the Community's aid has been devoted to building up their economic infrastructure and to their general economic development. It will be the same in the future with the new development funds, which in all likelihood will be increased. Moreover, although the Community imports the products of its associates freely, it gives them a unilateral right to protect their nascent industries against exports from the Community. All this has surely nothing to do with colonialism.

Nothing is more foolish than to pretend that our enterprise is directed against the Eastern bloc. What we are doing we are doing for ourselves and for the whole free world together. We are doing it by the most peaceful means that can be imagined. And we are doing it, finally, in the hope that one day we will be able to convince even those who today believe it necessary to be our opponents that there are advantages in cooperation.

DOCUMENT 7.6

Walter Hallstein, 'A New Path to Peaceful Union', 1962

The following, from a lecture given in India in 1962, examines the institutional nature of the new European Community.

What sort of government is the government which we see in embryo in the European Economic Community? It is not, as I said, a further development of normal diplomatic methods of consultation and co-operation as seen in traditional international organisations. Instead, the fusion of interests in the European Community is being achieved through a new mechanism of institutions which it is only a slight exaggeration to call a constitutional framework.

Of course, the European Community is not just a new power-bloc or a new coalition. although it has its pride, it is not a swollen version of 19th century nationalism, taking a continent rather than a country as its basis. In fact, it is the concrete embodiment of a new approach to the relations between states. It is not merely international: it is not yet fully federal. But it is an attempt to build on the federal pattern a democratically constituted Europe – what I have called elsewhere a federation in the making.

No practical statesman would I think be prepared to endorse unreservedly the doctrine of the separation of powers: but classical democratic theory, with its division of the organs of government into executive, legislative and judiciary, certainly underlines the constitutional structure of the European Economic Community. The Executive is the Commission – nine men, many of them former ministers in national governments, who are now no longer national, but European, responsible to the Community as a whole. They are not permitted to take national instructions, and once appointed for their term of office by common agreement of the member governments, they can only be removed by a vote of no confidence from the Community Parliament, of which I shall speak in a moment. The Commission has broadly three main tasks. First, it draws up proposals to be decided by the Council of Ministers. Secondly, it watches over the execution of the Treaty and may call firms and governments to account. Thirdly, it mediates between the governments and seeks to reconcile national interests with the Community interests; and a fourth task, whose importance is growing, is that of executing those decisions of detail which for the sake of rapid and impartial treatment it is empowered to take itself.

The legislative body of the Community is its Council of Ministers – one representing each Member State – which meets at fairly frequent intervals to take the major decisions on proposals from the Commission. The Council is not simply an international conference: it is an organ of the Community whose status is on a level with that of the Commission, and whose decisions are normally taken by qualified majority vote – a procedure which extends to more and more subjects as the Community moves through its twelve-year transition period. This means that the veto of a single Member State can less and less hinder progress. What is more, the Council can only modify the Commission's proposals by means of a unanimous vote: so that here the veto works on the side of progress rather than against anything being done.

The judiciary branch of the Community's embryo constitution is the Court of Justice, which bears some resemblance to a constitutional court – a supreme court. It has seven judges, appointed by common accord of the member governments, and like members of the Commission completely independent of the national states. Their judgments are binding throughout the Community's territory, and there has never been a case in which they have been defied.

I have left until last the European Parliament which represents and exercises democratic control over all the actions of the Community. The national minsters who meet in the Council are of course subject to control by their national parliaments: but the Commissioners, by definition, cannot be subject to national control and must therefore be answerable to a Community parliament. So far, the Parliament's powers are limited. Its 142 members, at present elected by and from the national parliaments, may one day be elected directly: but already they have the power to dismiss the Commission by a two-thirds majority vote. Their questions, addressed to both Council and Commission, have to be answered in public: each year, the Commission has to report to the Parliament's plenary session which scrutinizes and debates Community activities on that occasion and on several others at intervals throughout the year. Meanwhile, almost every week the Parliament's thirteen standing committees hold very searching 'hearings' at which members of the Commission explain and defend their policies and are subject to the full, shrewd scrutiny of very experienced representatives of the democratic political life.

I should not wish to claim that this constitutional mechanism was perfect. But it does introduce into the relations between Member States several new elements. First, it means that there is a Community interest independent of those of the states themselves. Secondly, Community decisions are reached by a constitutional process rather than just by traditional horsetrading among transient coalitions. Thirdly, the international relations between the Member States – and the fact of calling them international reveals by its strangeness how far removed the Community's internal workings are from those of traditional diplomacy – are subject to the rule of law in a very concrete and immediate sense. Finally, and most importantly, they are subject also to a degree of democratic control greater than that ever imposed upon traditional international relations. In a word, while the Community, like India, is 'a Union of States', it is also, in many respects already, a 'Sovereign Democratic Republic'.

DOCUMENT 7.7

The British Prime Minister, Harold Macmillan, in the House of Commons, 31 July 1961

This speech signalled the British government's decision to apply to become a member of the Community.

With permission, I wish to make a statement on the policy of Her Majesty's Government towards the European Economic Community.

The future relations between the European Economic Community, the United Kingdom, the Commonwealth and the rest of Europe are clearly matters of capital importance in the life of our country and, indeed, of all countries of the free world.

This is a political as well as an economic issue. Although the Treaty of Rome is concerned with economic matters, it has an important political objective, namely, to promote unity and stability in Europe which is so essential a factor in the struggle for freedom and progress throughout the world. In this modern world the tendency towards larger groups of nations acting together in the common interest leads to greater unity and thus adds to our strength.

I believe that it is both our duty and our interest to contribute towards that strength by securing the closest possible unity within Europe. At the same time, if a closer relationship between the United Kingdom and the countries of the European Economic Community were to disrupt the long-standing and historic ties between the United Kingdom and the other nations of the Commonwealth the loss would be greater than the gain. The Commonwealth is a great source of stability and strength both to Western Europe and to the world as a whole, and I am sure that its value is fully appreciated by the member Governments of the European Economic Community. I do not think that Britain's contribution to the Commonwealth will be reduced if Europe unites. On the contrary, I think that its value will be enhanced.

On the economic side, a community comprising, as members or in association, the countries of free Europe, could have a very rapidly expanding economy supplying, as eventually it would, a single market of approaching 300 million people. This rapidly expanding economy could, in turn, lead to an increased demand for products from other parts of the world and so help to expand world trade and improve the prospects of the less developed areas of the world.

No British Government could join the European Economic Community without prior negotiation with a view to meeting the needs of the Commonwealth countries, of our European Free Trade Association partners, and of British agriculture consistently with the broad principles and purposes which have inspired the concept of European unity and which are embodied in the Rome Treaty. . .

Therefore, after long and earnest consideration, Her Majesty's Government have come to the conclusion that it would be right for Britain to make a formal application under Article 237 of the Treaty for negotiations with a view to joining the Community if satisfactory arrangements can be made to meet the special needs of the United Kingdom, of the Commonwealth and of the European Free Trade Association.

If, as I earnestly hope, our offer to enter into negotiations with the European Economic Community is accepted, we shall spare no efforts to reach a satisfactory agreement. These negotiations must inevitably be of a detailed and technical character, covering a very large number of the most delicate and difficult matters. They may, therefore, be protracted and there can, of course, be no guarantee of success. When any negotiations are brought to a conclusion then it will be the duty of the Government to recommend to the House what course we should pursue. . .

DOCUMENT 7.8

Press release from the US 'National Committee for an Effective Congress', 27 December 1961

This extract provides an interesting comment on the desirability of British membership from the American viewpoint.

Today this simple truth is becoming apparent to Washington as well as to Wall Street: that a Europe organised without the United States would be a Europe organised against the United States. This is why we are pushing hard for Britain to join the Common Market without delay. We need Britain as a broker and to ensure an Open Door. For if we fail to strengthen our political ties with NATO and don't establish a free world Common Market, we may see the economic community of continental Europe and Africa become a separate political bloc, which could be a third great power, equal in strength to Russia and to the United States, and uncommitted between the two. The emergence of such a fortress Europe would crack the historic unity of Western Civilisation, upon which rest the hopes of free men and free institutions.

DOCUMENT 7.9

The French President, Charles de Gaulle, press conference at the Elysée Palace, Paris, 14 January 1963

This extract offers justification for his rejection of Britain's application to join the Community. He was also subsequently to veto the attempt by the Labour Government under Harold Wilson in 1967.

Could you define explicitly France's position towards Britain's entry into the Common Market and the political evolution of Europe?

A very clear question, to which I shall endeavour to reply clearly.

I believe that when you talk about economies – and much more so when you practise them – what you say and what you do must conform to realities, because without that you can get into impasses and, sometimes, you even head for ruin. In this very great affair of the European Economic Community and also in that of eventual adhesion of Great Britain, it is the facts that must first be considered. Feelings, favourable though they might be and are, these feelings cannot be invoked against the real facts of the problem. What are these facts?

The Treaty of Rome was concluded between six continental States – States which are, economically speaking, one may say, of the same nature. Indeed, whether it be a matter of their industrial or agricultural production, their external exchanges, their habits or their commercial clientele, their living or working conditions, there is between them much more resemblance than difference. Moreover, they are adjacent, they inter-penetrate, they prolong each other through their communications. It is therefore a fact to group them and to link them in such a way that what they have to produce, to buy, to sell, to consume – well, they do produce, buy, sell, consume, in preference in their own ensemble. Doing that is conforming to realities.

Moreover, it must be added that from the point of view of their economic development, their social progress, their technical capacity, they are, in short, keeping pace. They are marching in similar fashion. It so happens, too, that there is between them no kind of political grievance, no frontier question, no rivalry in domination or power. On the contrary, they are joined in solidarity, especially and primarily, from the aspect of the consciousness they have, of defining together an important part of the sources of our civilisation; and also as concerns their security, because they are continentals and have before them one and the same menace from one extremity to the other of their territories; finally, they are in solidarity through the fact that not one among them is bound abroad by any particular political or military accord.

Thus, it was psychologically and materially possible to make an economic community of the Six, though not without difficulties. When the Treaty of Rome was signed in 1957, it was after long discussions; and when it was concluded, it was necessary in order to achieve something that we French put in order our economic, financial, and monetary affairs . . . and that was done in 1959.

From that moment the community was in principle viable, but then the treaty had to be applied. However, this treaty, which was precise and complete enough concerning industry, was not at all so on the subject of agriculture. However, for our country this had to be settled.

Indeed, it is obvious that agriculture is an essential element in the whole of our national activity. We cannot conceive, and will not conceive, of a Common Market in which French agriculture would not find outlets in keeping with its production. And we agree, further, that of the Six we are the country on which this necessity is imposed in the most imperative manner.

This is why when, last January, thought was given to the setting in motion of the second phase of the treaty – in other words a practical start in application – we were led to pose the entry of agriculture into the Common Market as a formal condition.

This was finally accepted by our partners but very difficult and very complex arrangements were needed – and some rulings are still outstanding. I note in passing that in this vast undertaking it was the governments that took all the decisions, because authority and responsibility are not to be found elsewhere. But I must say that in preparing and untangling these matters, the Commission in Brussels did some very objective and fitting work.

Thereupon Great Britain posed her candidature to the Common Market. She did it after having earlier refused to participate in the communities we are now building, as well as after creating a free trade area with six other States, and, finally, after having – I may well say it, the negotiations held at such length on this subject will be recalled – after having put some pressure on the Six to prevent a real beginning being made in the application of the Common Market. If England asks in turn to enter, but on her own conditions, this poses without doubt to each of the six States, and poses to England, problems of a very great dimension.

England in effect is insular, she is maritime, she is linked through her exchanges, her markets, her supply lines to the most diverse and often the most distant countries; she pursues essentially industrial and commercial activities, and only slight agricultural ones. She has in all her doings very marked and very original habits and traditions.

In short, the nature, the structure, the very situation (conjuncture) that are England's differ profoundly from those of the continentals.

What is to be done in order that England, as she lives, produces and trades, can be incorporated into the Common Market, as it has been conceived and as it functions?

For example, the means by which the people of Great Britain are fed and which are in fact the importation of foodstuffs bought cheaply in the two Americas and in the former dominions, at the same time giving, granting considerable subsidies to English farmers? These means are obviously incompatible with the system which the Six have established quite naturally for themselves.

The system of the Six – this constitutes making a whole of the agricultural produce of the whole Community, in strictly fixing their prices, in prohibiting subsidies, in organising their consumption between all the participants, and in imposing on each of its participants payment to the Community of any saving they would achieve in fetching their food from outside instead of eating what the Common Market has to offer.

Once again, what is to be done to bring England, as she is, into this system?

One might sometimes have believed that our English friends, in posing their candidature to the Common Market, were agreeing to transform themselves to the point of applying all the conditions which are accepted and practised by the Six. But the question, to know whether Great Britain can now place herself like the Continent and with it inside a tariff which is genuinely common, to renounce all Commonwealth preferences, to cease any pretence that her agriculture be privileged, and, more than that, to treat her engagements with other countries of the free trade area as null and void – that question is the whole question.

It cannot be said that it is yet resolved. Will it be so one day? Obviously only England can answer.

The question is even further posed since after England other States which are, I repeat, linked to her through the free trade area, for the same reasons as Britain, would like or wish to enter the Common Market.

It must be agreed that first the entry of Great Britain, and then these States, will completely change the whole of the actions, the agreements, the compensations, the rules which have already been established between the Six, because all these States, like Britain, have very important peculiarities. Then it will be another Common Market whose constructions ought to be envisaged; but one which would be taken to 11 and then 13 and then perhaps 18 would no longer resemble, without any doubt, the one which the Six built.

Further, this community, increasing in such fashion, would see itself faced with problems of economic relations with all kinds of other States, and first with the United States.

It is to be foreseen that the cohesion of its members, who would be very numerous and diverse, would not endure for long, and that ultimately it would appear as a colossal Atlantic community under American dependence and direction, and which would quickly have absorbed the community of Europe.

It is a hypothesis which in the eyes of some can be perfectly justified, but it is not at all what France is doing or wanted to do – and which is a properly European construction.

DOCUMENT 7.10

Paul-Henri Spaak on the de Gaulle veto, as recorded in his memoirs, 'The Continuing Battle'

At the final meeting of the Brussels Conference on 29 January 1963 Spaak had commented: 'If there were some other reason at present for rejecting Great Britain, it seems to me that the duty of those, who suddenly had discovered some motives for putting an end to the negotiations, would have been to tell us in order that we would have been able to discuss them. These new motives have not been placed before us. We have been asked to halt in a brutal manner an effort that we had undertaken for more than a year . . . At a time when, in a community, a single partner wants to compel all the others to take decisions which are of a capital importance in the life of the community, the community spirit no longer exists'.

During the afternoon of the 14th of January 1963, while we were in session, the official messengers brought us news flashes of the press conference General de Gaulle was just holding in Paris. Once we had seen these dispatches we could no longer keep our minds on the technical issues before us. A new political event of extreme importance was in the making: General de Gaulle had torpedoed our negotiations without having warned either his partners or the British. He had acted with a lack of consideration unexampled in the history of the EEC, showing utter contempt for his negotiating partners, allies and opponents alike. He had brought to a halt negotiations which he himself put in train in full agreement with his partners, and had done so on the flimsiest of pretexts.

What had happened? There is every reason to believe that it was the attitude adopted by Macmillan at his meeting with Kennedy in Bermuda which so upset the President of the French Republic. Macmillan's crime was to have reached agreement with the President of the United States on Britain's nuclear, weaponry. He had in fact arranged for the purchase of Polaris missiles from the United States. In General de Gaulle's eyes the cooperation with the Americans was tantamount to treason against Europe's interests and justified his refusal to allow Britain into the Common Market. The General's resentment was all the greater because a few days before the Bermuda meeting he had received Macmillan at Rambouillet. The British Prime Minister, he claimed, had told him nothing of his nuclear plans. On the other hand, de Gaulle gave Macmillan no warning that he was about to torpedo the negotiations in

Brussels. I think the full truth about these events still remains to be told. The French and British versions which have been circulating in the chancelleries differ, but what is certain is that France, without consulting her partners, unilaterally withdrew from negotiations to which she had earlier agreed and that she did so, moreover, after first insisting that the Six must present a united front.

We were faced with a complete volte-face. Stunned and angry, our first reaction was to ignore what had been said in Paris and to continue the negotiation as if nothing had happened. The British showed extraordinary sang-froid. Though, deep down, they were greatly shocked, they gave no outward sign of this and continued to present their arguments at the negotiating table with imperturbable calm.

DOCUMENT 7.11

President de Gaulle on European integration – press conference, 15 May 1962

The French President, Charles de Gaulle, offered the following comments on Western European integration in his press conference on Europe of 15 May 1962. His objection to the Jean Monnet approach is clear, as is his fear of the extension of US influence in Europe.

I should like to speak particularly about the objection to integration. People counter this by saying: 'Why not merge the six states together into a single supranational entity? That would be very simple and practical'. But such an entity is impossible to achieve in the absence in Europe today of a federator who has the necessary power, reputation and ability. Thus one has to fall back on a sort of hybrid arrangement under which the six states agree to submit to the decisions of a qualified majority. At the same time, although there are already six national Parliaments as well as the European Parliament and, in addition the Consultative Assembly of the Council of Europe . . . it would be necessary to elect over and above this, yet a further Parliament, described as European, which would lay down the law to the six states.

These are ideas that might appeal to certain minds but I entirely fail to see how they could be put into practice, even with six signatures at the foot of a document. Can we imagine France, Germany, Italy, the Netherlands, Belgium, Luxembourg being prepared on a matter of importance to them in the national or international sphere, to do something that appeared wrong to them, merely because others had ordered them to do so? Would the peoples of France, of Germany, of Italy, of the Netherlands, of

Belgium or of Luxembourg ever dream of submitting to laws passed by foreign parliamentarians if such laws ran counter to their deepest convictions? Clearly not. It is impossible nowadays for a foreign majority to impose their will on reluctant nations. It is true, perhaps, that in this 'integrated' Europe as it is called there might be no policy at all. This would simplify a great many things. Indeed, once there was no France, no Europe; once there was no policy – since one could not be imposed on each of the six states, attempts to formulate a policy would cease. But then, perhaps, these peoples would follow in the wake of some outsider who had a policy. There would, perhaps, be a federator, but he would not be European. And Europe would not be an integrated Europe but something vaster by far and, I repeat, with a federator. Perhaps to some extent it is this that at times inspires the utterances of certain advocates of European integration. If so, then it would be better to say so.

DOCUMENT 7.12

The Luxembourg Agreement (Compromise) of 29 January 1966

This resolved the 'empty chair crisis' between France and the other Five. It also reduced the institutional importance of the Commission and hindered the process of integration until the mid-1980s. See also Document 9.5.

Relations between the Commission and the Council

Close co-operation between the Council and the Commission is essential for the functioning and development of the Community. In order to improve and strengthen this co-operation at every level, the Council considers that the following practical methods of co-operation should be applied, these methods to be adopted by joint agreement, on the basis of Article 162 of the EEC Treaty, without compromising the respective competences and powers of the two Institutions.

1. Before adopting any particularly important proposal, it is desirable that the Commission should take up the appropriate contacts with the Governments of the Member States, through the Permanent Representatives, without this procedure compromising the right of initiative which the Commission derives from the Treaty.
2. Proposals and any other official acts which the Commission submits to the Council and to the Member States are not to be made public until the recipients have had formal notice of them and are in possession of the texts.

    The 'Journal Officiel' (official gazette) should be arranged so as to show clearly which acts are of binding force. The methods to be employed for publishing those texts whose publication is required will be adopted in the context of the current work on the re-organisation of the 'Journal Officiel'.

3. The credentials of Heads of Missions of non-member states accredited to the Community will be submitted jointly to the President of the Council and to the President of the Commission, meeting together for this purpose.

4. The Council and the Commission will inform each other rapidly and fully of any approaches relating to fundamental questions made to either institution by the representatives of non-member states.

5. Within the scope of application of Article 162, the Council and the Commission will consult together on the advisability of, the procedure for, and the nature of any links which the Commission might establish with international organisations pursuant to Article 229 of the Treaty.

6. Co-operation between the Council and the Commission on the Community's information policy, which was the subject of the Council's discussions on 24 September 1963, will be strengthened in such a way that the programme of the Joint Information Service will be drawn up and carried out in accordance with procedures which are to be decided upon at a later date, and which may include the establishment of an *ad hoc* body.

7. Within the framework of the financial regulations relating to the drawing up and execution of the Communities' budgets, the Council and the Commission will decide on means for more effective control over the commitment and expenditure of Community funds.

Majority voting procedure

1. Where, in the case of decisions which may be taken by majority vote on a proposal of the Commission, very important interests of one or more partners are at stake, the Members of the Council will endeavour, within a reasonable time, to reach solutions which can be adopted by all the Members of the Council while respecting their mutual interests and those of the Community, in accordance with Article 2 of the Treaty.

2. With regard to the preceding paragraph, the French delegation considers that where very important interests are at stake the discussion must be continued until unanimous agreement is reached.

3. The six delegations note that there is a divergence of views on what should be done in the event of a failure to reach complete agreement.

4. The six delegations nevertheless consider that this divergence does not prevent the Community's work being resumed in accordance with the normal procedure.

DOCUMENT 7.13

Sicco Mansholt on the reform of the Common Agricultural Policy

Dr Mansholt was Vice-President of the Commission. The plan named after him was the origin of the Common Agricultural Policy (CAP). The following was written in 1970 and describes the difficulties he faced. The CAP remains one of the major problems of the Community. See also Document 9.6.

On 10 December 1968, I put before the European Community's Council of Ministers a memorandum on the reform of Community agriculture. Hitherto, the policy followed in the Six had led to an absurd state of affairs. Huge sums were being spent by the member Governments on structural improvements. Yet these did nothing to remedy our real agricultural problem – farms were too small, and farmers' incomes and living standards were lagging further and further behind those of other population groups.

To try to remedy this, I drew up for the Commission a programme entitled 'Agriculture 1980', which provided for:

1. A different price policy, aimed at restoring a more normal relationship between market and price trends.
2. Radical land-reform measures to bring farms up to a viable size and enable farmers to live as comfortably as everybody else.

The plan's basic premise was that the Community's farming population of 10–6 million should be reduced by five million. This exodus was to take place in an orderly manner, accompanied by all the measures necessary to provide financial assistance and create new jobs. The allocation of structural improvement aid among those who did not leave the land would be progressively concentrated on farms large enough to pay their way. . .

It shocked the public and brought an avalanche of criticism from politicians . . . This memorandum, however, was only a proposal for discussion . . . We received many highly favourable reactions, but a great deal of criticism still persists on certain points, which need some clarification. . .

Why didn't we present a plan earlier? Mainly because the member Governments would not hear of it. In its first memorandum, the so-called Green Bible of 1960, the Commission proposed a comprehensive policy, covering not only prices and market organisation, but also structural reform – which the Council never tackled. When the common agricultural policy took shape, it covered only prices and market organisation. The Governments had jealously kept the structural side in their own domain, thereby depriving farm policy of an essential element for its success.

The price policy, based on consensus politics rather than economics, has taken us almost to the end of the road, with structural surpluses costing astronomical amounts. Dairies churn out subsidised butter regardless of market needs; no one worries about packing the stuff, because no matter whether it is bought, stored, sold cheaply or destroyed, the producer gets the guaranteed price.

At the same time, the Member States spend their own money to nobody's advantage on farms so small as to condemn their occupants to constant want . . . There are many examples: one country provides grants to build stalls for fifteen cows, when no farm can possibly make a profit on fewer than forty. Others offer easy terms to buy tractors or subsidise the purchase of threshing-machines, when most tractors in the Community are utilised to barely half their capacity and threshers to only a third. Eight out of ten Community farms have fewer than ten cows, and two-thirds have fewer than five, although on a fair-sized modern farm one cowman can tend a herd of forty to sixty head. At the current rate of increase in average size, it would take our structural policy a century to make the average farm big enough to provide all Community farmers with a decent livelihood. . .

Accordingly, we decided to tell the public the truth and show the Member States where their duty lies. . .

We are out to enable modern, lucrative farms to be set up, capable of providing farmers and farm workers with the same standard of living as the rest of the population. Farmers' wives should not have to toil in the fields, cowhouses or pigsties, but rather look after their families and keep the accounts. Normal working hours, weekly days off and the usual holidays should be the rule on the land, as they are everywhere else. Farms must be large enough to make the capital investments necessary for moderinisation. Financing farms with five cows is tantamount to financing chronic destitution. . .

The plan is not supposed to do away with family farms. We have no special preference for collective rather than individual ventures, though collective farming seems to be more suitable, for instance, for stock farming, while individuals often do best at crop-raising. The plan provides for the possibility of enlarging individual farms as well as for amalgamations . . . At the same time, anyone who wants to carry on alone with an uneconomic smallholding can remain an 'independent yeoman farmer', at the cost of living poorly. The choice will be up to the individual. . .

The Commission's plan presupposes a halving of the current agricultural population to five million people. . .

In contrast to the past *laissez-faire* attitude to the flight from the land, we offer farmers and farm workers a choice, on terms. They can stay if they co-operate in a programme enabling them to run a fair-sized modern farm, live as comfortably as the rest of the population and work at a profit. Or they can leave, in which case they will receive financial compensation, occupational retraining and arrangements to have their children trained for other jobs.

Eight in ten holdings are now too small to keep one efficient man busy full-time. One new idea in the plan is that the land of farmers who pull out should be either sold or rented to those who stay on. . .

More than half the Community's farmers are over fifty-seven, and of the estimated total departures in the next ten years, a substantial proportion (three million) will be of farmers over fifty-five. Most of these men will not be seeking other work, particularly as the plan offers them security for their old age. For younger ex-farmers the plan specifies that at least 80,000 new jobs should be created each year in the less industrialised parts of the Community.

Some critics maintain that reorganising agriculture on modern lines will aggravate the farm-surplus problem instead of solving it. . .

Since estimated production in 1980 was higher than consumption, we concluded that about 12.5 million acres would have to be taken out of cultivation. These figures may have to be revised as the plan goes forward. . .

Prices are a psychologically charged question to be treated with caution. Here is an example of how the different aspects of the plan dovetail: action on prices will be practicable only when modern, viable farms have replaced the million little ones now entirely dependent on the price of milk for a living. . . Again, the producers themselves may be called upon to part-finance the support and guarantee systems through farmers' unions. . .

Finally, the plan would be carried out in stages, to ease the change.

Anyone who thinks it will cost too much should look at the facts. The current policy condemns three-quarters of Europe's farmers to stagnate on unprofitable holdings while producing utterly unmarketable surpluses. It costs as much each year as the Americans were spending on reaching the moon, and if the money we are wasting on the present system keeps increasing at the current rate, it should soon be enough to put a man on Mars.

Under our plan the costs would be halved by 1980, after reaching a peak in 1973–4. We are now spending $4,000 million a year on structural improvements and price guarantees. The aim is to cut this by 1980 to $1,800 million ($670 million for price support, the rest for structural outlay). The Community and Member States would share the costs.

In France and Italy particularly, farmers are beginning to realise that our programme offers them a fair deal and their only chance of prospering in the future . . . The means of reform are open to discussion, but one can scarcely contest our account of the present state of affairs, our insistence that reform is vital and our objective of modernising the structure of agriculture. Those with whom the decisions rest – the Governments of the six countries – can no longer shirk their responsibility.

Suggested reading

A quite invaluable guide to publications on the institutions, policies and decision-making processes of the EC is J. Lodge (ed.), *The European Community: Bibliographical Excursions* (London, 1983). A very good and popular account of the economics of the EC is D. Swann, *The Economics of the Common Market*, 6th edn (London, 1988). Different interpretations of the integration process may be found in C.C. Pentland, *International Theory and European Integration* (New York, 1973); A.J.R. Groom and P. Taylor, *Functionalism* (London, 1975); B. Balassa, *The Theory of Economic Integration* (London, 1962); L. Lindberg, *The Political Dynamics of European Economic Integration* (Stanford, California, 1963); E.B. Haas, *The Uniting of Europe* (London, 1958); C.J. Friedrich, *Europe an Emergent Nation* (New York, 1967); and R.J. Harrison, *Europe in Question* (London, 1974). On the question of enlargement of the Community, see S. George, *Awkward Partner* (Oxford, 1990). The standard account of the first British application (though long out of print) is M. Camps, *Britain and the European Community 1955-63* (London, 1964). See also her *European Unification in the Sixties. From the Veto to the Crisis* (New York, 1966) which includes a perspective on the US role in the integration process. F.R. Willis, *France, Germany and the New Europe 1945-67* (New York, 1968) provides a sound account and J. Newhouse, *De Gaulle and the Anglo-Saxons* (London, 1970) a lively one of the difficulties of the mid-1960s in the Community. Other helpful studies are S. Bodenheimer, *Political Union: A Microcosm of European Politics 1960-66* (Leiden, 1967), R. Pryce, *The Politics of the European Community* (London, 1973) and his *The Dynamics of European Union* (London, 1987). A. Spinelli, *The Eurocrats* (Baltimore, 1966) is an interesting study. R.S. Jordan and W.J. Feld relate the Western European integration process to the wider strategic context of the Cold War in *Europe in the Balance: The Changing Context of European International Politics* (London, 1982). As an introduction, D.W. Irwin, *The Community of Europe* (London, 1991) is strongly recommended: highly informative and concise.

8 The first enlargement of the European Community

Introduction

In August 1947 the Senior Economic Adviser to the Foreign Secretary Ernest Bevin, Sir Edmund Hall-Patch, wrote as follows:

'There is a well-established prejudice in Whitehall against a European Customs Union. It goes back a long way and is rooted in the old days of Free Trade. It is a relic of a world which has disappeared, probably never to return. The Board of Trade is overstating the case against it. One of their most potent arguments is that we have to choose between a European Customs Union and the Commonwealth. However that may be, the Board of Trade have successfully blocked for two years our efforts to look at these proposals objectively.'

On the Continent, though, he noted, as a result of the Marshall Plan and the OEEC,

'European imaginations have been fired. It may be possible to integrate in some measure comparable with the vast industrial integration and potential of the US, which the Russians are trying to emulate. If some such integration does not take place Europe will gradually decline in the face of pressure from the US on the one hand and USSR on the other'.

This prejudice remained for many years in official circles.

For the first 15 years after World War II, as we have seen, Britain held aloof from the integration process. She favoured cooperation and a wide free trade area, but resisted supranationalism. This reflected what she regarded (but with diminishing justification) as her real economic interests and also a popular distrust of the Continent conditioned by insularity, the experience of two world wars during which British national sentiment was enhanced, and complacency about the future. Jean Monnet commented:

'the price of victory was the illusion that you could maintain what you had without change'.

Popular attitudes in Britain long outlasted the British government's decision to apply for membership. The question as to whether Britain should or should not join the Community and then, once having joined in 1973, whether it should remain in, were live political issues until the mid-1980s, dividing both the Labour and Conservative Parties. More recently the debate over what kind of Europe, how supranational, federal or intergovernmental, has been widely publicised (see Chapter 9).

In January 1963, as we have seen, the Macmillan initiative was thwarted by President de Gaulle. This also meant that the Danish, Irish and Norwegian applications to join lapsed. They too would have to wait for de Gaulle's departure from office. Four years later, in 1967, Harold Wilson, Labour Prime Minister, applied again. 'Over the next year,' he said, 'the next ten years, the next twenty years, the unity of Europe is going to be forged, and geography and history and interest and sentiment alike demand that we play a part in forging it, and in working it.' De Gaulle again vetoed the application. It was only after the President's resignation in April 1969 and the Hague Conference in December of that year (see Document 8.2) that the way opened for Britain with the new President Georges Pompidou and the new Conservative Prime Minister Edward Heath. Heath had argued for British participation in the integration process throughout his parliamentary career, from the time of the foundation of the ECSC. Of all the British Prime Ministers to date he was to be the most consistently 'pro-European'.

From the French standpoint, by the end of the 1960s German economic preponderance was causing concern. British accession, providing the terms were satisfactory, would open up an additional market, and offer a counterbalance to Germany. The Warsaw Pact invasion of Czechoslovakia in 1968 had robbed de Gaulle's idea of 'Europe from the Atlantic to the Urals' of credibility, just as the events of 1968 in Paris had weakened his authority. Pompidou was willing to consider a Europe from the Thames to the Elbe and to seek *rapprochement* with the United Kingdom. Another consequence of the French wish to contain German dominance was the establishment of Economic and Monetary Union (EMU) in 1973, though the weakness of the Franc forced France to leave the EMU 'Snake' in 1974.

The enlargement of the Community in 1973 removed a major cause of contention which had divided the Six for ten years. The Six became the Nine with the accession at the same time of Ireland and Denmark. Norway had also applied but in 1972 the Norwegian electorate had rejected membership in a referendum. Within Britain, though, there was very considerable argument over the economic benefits or disadvantages of membership. In particular, the CAP had been designed for the Six. It was

ill-adapted to the needs of Britain with its relatively small and highly efficient agricultural sector and large imports of foodstuffs. She had a defi-
ciency payment subsidy system, whereas the CAP was based on a scheme
of guaranteed prices. Britain had also had endemic balance-of-payments
difficulties and a number of economists argued that membership was likely
to aggravate this problem and did not accept the optimism of the White
Paper (see Document 8.4). In the event, a transition period of seven years
was agreed during which Britain was to be eased gradually into full
participation. However the question of budget contributions remained a
vexed one and was to be the major point at issue between Britain and the
Community during the first two administrations of Mrs. Thatcher. Other
key considerations in the negotiations were the questions of
Commonwealth produce and the role of sterling.

There was widespread hostility to membership in the Labour Party,
particularly among the Left wing and Trade Unions (see Document 8.6).
In February 1974 Edward Heath called an election. Labour won, and won
again in October. The Labour Party manifesto for October promised that
within a year the people would decide 'through the ballot box' whether
Britain should stay in the Community on terms to be renegotiated by
Labour. The following year the Government announced a Referendum on
whether or not to remain in the Community. Harold Wilson announced
that the Government would recommend a 'yes' vote. Even his Cabinet was
split 16 for to 7 against. In the event 67.2 per cent of those voting were
in favour. For examples of the arguments advanced for and against by the
two major campaigns 'Britain in Europe' and 'The National Referendum
Campaign' see Documents 8.7 and 8.8.

After this there was the disputed issue of Direct Elections to the European Parliament. Article 138 of the Treaty of Rome had specified: 'The
Assembly shall draw up proposals for elections by direct universal suffrage
in accordance with a uniform procedure in all Member States . . . The
Council shall, acting unanimously, lay down the appropriate provisions,
which it shall recommend to Member States for adoption in accordance
with their respective constitutional requirements'. There had been
considerable pressure for such elections (see Document 8.9) but a Draft
Convention was not adopted until January 1976 and elections were not
held until 1979. One of the main stumbling blocks had been the Treaty
requirement for a uniform electoral procedure. It proved impossible,
however, to reach agreement on either a single day or single electoral
system. All the Direct Elections to date have been fought under divergent
systems, with Britain retaining the first-past-the-post system (see Document
8.10). Until 1979 the European Parliament had consisted of nominated
representatives from the national parliaments. The number of representatives increased from 198 to 410 with Direct Elections. Now, after the
accession of Greece, Spain and Portugal the number stands at 518.

Already in the first decade after this enlargement, the issue of widening-versus-deepening of the Community was emerging. The Community was enlarged just before the oil crisis which followed the Arab–Israeli war. A long period of high and stable economic growth was now followed by the deceleration of growth, declining investment and productivity, high inflation and rising unemployment. This encouraged a mood of protectionism among the Member States of the Community, and later it was to raise the spectre of trade war between the Community and the United States and Japan.

Hopes of monetary integration (see Document 8.3) were also diminished, though the creation of the European Monetary System (EMS) with the Exchange Rate Mechanism (ERM) was introduced to help stabilise a Community faced with considerable fluctuations in the world money markets. The new French President, Giscard d'Estaing, and the German Chancellor, Helmut Schmidt, had called for a 'zone of monetary stability' at the meeting of the European Council in Copenhagen. It was hoped, too, that a common discipline of exchange rates would impose convergence upon the economies of the Community.

Two further developments were the institution of the financial independence of the Community through the introduction of its own sources of revenue, consisting of customs duties, agricultural levies and a percentage of Value Added Tax, and the creation of an intergovernmental system of foreign policy coordination, European Political Cooperation.

Another important aspect of the Community was its developing relationship with the Third World. Throughout the 1960s and 1970s association or cooperation agreements were signed with large numbers of developing countries. The First Yaoundé Convention, signed on 20 July 1963, extended tariff reductions and development aid to 18 former French colonies in Africa. This was widened to include several more African states in the Second Yaoundé Convention of 29 July 1969. These were replaced on 28 February 1975 by the First Lomé Convention. This established a privileged relationship between the Community and 46 states in Africa, the Caribbean and the Pacific, known collectively as the APC States. Under this agreement 99 per cent of APC exports entered the Community duty-free. The convention also provided for development aid. The Lomé Convention was extended in 1979 and 1984 with the Second and Third Lomé Conventions.

Documents

DOCUMENT 8.1

Extract from the Declaration by the European Commission on the Occasion of the Achievement of the Customs Union on 1 July 1968

Customs duties within the Common Market were abolished 18 months ahead of schedule. This declaration looks ahead to future achievements in European integration.

II The Objectives

The Europeans face immense tasks.

A. The Economic Union

The Customs Union being complete, work on the achievement of economic union must be continued. This means that the common economic policies designed to transform the customs territory into an economically organised continent must be built up or completed. We must put the finishing touches to the common agricultural policy, much of which is already in place, and finish work on policies for harmonisation or unification in the commercial, fiscal, social, transport, and other fields, as provided for in the Treaties. We must gradually replace the old national policies with Community policies, changing the European area into an organised European society, with a general economic policy thought out and built up to the scale of the continent.

Three of these policies deserve special mention. In the first place, after having abolished the customs frontiers within the Community, the tax frontiers must also be gradually eliminated so that men and goods can move freely without formalities or controls at the frontiers. In addition, we must make progress in the field of monetary union, first by harmonising the monetary policies of our six Member States, and then by creating between them a degree of monetary solidarity which will lead stage by stage to the coping-stone of the economic edifice – a common currency superseding the old national currencies. Lastly, Europe must be led to make decisive progress in the field of research and technology, so that it can stand on an equal footing with the other great world economic areas.

B. Political union

A political Europe – the aim of Robert Schuman, Konrad Adenauer and de Gasperi – must be built up in the same way as our large countries, Germany, France, and Italy, were gradually unified by major political decisions. Europe must have institutions enabling it to become a politically organised continent, having not only its economic institutions – which are already well on the road to completion – but also political institutions

enabling it to act and become what the declaration of 9 May 1950 called
the European Federation.

If this is to be done, Europe must not only have genuine federal institutions; it must also be unified and the other countries of Europe which are
willing to accept the same rights and the same duties must gather around
the nucleus formed by the Europe of the Six. At the same time political
integration must facilitate a *détente* and co-operation between the East and
the West, thus making an essential contribution to the establishment of a
pacific order in Europe.

C. Europe and the rest of the world

Europe bears major international responsibilities. The Europe of the Six,
inferior to the United States in military, industrial and financial power, is
already its equal in the field of trade. It is the world's leading importer of
manufactured and agricultural produce. It is the leading importer of
products from the countries of the third world. Today, in its present form,
it already has major responsibilities to the developing countries – and these
will be even more important tomorrow when Europe is a larger entity.

In addition, at a time when the organisation of the world on the scale
of the old sovereign nations is yielding place to organisation at the level
of continents, it is important that the errors of the past should not be
repeated at this higher level, that the clash of nations should not give way
to the clash of entire continents. Consequently, it is Europe's duty to
organise co-operation and association with the other main groups in the
world.

D. Human problems

Lastly, the great social changes in a world dominated by technology and
speed raise immense questions for our generation: the transformation of
society, the organisation of social life, the environment and the destiny of
man, his liberty, his security, his health, his life itself.

None of all this, none of these fundamental political, economic, social
and human problems can be solved by our old States imprisoned within
their narrow frontiers. It is just as impossible to solve them without breaking through the old structures inherited from the past and without creating
the European structures which are vital to the work of renewal as it is
necessary to retain the old cultures, traditions, languages, originality,
everything which gives the States their personalities and which constitutes
the beauty, the diversity, the charm, and the immanent value of Europe,
and in place of which nobody could possibly desire to set up colourless and
impersonal machinery.

III The Means

What is the right approach to these tasks and how are they to be carried out? This is work on a grand scale which will keep a whole generation busy – but there has to be a beginning. Starting from what has already been done, starting from the 1 July deadline, and without looking too far ahead, let us inquire what we can, what we must, do in the next five years.

(a)   We must take a step forward in the field of political union. A single Treaty, enabling a new stage forward to be begun must take the place of the Treaty of Paris (1951) and the two Treaties of Rome (1957), which created our three European Communities. The Council of Ministers of the Community must be re-established in its normal functioning as a body which can take majority decisions. The out-of-date system of the right of veto, which paralyses action, must be done away with. The single Commission must be given the implementing powers enabling it not only to take the initiative in Community progress but genuinely to manage the Community, with the task of management growing as the new Community policies gradually enter into force.

At the same time, the authority entrusted to European Institutions must be steadily given a wider democratic basis – and this must be done more rapidly. The European Parliament must be given greater budgetary and legislative powers. The European peoples must participate increasingly, through direct elections and all other appropriate methods, in Community life at the European level.

(b)   In coming years we must work through the stages in the construction of the economic union. Stimulated by the results already obtained, particularly in agriculture (here it has made an enormous effort), the European Commission intends to speed up and multiply its proposals to the Council of Ministers, so that the Community may make early and decisive progress in working out the economic, monetary, fiscal, social and other policies, which, in the five coming years, will need to have achieved most of their objectives.

(c)   The efforts to enlarge the Community and unify the European continent must be resumed. The profound economic and social crisis in some of our countries, both within and without the community, has shown how far the destinies of the European States have become intermingled. The moment has come to face the implications of this fact.

(d)   The major economic, social and intellectual forces of Europe must be persuaded to take part more fully in the construction of the European continent.

It would be wrong to wait until the European people as a whole is officially consulted and takes part constitutionally and organically in the political life of the European continent. The major social groups in the Community must be called upon more urgently to help here and now.

This is why the Commission has decided to propose to the Economic and Social Committee that the Committee and the Commission should embark in the autumn on a far-reaching examination of the Community situation considered as a whole.

DOCUMENT 8.2

Extract from the Communiqué of the Meeting of the Heads of State or Government at The Hague, 1–2 December 1969

This summit meeting was convoked by the French President, Georges Pompidou. It was the prelude to the first enlargement of the Community and prefigured other key developments in the 1970s. This extract is from a press release from the Dutch Ministry of Foreign Affairs.

5. As regards the completion of the Communities, the Heads of State or Government reaffirmed the will of their governments to pass from the transitional period to the final stage of the European Community and accordingly to lay down a definitive financial arrangement for the common agricultural policy by the end of 1969.

   They agreed to replace progressively, within the framework of this financial arrangement, the contributions of member countries by their own resources, taking into account all the interests concerned, with the object of achieving in due course the integral financing of the communities' budgets in accordance with the procedure provided for in Article 201 of the Treaty establishing the EEC and of strengthening the budgetary powers of the European Parliament.

   The problem of the method of direct elections is still being studied by the Council of Ministers.

6. They asked the Governments to continue without delay within the Council the efforts already made to ensure a better control of the market by a policy of agricultural production making it possible to limit budgetary charges.

7. The acceptance of a financial arrangement for the final stage does not exclude its adaption by unanimous vote, in particular in the light of an enlarged community and on condition that the principles of this arrangement are not infringed.

8. They reaffirmed their readiness to further the more rapid progress of the later development needed to strengthen the Community and promote its development into an economic union. They are of the opinion that the integration process should result in a community of stability and growth. To this end they agreed that within the Council,

on the basis of the memorandum presented by the Commission on 12 February 1969 and in close collaboration with the latter, a plan in stages should be worked out during 1970 with a view to the creation of an economic and monetary union.

The development of monetary cooperation should depend on the harmonisation of economic policies.

They agreed to arrange for the investigation of the possibility of setting up a European reserve fund in which a joint economic and monetary policy would have to result.

9. As regards the technological activity of the community, they reaffirmed their readiness to continue more intensively the activities of the Community with a view to coordinating and promoting industrial research and development in the principal sectors concerned, in particular by means of common programmes, and to supply the financial means for the purpose.

10. They further agreed on the necessity of making fresh efforts to work out in the near future a research programme for the European Atomic Energy Community designed in accordance with the exigencies of modern industrial management, and making it possible to ensure the most effective use of the Common Research Centre.

11. They reaffirmed their interest in the establishment of a European university.

12. The Heads of State or Government acknowledged the desirability of reforming the Social Fund, within the framework of a closely concerted social policy.

13. They reaffirmed their agreement on the principle of the enlargement of the Community, as provided by Article 237 of the Treaty of Rome.

In so far as the applicant States accept the Treaties and their political finality, the decisions taken since the entry into force of the treaties and the options made in the sphere of development, the Heads of State or Government have indicated their agreement to the opening of negotiations between the Community on the one hand and the applicant States on the other.

They agreed that the essential preparatory work could be undertaken as soon as practically and conveniently possible; by common consent, the preparations would take place in a most positive spirit.

14. As soon as negotiations with the applicant countries have been opened, discussions will be started with such other EFTA members as may request them on their position in relation to the EEC.

15. They agreed to instruct the Ministers for Foreign Affairs to study the best way of achieving progress in the matter of political unification, within the context of enlargement. The Ministers would be expected to report before the end of July 1970.

DOCUMENT 8.3

Conclusions of the Werner Report on Economic and Monetary Union, 11 October 1970

This report followed the decision of the Hague Summit (see Document 8.2) which called for Economic and Monetary Union (EMU). It was intended that this should be introduced by 1980. Pierre Werner was Prime Minister of Luxembourg. A modified report was accepted by the Council of Ministers in 1971.

The Group, recalling that the Council adopted on 8 and 9 June 1970 the conclusions presented by the Group in its interim report, suggests to the Council that it should accept the contents of the present report and approve the following conclusions:

A. Economic and monetary union is an objective realisable in the course of the present decade provided only that the political will of the Member States to realise this objective, as solemnly declared at the Conference at the Hague, is present. The union will make it possible to ensure growth and stability within the Community and reinforce the contribution it can make to economic and monetary equilibrium in the world and make it a pillar of stability.

B. Economic and monetary union means that the principal decisions of economic policy will be taken at Community level and therefore that the necessary powers will be transferred from the national plane to the Community plane. These transfers of responsibility and the creation of the corresponding Community institutions represent a process of fundamental political significance which entails the progressive development of political cooperation. The economic and monetary union thus appears as a leaven for the development of political union which in the long run it will be unable to do without.

C. A monetary union implies, internally, the total and irreversible convertibility of currencies, the elimination of margins of fluctuation in rates of exchange, the irrevocable fixing of parity ratios and the total liberation of movements of capital. It may be accompanied by the maintenance of national monetary symbols, but considerations of a psychological and political order militate in favour of the adoption of a single currency which would guarantee the irreversibility of the undertaking.

D. On the institutional plane, in the final stage, two Community organs are indispensable: a centre of decision for economic policy and a Community system for the central banks. These institutions, while safeguarding their own responsibilities, must be furnished with

effective powers of decision and must work together for the realisation
of the same objectives. The centre of economic decision will be
politically responsible to a European Parliament.

E.   Throughout the process, as progress is achieved Community instruments will be created to carry out or complete the action of the national
instruments. In all fields the steps to be taken will be interdependent and
will reinforce one another; in particular the development of monetary
unification will have to be combined with parallel progress towards the
harmonization and finally the unification of economic policies.

DOCUMENT 8.4

**Extract from the White Paper, 'The United Kingdom and the
European Communities', London, 1971**

*This assessment of economic effects of British membership of the Community accom-
panied Britain's final and successful attempt to join.*

44.   The effects of membership on British industry will stem principally
from the creation of an enlarged European market by the removal of
tariffs between the United Kingdom and the Community countries,
and, less importantly, from other tariff changes.* The response of
British industry will be broadly of two different kinds. First, there will
be the immediate reaction of a British exporter to each annual reduction in the tariff on his exports to the Community. This response will
involve a decision whether, for example, to maintain his prices and
so increase his profit margins, or reduce his prices and so expand his
sales. But secondly, and in the long run far more significant than his
response to relatively small annual changes in tariffs, will be
industry's decisions on how to take advantage by structural changes
of the opportunities opened up by the creation at the end of the transitional period of a permanent, assured and greatly enlarged market.
Manufacturers will be operating in a 'domestic market' perhaps five
times as large as at present, in which tariff barriers cannot be put up
against them however well they do. There will in consequence be a
radical change in planning, investment, production and sales effort.

45.   Any calculation of the effects on the balance of trade of these tariff

---

* British exporters will benefit from preferential access to those markets associated, or having
special trade arrangements, with the Community. On the other hand they will share with
Community exporters their present preferential position in other EFTA countries and in the
Irish Republic; and must expect a faster erosion of existing Commonwealth preferences, which
have, however, been steadily eroded over recent years and which would probably continue to
diminish in future even if we remained outside the Community.

changes will only produce a valid estimate if it takes account of the parallel existence of both these influences operating on industry. And a simple summation of estimates of industry's immediate responses to the small annual tariff changes involved would reflect only the false assumption that no other changes were taking place. The Government do not believe that the overall response of British industry to membership can be quantified in terms of its effect upon the balance of trade. They are confident that this effect will be positive and substantial, as it has been for the Community.

46. Growth and prosperity in any country, including of course each of the six Community countries, depend first and foremost upon the size and effective use of its resources of manpower, plant, equipment and managerial skill. It is essential to deploy these resources to the maximum benefit, and this requires the pursuit of appropriate economic policies. This requirement would be mandatory upon the United Kingdom in any event. However, the general economic and commercial environment within which a country operates is also a vital element in its success in creating wealth and promoting welfare. The environment can be conducive to growth, or it can be unfavourable to growth. It is generally agreed that for advanced industrial countries the most favourable environment is one where markets are large, and are free from barriers to trade. These conditions favour specialisation, the exploitation of economies of scale, the developing and marketing of new products and a high level of investment in the most modern and up-to-date equipment. Through increased competition, they foster the more efficient use of resources over a wide area of industry and help to check the trend to monopoly positions on the part of large-scale organisations.

47. In particular, the development and exploitation of modern industrial technology, upon which so much of our employment and income increasingly depends, requires greater resources for research and development and wider markets than any one Western European nation can provide. The different national systems of corporate law and taxation in Western Europe make it difficult for European firms to combine and co-operate effectively to meet competition from the great firms whose resources are based on the much larger home markets of the United States and, more recently, of Japan. In recent years Western European markets for jet aircraft and aero engines, for computers and advanced electronic equipment, for nuclear fuel and power, for motor vehicles and for many other products have been increasingly dominated or penetrated by the much larger international corporations based outside Europe. Together, the Western European nations can organise themselves to compete with these

giants, which are otherwise bound to go on increasing their share of European industrial markets.

48. If we enter the Communities we shall be able to profit from the general advantages of a larger market and, in particular, to play a full part in the development of industries based on advanced technology. If we do not join, we shall forgo these opportunities which the members of the Communities will increasingly enjoy. Their industries will have a home market of some 190 million people, with preferential markets in other European and overseas countries. Our industries would have a home market of some 55 million people, with perhaps another 45 million in EFTA, as against the home market of some 299 million people we should have if we joined the Communities.

Experience of the Six

49. The economic growth of the Six countries had already been considerable in the 1950s, as they recovered from the disruptions of war and occupation. The formation of the European Economic Community then created an environment within which they have each made further and striking progress over the past decade. In considering the likely effect upon our economy of membership of an enlarged Community we must first examine the evidence of that decade.

50. The members of the Community created a common market in industrial goods by steadily eliminating the tariffs on imports from one another over the years 1959–68. The abolition of tariffs provided a strong and growing stimulus of the mutual trade of Community countries. It is estimated that by 1969 the value of this 'intra-trade' in manufactured products was about 50 per cent higher than it would have been, had the Community not been formed; moreover it appears that the stimulus to intra-trade is continuing. The abolition of tariffs and this consequent increase in intra-trade were accompanied by important changes in the performance of manufacturing industries in the Six countries. Those industries which competed with imports faced an intensification of competitive pressure as tariffs fell, obliging them to seek ways of raising efficiency and reducing costs. By the same token, prospects for exporting dramatically improved. Import competition and export expansion were closely associated with a growth in investment. The outcome of these processes was a significant improvement in the rate of growth of manufacturing productivity, and, therefore, higher national incomes in the Community than the member countries believe they would have enjoyed otherwise. Moreover, the increase in productivity was accompanied by a

low level of unemployment, even though large numbers of farm workers left the land for industry.

51.　The rate of growth of manufacturing output per head in the five major Community countries had already been at a generally high level over the 1950s and early 1960s, faster than in nearly all other comparable industrial economies. In the latter half of the 1960s, however, this growth rate showed a further marked increase (with the one exception of Italy, where the very high rate achieved in the earlier period was not quite maintained).

52.　The rapid growth in manufacturing productivity in the Six was a key factor in their impressive economic record in the past decade. But other indicators also show clearly the extent of the advances made by comparison with the United Kingdom. For example, in 1958 average earnings in Britain were similar to those in France, Germany, Belgium and the Netherlands and well over half as high again as those in Italy. By 1969 average earnings in Italy had caught up with British earnings, and in the other Community countries, earnings were now between a quarter and a half higher on average than those in Britain. In real terms (i.e., after allowing for price inflation), average British earnings had increased by less than 40 per cent between 1958 and 1969, while in the Community countries average real earnings had gone up over 75 per cent. Similarly, all the Community countries enjoyed rates of growth of gross national product (GNP) per head of population, or of private consumption per head, roughly twice as great as Britain's.

53.　Moreover, at the same time a high proportion of the Community's output continued to be channelled into investment, so providing the basis for further rapid growth. In the period 1959–69, the Six devoted 24 per cent of their GNP to investment, whereas the figure for Britain was 17 per cent.

54.　Finally, the Community as a whole have maintained a strong balance of payments position, earning a surplus on current account of more than $25,000 million over the period 1958 to 1969; by comparison the United Kingdom had a small cumulative deficit on current account over these years.

Prospects for Our Economy

55.　This, then, has been the experience of the Community. It is the conviction of the Governments, of the industries and of the trade unions in the Six countries that their economic progress has been promoted in large measure by the changes brought about by the creation of the Community. The economic structure of the United Kingdom is in many respects similar to that of the member countries of the Community. We, like they, are a highly industrialised society, without large indigenous resources of raw materials, and thus heavily dependent upon foreign trade. Like the three larger members of the Community – which in size of population are closely comparable to ourselves – we have a widely diversified industrial structure, which has great potential for development in a larger market.

56.   In the light of the experience of the Six themselves their conviction that the creation of the Community materially contributed to their growth, and of the essential similarity of our economies, the Government are confident that membership of the enlarged Community will lead to much improved efficiency and productivity in British industry, with a higher rate of investment and a faster growth of real wages. The studies, mentioned earlier, made by the Confederation of British Industries show that this belief is shared by a substantial majority of British industry, whose own interests are at stake, and who are in the best position to judge. A more efficient United Kingdom industry will be more competitive not only within the enlarged Community but also in world markets generally.

DOCUMENT 8.5

A comparative poll on the EEC in seven countries, 1970

The response to the following questions illustrates very clearly the gap between British and Continental public opinion on the question of Western European integration.

Are you in favour of, or against, Britain joining the European Common Market?

	Holland	Luxem-bourg	West Germany	France	Belgium	Italy	EEC	Britain
In favour	79	70	69	66	63	51	64	19
Against	8	6	7	11	8	9	8	63
Don't know	13	24	24	23	29	40	28	18

Assuming that Britain did join, would you be for or against the evolution of the Common Market towards the political formation of a United States of Europe?

	Holland	Luxem-bourg	West Germany	France	Belgium	Italy	EEC	Britain
For	64	75	69	67	60	60	65	30
Against	17	5	9	11	10	7	9	48
Don't know	19	20	22	22	30	33	26	22

Would you be in favour of or against the election of a European Parliament by direct universal suffrage; that is a parliament elected by all the voters in the member countries?

	Holland	Luxem-bourg	West Germany	France	Belgium	Italy	EEC	Britain
In favour	59	71	66	59	56	55	59	25
Against	21	10	9	15	11	6	11	55
Don't know	20	19	25	26	33	39	30	20

Would you be willing to accept, over and above your own government, a European Government responsible for a common policy in foreign affairs, defence and the economy?

	Holland	Luxem-bourg	West Germany	France	Belgium	Italy	EEC	Britain
Willing	50	47	57	49	51	51	53	22
Not willing	32	35	19	28	19	10	20	60
Don't know	18	18	24	23	30	39	27	18

If a President of a United States of Europe were being elected by popular vote, would you be willing to vote for a candidate not of your own country – if his personality and programme corresponded more closely to your ideas than those of the candidates of your own country?

	Holland	Luxem-bourg	West Germany	France	Belgium	Italy	EEC	Britain
Willing	63	67	69	61	52	45	59	39
Not willing	18	20	20	22	24	19	18	41
Don't know	19	13	19	17	24	36	23	20

DOCUMENT 8.6

Labour Party Conference resolution, passed October 1972

This resolution articulates the view widespread in the Labour Party in Britain that Community policies and the achievement of Socialist objectives were not compatible.

This Conference declares its opposition to entry to the Common Market on the terms negotiated by the Tories and calls on a future Labour Government to reverse any decision for Britain to join unless new terms have been negotiated including the abandonment of the Common Agricultural Policy and the Value Added Tax, no limitations on the freedom of a Labour Government to carry out economic plans, regional development, extension of the Public Sector, control of Capital Movements, and the preservation of the power of the British Parliament over its legislation and taxation, and, meanwhile to halt immediately the entry arrangements, including all payments to the European Communities, and participation in their Institutions, in particular the European Parliament, until such terms have been negotiated and the assent of the British electorate has been given.

DOCUMENT 8.7

'Why You Should Vote Yes'

The following are extracts from the 'Britain in Europe' campaign leaflet issued in May 1975. The British Referendum posed the question: 'Do you think the United Kingdom should stay in the European Community?'

It makes good sense for our jobs and prosperity. It makes good sense for world peace. It makes good sense for the Commonwealth. It makes good sense for our children's future. Being in does not in itself solve our problems. No one pretends it could. It doesn't guarantee us a prosperous future. Only our own efforts will do that. But it offers the best framework for success, the best protection for our standard of living, the best foundation for greater prosperity. All the original six members have found that. They have done well – much better than we have – over the past 15 years. . .

Our friends want us to stay in. If we left we would not go back to the world as it was when we joined, still less to the old world of Britain's imperial heyday. The world has been changing fast. And the changes have made things more difficult and more dangerous for this country. It is a time when we need friends. What do our friends think? The old Commonwealth wants us to stay in, Australia does, Canada does. New Zealand does. The new Commonwealth wants us to stay in. Not a single one of their 34 governments wants us to leave. The United States wants us to stay in. They want a close Atlantic relationship (upon which our whole security depends) with a Europe of which we are part; but not with us alone. The other members of the European Community want us to stay in. That is why they have been flexible in the recent re-negotiations and so made possible the improved terms which have converted many former doubters. Outside, we should be alone in a harsh, cold world, with none of our friends offering to revive old partnerships. . .

Why can't we go it alone? To some this sounds attractive. Mind our own business. Make our own decisions. Pull up the drawbridge. In the modern world it just is not practicable. It wasn't so even 40 or 60 years ago. The world's troubles, the world's wars inevitably dragged us in. Much better to work together to prevent them happening. Today we are even more dependent on what happens outside. Our trade, our jobs, our food, our defence cannot be wholly within our own control. That is why so much of the argument about sovereignty is a false one. It's not a matter of dry legal theory. The real test is how we can protect our own interests and exercise British influence in the world. The best way is to work with our friends and neighbours. If we came out, the Community would go on taking decisions which affect us vitally – but we should have no say in them. We would be clinging to the shadow of British sovereignty while its substance flies out of the window. The European Community does not pretend that each member nation is not different. It strikes a balance between the wish to express our own national personalities and the need for common action. All decisions of any importance must be agreed by every member.

Our traditions are safe. We can work together and still stay British. The Community does not mean dull uniformity. It hasn't made the French eat German food or the Dutch drink Italian beer. Nor will it damage our British traditions and way of life. The position of the Queen is not affected. She will remain Sovereign of the United Kingdom and Head of the Commonwealth. Four of the other Community countries have monarchies of their own.

English Common Law is not affected. For a few commercial and industrial purposes there is need for Community Law. But our criminal law, trial by jury, presumption of innocence remain unaltered. So do our civil rights. Scotland, after 250 years of much closer union with England, still keeps its own legal system. . .

Staying in protects our jobs. Jobs depend upon our industries investing more and being able to sell in the world. If we came out, our industry would be based on the smallest home market of any major exporting country in the world, instead of on the Community market of 250 million people. It is very doubtful if we could then negotiate a free trade agreement with the Community. Even if we could it would have damaging limitations and we would have to accept many Community rules without having the say we now have in their making. So we could lose free access not only to the Community market itself but to the 60 or more other countries with which the Community has trade agreements. The immediate effect on trade, on industrial confidence, on investment prospects, and hence on jobs, could well be disastrous. . .

Secure food at fair prices. Before we joined the Community everyone feared that membership would mean paying more for our food than if we were outside. This fear has proved wrong. If anything, the Community has saved us money on food in the past two years. Why? Not just by accident, but because stronger world demand has meant that the days when there were big surpluses of cheap food to be bought around the world have gone, and almost certainly gone for good. Sometimes Community prices may be a little above world prices, sometimes a little below. But Britain, as a country which cannot feed itself, will be safer in the Community which is almost self-sufficient in food. Otherwise we may find ourselves standing at the end of a world food queue. It also makes sense to grow more of our food. That we can do in the Community, and it's one reason why most British farmers want to stay in. . .

Britain's choice: the alternatives. The Community is not perfect. Far from it. It makes mistakes and needs improvement. But that's no reason for contracting out. What are the alternatives? Those who want us to come out are deeply divided. Some want an isolationist Britain with a 'siege economy' – controls and rationing. Some want a Communist Britain – part of the Soviet bloc. Some want us even closer to the United States than to Europe – but America itself doesn't want that. Some want us to fall back on the Commonwealth – but the Commonwealth itself doesn't want that. Some want us to be half linked to Europe, as part of a free trade area – but the European Community itself doesn't want that. So when people say we should leave, ask them what positive way ahead they propose for Britain. You will get some very confusing answers. There are also differences amongst those of us who say 'stay in'. Some of us are Labour, some are Conservative, some are Liberal, some are non-party. But we all agree on the fundamental question before us. The safety and prosperity of this country demand that we stay in the European Community. So do our duty to the world and our hope for the new greatness of Britain. We believe in Britain – in Britain in Europe. For your own and your children's future it makes good sense to stay in. . .

DOCUMENT 8.8

'Why You Should Vote No'

The following is extracted from the 'National Referendum Campaign' leaflet, also issued in May 1975. In the event 67.2 per cent of the votes cast in the Referendum were in favour of staying in the Community.

Re-negotiation. The present Government, though it tried, has on its own admission failed to achieve the 'fundamental re-negotiation' it promised at the last two General Elections. All it has gained are a few concessions for Britain, some of them only temporary. The real choice before the British peoples has been scarcely altered by re-negotiation.

What did the pro-Marketers say? Before we joined the Common Market the Government forecast that we should enjoy – A rapid rise in our living standards; A trade surplus with the Common Market; Better productivity; Higher investment; More employment; Faster industrial growth.

In every case the opposite is now happening, according to the Government's figures. . .

Our legal right to come out. It was agreed during the debates which took us into the Common Market that the British Parliament had the absolute right to repeal the European Communities Act and take us out. There is nothing in the Treaty of Rome which says a country cannot come out.

The right to rule ourselves. The fundamental question is whether or not we remain free to rule ourselves in our own way. For the British people, membership of the Common Market has already been a bad bargain. What is worse, it sets out by stages to merge Britain with France, Germany, Italy and other countries into a single nation. This will take away from us the right to rule ourselves which we have enjoyed for centuries. . .

Your food, your jobs, our trade. We cannot afford to remain in the Common Market because: it must mean still higher food prices. Before we joined, we could buy our food at the lowest cost from the most efficient producers in the world. Since we joined, we are no longer allowed to buy all our food where it suits us best. . .

Your jobs at risk. If we stay in the Common Market, a British Government can no longer prevent the drift of industry southwards and increasingly to the Continent. This is already happening.

If it went on, it would be particularly damaging to Scotland, Wales, Northern Ireland and much of the North and West of England, which have suffered so much from unemployment already.

If we stay in the Common Market, our Government must increasingly abandon to them control over this drift of industry and employment. Far-reaching powers of interference in the control of British industry, particularly iron and steel, are possessed by the Market authorities.

Interference with the oil around our shores has already been threatened by the Brussels Commission.

Huge trade deficit with Common Market. The Common Market pattern of trade was never designed to suit Britain. . .

Taxes to keep prices up. The Common Market's dear food policy is designed to prop up inefficient farmers on the Continent by keeping food prices high. . .

Agriculture. It would be far better for us if we had our own national agricultural policy suited to our own country, as we had before we joined. . .

Commonwealth links. Our Commonwealth links are bound to be weakened much further if we stay in the Common Market. We are being forced to tax imported Commonwealth goods. And as we lose our national independence, we shall cease, in practice, to be a member of the Commonwealth.

Britain a mere province of the Common Market? The real aim of the Market is, of course, to become one single country in which Britain would be reduced to a mere province. The plan is to have a Common Market Parliament by 1978 or shortly thereafter.

What is the alternative? A far better course is open to us. If we withdraw from the Market, we could and should remain members of the wider Free Trade Area which now exists between the Common Market and the countries of the European Free Trade Association (EFTA) – Norway, Sweden, Finland, Austria, Switzerland, Portugal and Iceland. These countries are now to enjoy free entry for their industrial exports into the Common Market without having to carry the burden of the Market's dear food policy or suffer rule from Brussels. Britain already enjoys industrial free trade with these countries. If we withdrew from the Common Market, we should remain members of the wider group and enjoy, as the EFTA countries do, free or low-tariff entry into the Common Market countries without the burden of dear food or the loss of the British people's democratic rights. . .

DOCUMENT 8.9

Giuseppe Saragat, Italian Foreign Minister, on the question of direct elections to the European Parliament, April 1964

Direct Elections were not held until 1979 (see Document 8.10). Signor Saragat's proposal envisaged partial European elections in 1966 with a full election to be held before 1 January 1970, the original date proposed for the completion of the Common Market.

The election of Members of the European Parliament by universal suffrage is provided for . . . in the three Community Treaties: in the Treaty setting up the ECSC and in the Treaties setting up the Common Market and Euratom. This election was provided for because it was felt to be an essential condition for achieving that ever-closer political, economic and social union among the European peoples which is the ultimate objective of the three Treaties.

Direct elections will play a decisive part in awakening a real awareness of Europe both among the general public and in leading circles. It will fully justify a substantial widening of the European Parliament's powers of initiative and control and, leading as it would to the establishment of a real European and supranational legislative body; it will encourage and indeed necessitate the setting-up of a political institution of like nature. Any remaining opposition to the political integration of Europe is bound to vanish under the pressure of the democratically expressed will of the European peoples.

DOCUMENT 8.10

Direct elections and integration from 'Parliament for Europe' by David Marquand, 1979

David Marquand was a Labour politician and adviser to the European Commission before becoming a professor of history. The following extract examines the likely impact of direct elections. These elections were held in the same year.

In Community circles, It has sometimes been suggested – in terms implying that the suggestion is virtually self-evident – that integration is bound to benefit, since the mere holding of direct elections will in some way 'legitimise' the Community and the Community process. The Patijn Report claimed that direct elections to the European Parliament 'would

. . . lend to the exercise of power by the Communities a legitimacy which has hitherto been lacking'. The Tindemans Report said that direct elections would 'reinforce the democratic legitimacy of the whole European institutional apparatus'. The truth is more disturbing. The suggestion that direct elections are bound to make integration easier founders on the simple fact that the body which is to be elected – namely the Parliament – plays only a trivial role in the integration process. Parliament will indeed gain legitimacy from direct elections. But the institutions which determine what happens in the Community – namely, the Commission and the Council – will not be affected one way or the other. Direct elections will make a difference to the process of integration, and to the legitimacy of the Community as such, only if Parliament's new weight can somehow be brought to bear in favour of integration, and against the resistance of the national institutions whose positions are threatened by integration. There is no guarantee that this will happen. Indeed, it cannot happen unless the Community's present institutional structure is radically changed. For the hard fact is that, as things are at present, Parliament cannot bring any significant influence to bear on the national resistance to integration.

Indeed, if the present institutional structure remains intact, direct elections may make it even more difficult to achieve further integration than it is already. For the reasons discussed above, elected Members are almost certain to want to prove to their constituents and to themselves that they can influence Community decisions. They will soon discover that their influence is very limited. Though the European Parliament has certain powers over Community spending it has no power over Community revenue-raising. Its role in the legislative process, though not as negligible as is sometimes assumed in the United Kingdom, is merely consultative. Community legislation is proposed by the Commission and decided by the Council; though the Council consults Parliament, Parliament's opinion is not binding. The elaborate process of consultation in which the Commission engages before it makes proposals is not subject to parliamentary scrutiny. Nor are the weekly meetings of the powerful Committee of Permanent Representatives – normally known as COREPER after its acronym in French – which consists of the nine Ambassadors of the Member States to the Community, acting as a kind of legislative sieve, which sends controversial proposals through to the Council of Ministers, but holds back uncontroversial ones for decision by the Ambassadors themselves. In spheres unconnected with legislation or finance, Parliament's role is even more limited. In spite of the Community's growing importance as a negotiating bloc, Parliament plays no part in foreign-policy co-ordination – though its Political Affairs Committee has regular meetings with the foreign minister who holds the presidency of the Council – and does not have to approve the Community's line in trade negotiations. Direct elections will not change any of this. The elected Members will find that laboriously worked-out reports and eloquent speeches in the hemicycle produce no more results than they do at present. Some may sink back into frustrated apathy, but the ablest, the most energetic and the most ambitious can be expected to look for a scapegoat.

Suggested reading

F. Nicholson and R. East, *From the Six to the Twelve* (London, 1987) provides a very full chronological account, giving detailed attention to the accession of all the new Member States. The standard works on the United Kingdom's applications to join the Community are M. Camps, *Britain and the European Community 1955–63* (London, 1964) and U. Kitzinger, *Diplomacy and Persuasion: How Britain Joined the Common Market* (London, 1973). See also the latter's *The Second Try: Labour and the EEC* (Oxford, 1968). A good account of Britain and the Community up to recent times is S. George, *An Awkward Partner* (Oxford, 1990). See also M. Charlton, *The Price of Victory* (London, 1983) and R. Morgan and C. Bray (eds), *Partners and Rivals in Western Europe: Britain, France and Germany* (London, 1986). An interesting account of the Labour Party and the Community can be found in M. Newman, *Socialism and European Unity: The Dilemma of the Left in Britain and France* (London, 1983). R. Jowell and G. Hoinville (eds) examine public attitudes in *Britain into Europe: Public Opinion and the EEC 1961–75* (London, 1976). For the 1975 United Kingdom Referendum see D. Butler and U. Kitzinger, *The Referendum* (London, 1976).

9 From the Nine to 1992

Introduction

In 1979 an article entitled 'Fragments Floating in the Here and Now', an American observer of the EC, Professor Stanley Hoffman, wrote: 'Western Europe remains a collection of largely self-encased nation-states. The various governments of Western Europe have found it useful to establish common institutions to deal with their common problems . . . the basic unit of concern remains the nation-state, however inadequate'. Three years later, 25 years after the signature of the Rome Treaties the President of the European Parliament, Pieter Dankert, asked: 'Why has the infant which held out so much promise 25 years ago changed into a feeble cardiac patient whose condition is so poor that he cannot even be disturbed by a birthday party?'

In the early 1980s there was widespread concern that the Community economies might become perilously uncompetitive in the world market. The word 'Eurosclerosis' was coined. There were grave economic problems and there was a sense of institutional drift (see Document 9.5). The question of further expansion of the Community – Greece joined in 1981 and Spain and Portugal were to become members in 1986 – and institutional reform were closely linked (see Documents 9.3 and 9.4). Recession, regional imbalance and divergence of the economies, unemployment and inflation, and growing concern for the environment all demanded attention. At the same time the question of reform of the Common Agricultural Policy (CAP) and the size of budget contributions, particularly that of the United Kingdom, led to protracted wrangling and heated exchanges. . . (See Document 9.6.)

The objectives set by the EEC Treaty of Rome had only been partly fulfilled, but with the further enlargement of the Community to include Greece, Spain and Portugal, with a Community with now double the original number of Member States, decision-making would become more difficult. References to the probability of a Community 'à deux vitesses', a 'two-tier' or 'two-speed' Community became frequent. On the other hand, the idea of further advance towards what was called 'European

Union' or 'Political Union' and the feeling that the Community must either advance or stagnate, or even disintegrate, was nothing new (see Documents 9.1 and 9.2). There were repeated declarations by national leaders that the unification process must continue. For example, in 1982 Hans-Dietrich Genscher, Foreign Minister of the Federal Republic, and Emilio Colombo his, Italian counterpart, proposed a 'European Act' and in 1984 the European Parliament produced a 'Draft Treaty for European Union'.

In 1985 the Commission produced a paper 'Completing the Internal Market' and recommended 300 measures for the removal of non-tariff barriers (NTBs). There were still a large number of obstacles to the free movement of goods in the Community, such as discriminatory technical specifications and preferential public procurement by governments of their own nations' products. Though the Treaty of Rome had stated that such things should not be allowed to restrict trade, no time had been specified for their abolition. Nor did the institutional mechanism exist for guaranteeing their abolition as long as any Member State could exercise a veto. The Luxembourg Compromise has cast a long shadow (see Document 9.5). It was clear that the further liberalisation of the market could not be accomplished within any reasonable time scale without other changes.

In 1978 the *Cassis de Dijon* case had already cleared the way for further liberalisation of the market. By upholding the right of this French liqueur to be sold in Germany (the German authorities had banned its sale on the grounds that its alcoholic content was too small) this ruling established the general principle that all goods lawfully produced and marketed in one member country should be accepted also by the other member countries. The Single European Act (SEA) which came into force on 1 July 1987 set the target date for the completion of the internal market by the end of 1992. It also introduced qualified majority voting for a wide range of measures and it enhanced the role of the European Parliament by the introduction of the cooperation procedure. (See Appendix B for further details on the SEA.)

Though not an explicit objective in the Treaty of Rome, the idea of monetary union had become an accepted element in Community policy-making at the Hague in 1969 (see Document 8.2) and with the submission of the Werner Report (see Document 8.3). The subsequent creation of the EMS was a significant step forward. According to the Werner Report the test by which to judge whether monetary union had been achieved was total and irreversible convertibility of currencies, liberalisation of capital transactions and financial services, an irrevocably fixed exchange rate or a single currency. The creation of the Single European Market (SEM) would bring about the first two. The Delors Committee Report of 1989 focused its attention on the third.

The British Prime Minister, Mrs. Thatcher, was an enthusiastic supporter of the removal of non-tariff barriers which she regarded as a laudable extension of her own liberal economic principles to the Continent, but was strongly opposed to anything that suggested further inroads on national sovereignty. (See Documents 9.9 and 9.10.) Document 9.7 on the question of the powers of the directly elected European Parliament is another example of nationalistic opposition to integration.

There are now frequent references in Community documents to what is called 'subsidiarity'. In the Draft Treaty Establishing the European Union it means entrusting 'common institutions . . . only with those powers required to complete successfully the tasks they may carry out more satisfactorily than the States acting independently'. Sir Leon Brittan, as a Commissioner, described it as doing 'at Community level only what needs to be done at Community level'. There is obviously ample scope for debate here as to where exactly to draw the line between Community and national responsibilities.

Another word which has come to be used commonly is 'cohesion'. The Single European Act specified a policy of 'cohesion' for 'reducing disparities between the various regions and the backwardness of the least favoured regions' (Article 23). A doubling of what are called 'Structural Funds' has been promised. This raises the whole question of the budget and again brings to the fore the overspend on agriculture. Liberalisation of the market, institutional reform and the financing of the Community are therefore interrelated questions.

Enlargement of the Community has imposed additional strains. There was a strong political motivation in the decision of Greece, Spain and Portugal to join. In the 1970s the dictatorships of Franco, Salazar and the Greek Colonels had become democracies. Membership of the Community was intended to ensure that they remained democracies. At the same time, there were economic fears. Some of the Nine feared that they would be undercut by cheap labour and cheap produce from the new states. France, for instance, was hesitant about Spanish membership because of her agricultural interests. On the other hand, the new Member States were afraid that their developing industries would find it hard to compete with the other states. They feared that they might suffer the same fate as the *Mezzogiorno* after the unification of Italy in the nineteenth century. In addition, the events since 1989 in Eastern Europe, the reunification of Germany and the desire of other countries, such as Austria and Turkey to join the Community have forced a searching reappraisal of institutions and policies. (See Chapter 10.)

The Maastricht meeting on 9 and 10 December 1991 concluded the intergovernmental conferences on European Political Union and Economic and Monetary Union which had been going on for a year. At the time of writing the agreements reached at Maastricht have still to be ratified by the national parliaments. As this goes to press the Danish electorate have just rejected Maastricht in a referendum by a small majority. This presents considerable problems. Eire in a similar referendum have voted acceptance. Some interpret these agreements as laying down, albeit in outline only, the main elements of what might become a future European government, common defence and foreign policy, a single currency, common citizenship and a European Parliament whose powers have been steadily increasing. This is the federal perspective. Others see Maastricht more as a pragmatic response to fast-changing circumstances. It is argued that a Europe which is to compete effectively in world markets needs a unified currency and that closer policy coordination in foreign and defence matters is essential given the events in Russia and Eastern Europe, or, as last year, in the Gulf. (For further details on the Maastricht agreements see Appendix C.) The Community now faces a wider range of challenges than at any time since its foundation.

Documents

DOCUMENT 9.1

The Tindemans Report on European Union 1975–6

The following document is the questionnaire sent out in the preparation of this report. Leo Tindemans was Prime Minister of Belgium. His report raised issues which were increasingly to be discussed in future assessments of the progress of European integration. It proposed economic and monetary union, a common foreign policy, and the development of social, regional and industrial policies among other things.

Questionnaire on European Union Preliminary Questions

1. What does Europe stand for? What are its *raisons d'être* and its specificity in 1975?
2. What experience can be gained from the first twenty years of European construction?

II Content of European Union

1. As regards the fields of application of the Treaties, do you envisage a development of the policies which have been provided for, and an improvement in the actions and procedures currently in use? If so, in what way?
2. In certain areas not explicitly provided for in the text of the Treaties, common action has been undertaken by the Member States. Should the scope and content of the policies in question be further clarified?

Should more binding commitments be envisaged in the application of the common actions which have been decided upon?

3. More particularly, would you like to say what Economic and Monetary Union implies? What are the conditions for its attainment?

4. Beyond Economic and Monetary Union, what does European Union entail?

5. Would it be useful to provide – in the relatively short term – for the insertion of certain areas into the framework and procedures of the Community? If so, which ones?

6. In certain areas, it is possible to envisage a division of powers between the States and the Institutions of the Community: what should these areas be? How should the division of powers be envisaged in practical terms?

7. Regarding the extension of the decisions taken by the Heads of State and Government in their meeting in Paris on 7 December 1974, what initiatives could be taken to concretise the European reality in individual everyday life?

III The Institutions

A. Generalities

1. Should the objectives of European Union be attained through the existing institutions, or must parallel institutions be created? If so, which?

2. Is it possible to conceive of a single institutional structure, having recourse to different procedures – Community and intergovernmental – depending on the matters in question?

B. The European Council (meeting of the Heads of Government in the Council of Ministers and in the context of Political Cooperation)

What role can be played by the European Council? What missions should eventually be entrusted to it: coordination, impetus, arbitration. . .?

C. The Parliamentary Assembly

Starting from the principle of election to the Assembly by direct universal suffrage.

1. What kind of power should be acknowledged for it? Participation in the normative power of the Council? If so, following which modes? Control over the activities of the Commission? The right to initiate legislation? Intervention in the investiture of the Commission?

2. In which areas could it exercise its powers?

3. Structure of the Assembly and election methods. (See the general document drawn up following the debates in the European Parliament on January 14th 1975, concerning the adoption of a draft Convention instituting the election of the members of the European Parliament by direct universal suffrage.)

D. The Council

1. Should adjustments be made to the execution of the legislative function?
2. Should provision be made for delegation by the Council to the Commission of wider powers in the management of the common policies?

E. The Commission

1. Should its powers be strengthened? How? In which areas?
2. What sort of procedure should be envisaged for the nomination of the members of the Commission?
3. What should be the composition of the Commission?

F. The Court of Justice

Do you have any observations regarding the fields of competence and powers of the Court of Justice?

G. The Economic and Social Committee

How can the representation of economic and social interests within the Community be improved?

IV. Method

1. Should the exact content of the Union be fixed at the point of departure, or should the institutions of the Community be instructed to define the content, taking as their starting point a general concept to be agreed upon beforehand?
2. Should progress be made in stages, following a schedule of fixed deadlines?
3. What should be the legal foundations upon which European Union should be built? Certain clauses of the present Treaties? Additional clauses? New treaties?

V. Conclusion

In your view, what positive actions should be taken by the existing structures (political parties, trade union and employers' organisations, other professional organisations) in order to achieve the indicated objectives?

DOCUMENT 9.2

The conclusions of the European Council of 30 November 1976

This notes the response of the Council to the Tindemans Report.

1. The European Council examined the report on European Union submitted to it by Mr Tindemans at its request. It heard an account given by the Chairman of the work carried out, and approved the general lines of the comments by the Ministers for Foreign Affairs on the various Chapters of the Report.

2. The European Council indicated its very great interest in the analyses and proposals put forward by Mr Tindemans. It shared the views expressed by the Belgian Prime Minister on the need to build European Union by strengthening the practical solidarity of the nine Member States and their peoples, both internally and in their relations with the outside world, and gradually to provide the Union with the instruments and institutions necessary for its operation. It considered that European Union should make itself felt effectively in the daily life of individuals by assisting in the protection of their rights and the improvement of the circumstances of their life.

3. On this occasion the European Council had a wide-ranging discussion of the principles which must underlie the construction of European Union over the coming years. European Union will be built progressively by consolidating and developing what has been achieved within the Community, with the existing Treaties forming a basis for new policies. The achievement of Economic and Monetary Union is basic to the consolidation of Community solidarity and the establishment of European Union. Priority importance must be given to combating inflation and unemployment and to drawing up common energy and research policies and a genuine regional and social policy for the Community.

4. The construction of Europe must also make the best use of possibilities for cooperation between the nine Governments in those areas where the Member States are prepared to exercise their sovereignty in a progressively convergent manner. This form of cooperation in the field of foreign policy must lead to the search for a common external policy.

5. In the light of future developments as defined by the report on European Union, the Heads of Government, with the intention of establishing a comprehensive and coherent common political approach, reaffirm their desire to increase the authority and efficiency of the Community institutions, as well as the support of the peoples for them, and confirm the role of the European Council as a driving force.

6. On the basis of the conclusions reached by the Ministers for Foreign Affairs, the European Council invites them, and the Commission, in the sectors for which it is competent, to report to it once a year on the results obtained and the progress which can be achieved in the short term in the various sectors of the Union, thus translating into reality the common conception of European Union.

DOCUMENT 9.3

The enlargement of the Community: general considerations

The following points under the heading of 'Institutional Aspects and Adjustments to the Treaties' were contained in a communication from the Commission to the Council on 20 April 1978. They reflect some of the implications of greater enlargement.

Institutional aspects and adjustments to the treaties

48. The institutions and organs of the present Community cannot ensure that the process of integration will continue in an enlarged Community: on the contrary, there is reason to fear that the Community decision making procedures will deteriorate. If this happened, it would be difficult or even impossible to create a Community based on the rule of law, which is the foundation of the Community and the sole means of recognising in law the principle that to equal rights correspond equal obligations. The institutions and organs of the enlarged Community must accordingly be decisively strengthened.

49. Experience in the changeover from six to nine members has already revealed difficulties and deficiencies in the capacity to act and react jointly. With twelve members the institutions and decision-making procedures will be under considerable strain and the Community will be exposed to possible stalemate and dilution unless its practical *modus operandi* is improved. Extensive adjustments will therefore be essential if the enlarged Community is to work properly. The concept of adjustment will have to be interpreted more broadly than in the past, provided that any adjustment is a consequence of enlargement and as long as it is understood that any change in the fundamental principles of the Treaties can be made only by the special procedures laid down in the Treaties for that purpose.

50. With regard to the 'numerical' changes in the composition and operation of the institutions entailed by the increase in the number of Member States, the rule should be upheld that all the Member States, must be represented in every Community institution and organ. The Community must also avoid any appreciable shift in the existing balance, based on a combination of demographic factors and political considerations, between Member States.

51. Any adaptation of the Treaties will have to take account of the need to improve the functioning of the Community institutions in order to combat the tendency of the decision-making process to become more cumbersome as a result of the involvement of a larger number of

States. Such adaptation must be directed towards the use of majority voting, the Commission's powers and more judicious use of the legal instruments provided by the Treaties.

52.   In a twelve-member Community, more frequent use of majority voting is desirable, particularly to avoid a worsening of the holdups experienced in the present Community. In support of its argument the Commission would refer to the approach adopted by the Heads of State or Government at their Paris Summit in 1974 when they expressed the opinion that, in order to improve the functioning of the Council, it is necessary 'to renounce the practice which consists of making agreement on all questions conditional on the unanimous consent of the Member States, whatever their respective positions may be regarding the conclusions reached in Luxembourg on 28 January 1966'.

53.   The value of this approach has been confirmed by a practice which has been developing gradually since 1975. Majority voting in the Council has been extended pragmatically and a political code of conduct has gradually emerged which is now accepted by all the Member States. In the light of this trend and of the implications of enlargement, the Community would gain valuable room for manoeuvre if the areas where this code applies were extended, i.e. if unanimity were replaced by qualified majority in a few Treaty articles where the present insistence on unanimity does not appear objectively justified and has led in the past to considerable delays in the decision-making procedure.

54.   It will also be even more necessary to relieve the Council and its subsidiary bodies of preparatory work on the technical implementation matters and to use decision-making procedures which guarantee flexibility and speed. The simplest approach would be to alter the Treaties to provide that the Commission shall exercise administrative and executive powers whenever the Council does not decide otherwise. This would introduce into the Community legal order a method of action whose value has been recognised in many official statements in the past (the most important being the communiqué put out by the Heads of State or Government at the Summit in December 1974).

55.   As regards the problems that an enlarged Community will have to face as a result of greater diversity in its political, economic and social situations, these can already be tackled by applying the present principles of the Community legal system. The principle of the uniformity of Community law is tempered by the principle of non-discrimination and it is therefore possible for the Community institutions in adopting rules to take due account of the objective differences between the situations of the various Member States.

DOCUMENT 9.4

Extract from 'The European Community from the First Enlargement to the Second' by Roy Jenkins, President of the Commission

Roy Jenkins was President from 1977–81. The following points were made in a lecture to Edinburgh University in 1978.

The move towards enlargement is linked to the Commission's approach to economic and monetary union. What would clearly be unacceptable in any such desirable move is that only the strong should benefit and the weak should go further to the wall. This need not and must not be the result. There is as much mutual need between the strong and the weak in Europe as there was between the states of the American Union at the end of the nineteenth century. The strong need the underpinning of the unit of the Community market. The weak need the commitment to monetary discipline and the benefit in resource transfers that a powerful Community, socially-oriented, can provide.

These major issues . . . the balance between external strength and internal weakness and the pressing need for a new stimulus to our economies, and acceptable levels of employment, especially as we move towards new enlargement of the Community – are those which both in their political challenge and diversity of detail should dominate European discussion in Member States. They are linked the one to the other and it is our perspective of such major issues that should mould our conception of the Community as an organisation for deliberately acting in common in our mutual interest. We ought to eschew both an obsessive concentration on the largely outdated debate between federalism and the often illusory sovereignty of national institutions, and a myopic obsession with alleged bureaucracy and standardisation.

DOCUMENT 9.5

Extract from 'The European Community: What Kind of Future?' by Emile Noël, Secretary-General of the European Commission

These points about the 'institutional drift' of the Community were contained in a lecture to the Belgian Royal Institute of International Affairs, 20 November 1984.

I now turn to the Community's 'institutional drift' away from the spirit, and indeed the letter, of the Treaties of Rome. This is not a new development: it started with the so-called 'Luxembourg compromise' [see Document 7.12], and has of late been getting worse.

Rather oddly, the official admission of failure to agree in Luxembourg in January 1966 has been followed ever since by the systematic pursuit of unanimity on anything and everything, even though five of the six Member States then accepted that the Community had firmly stated that in the event of prolonged failure to agree, the matter was to be put to the vote wherever the Treaty so provided. This approach, which has become a still more regular practice since the first enlargement, has meant that the pursuit of unanimity dominates the proceedings not only of the Council but of the bodies doing the preparatory groundwork, the Permanent Representatives' Committee and the expert working parties. Even though the Council itself started to use voting two years ago, it still gets held up by the endless preparatory proceedings, striving for unanimity.

The European Council was throughout closely involved in dealing with the budget crisis, from the Strasbourg session when the crisis started, in June 1979, to the Fontainebleau session in June 1984. By the end of the process the Council of Ministers proper no longer even had any say in the preparations for the Heads of Government's meetings, it was so taken for granted that any ticklish matter (whatever it might be) could only be handled at the very top. In fact, since the Stuttgart session in June 1983 the European Council has ceased to be the organ of supreme political initiative originally intended: it is now doing the job of the Council of Ministers, and at the same time preventing the latter from doing its job itself. At Fontainebleau too, in spite of the wishes of the then President in office of the European Council, only a minute part of the proceedings was devoted to issues concerning the future – the institutional reactivation of the Community, its rehabilitation in the eyes of its citizens.

The fact that the Community system is gradually degenerating into intergovernmental negotiation must be fully recognised. The concentration on unanimity and the constant intervention of the European Council are to a great extent responsible for this degeneration. The European Council, when dealing with Community matters, acts – unsurprisingly – in its own way instead of 'sitting as the Council of the Community' as provided in the decision of 1973 which set it up.

What is more, at Stuttgart the Heads of Government decided, notwithstanding the Commission's objections, to depart from the prescribed Community procedures in their planned overall negotiations and set up the so-called 'Special Council', which could deliberate not only on Commission proposals but on any proposals from Member States. From then on there were constant bilateral talks between the Council Presidency and individual member governments, at the expense of multilateral discussions in the Institutions. I am not denying the admirable devotion of the Presidency of the Community, of the ministers and the Heads of State and Government and the hard work they put into securing the agreement that got the Community out of the rut but habits were formed – bad habits, as I see it – and those practices once begun tend to go on: multiplication of the compromises made by the Presidency on all sorts of subjects, thus supplanting Commission proposals, undue resort to bilateral talks, national glorification of the 'Presidency of the Community', although this is a new office with no legal basis. Something needs to be done about all this. It can still be done, but time is not on the side of the Institutions.

DOCUMENT 9.6

US–European Economic Relations 1981

The following points are from an address by the Assistant Secretary of State for Economic and Business Affairs, Joseph Hormats, to the Mid-America Committee, Chicago 16 December 1981. This extract gives some of the major reasons for the economic tension between the United States and the European Community.

Agriculture. The agricultural policies of the United States and the EC are inspired by different economic philosophies. The US farm program is designed to interfere as little as possible in international agricultural markets. When prices are low, the Commodity Credit Corporation (CCC) takes over, and along with farmers, holds surplus US production; it does not dampen world prices by subsidising exports. Our farmers hold the world's largest grain reserves, thus contributing to world food security and international price stability.

The EC's Common Agricultural Policy (CAP) is based on high price supports. It has no production controls and protects prices by variable levies at the border. It has created burdensome surpluses and serious budget problems for the Community. By subsidising exports, it has artificially stimulated large-scale European exports in such products as wheat, sugar, and meat. This limits market opportunities for products of such countries as the United States, which compete without subsidies.

We recognise the importance of the CAP to the origins of the Community and to its continued cohesion. Last week in Brussels, US Cabinet members stressed that we would not challenge the fundamental elements of the policies on which European unity is based. We also understand the political, social, and economic conditions under which European agriculture operates, which are quite different from those in the United States. But, we are seriously concerned about the effects of excesses in the CAP. We fear that the EC is seeking to solve its internal agricultural overproduction and budget problems by converting the CAP into a common export policy based on extensive subsidies. We are also deeply disturbed that the EC from time to time considers measures that would curb exports into the EC of soybeans and feed grain substitutes. This would violate their GATT bindings to us.

Some \$9 billion in US exports to the EC and more than \$40 billion in US world-wide sales are at issue in this area. Serious friction in our bilateral relations would result, as would increased instability in world markets, if present EC policy trends continue. We have made it clear to the Community that if our legitimate agricultural interests and rights are adversely affected, we will strongly defend them. However difficult Europe's internal situation, it cannot be resolved at the expense of US agricultural interests.

We welcome the effort within the Community to reform the CAP, make it less costly to the Community budget, and give it a greater market orientation. It will not be easy for 10 countries with diverse interests to agree on modifications to achieve greater efficiency and reduce cost. But it is a reasonable and sustainable course of action over the long run.

European Unity. We support the objective of European unity as embodied in the European Community. A strong, prosperous and united Europe is important to the security and the prosperity of the United States and the West.

While we may have difficulties with certain EC policies, the existence of the Community as the policy entity for, and representative of, the Ten on trade and other economic issues is much to be preferred to trying to maintain economic relations on these issues with ten countries, with constant friction among them. The Community makes trade and other economic issues more manageable than would be the case if it did not exist. And, its historical outward looking and constructive approach to the world economy has been essential to the success of the Tokyo Round, the creation of the International Energy Agency, and progress on a variety of international economic issues.

DOCUMENT 9.7

Enoch Powell on the European Parliament, speech to the House of Commons, 26 June 1986

The following is an extract from his speech on the European Communities (Amendment) Bill. Powell had earlier opposed the introduction of direct elections and Britain's accession to the Community in 1973.

When in 1978 the House ill-advisedly consented to convert the European Assembly into a directly elected body, it was predicted that a directly elected body, which was already endowed with the power to refuse assent to the budget of the Community and to dismiss the Commission, would soon discover and explore the potential powers which it would exercise, as in past centuries the House has made a similar discovery and exploration. The anxiety which was expressed on that score was strong on both sides of the House. As a result of that, what professed to be a protection was written into the European Assembly Act 1978, which enacted: 'No treaty which provides for any increase in the powers of the Assembly shall be ratified by the United Kingdom unless it has been approved by an Act of Parliament'.

Hon. Members who have looked at clause 3(4) of the Bill will notice that that is precisely what we are invited to do in approving the Bill. We do not need to argue whether the consequences of the Treaty and the Bill are an increase in the powers of the Assembly. The government say that this is so. The government may seek to argue that that increase of the powers of the Assembly is not at the expense of the powers of the Parliament of the United Kingdom. That proposition rests on an important fallacy about the nature of power. There is no vacuum of power unexercised, unavailable, which is ready to be dished out to new occupiers and exercisers.

At the moment, the power exists and it is shared between this Parliament and the institutions of the Community in accordance with a particular pattern. If the power of any portion of those institutions is increased, as the government tell the House it is increased in respect of the Assembly, by the Treaty and the Bill, it must follow that the effectiveness and real power – the political power – of the other elements, the other possessors, is diminished. Whatever is arrogated to the Assembly by the legislation and the Treaty is deducted from what is available to this Parliament and thus, to the people it represents.

No unoccupied ground or unexplored territory can be colonised by the Assembly without a diminution taking place in the control and powers of this House. We are discussing an actual deduction from the powers of this House so that those powers may be exercised by other bodies over which we do not have anything like the same opportunity of control.

There is a kind of tripod in the institutions of the Community – the Council, the Commission, and what was hitherto called the Assembly. It is only through the Council that this House can assert itself. It is only in the Council that the members of the government who are answerable to this House can assert themselves. Of course, in the last resort, they can only assert themselves in the Council when there is decision by unanimity. Whether they decide in the Council by unanimity or otherwise, it is through the Council that this House still exercises a degree of power, on behalf of the United Kingdom, in the institutions of the European Community.

A big shift is created in the relative power of the Council – its relative power in the tripod – by the Treaty and the Bill. That power is transferred and inures to the benefit of the other two elements – the Commission and the Assembly. Anyone who has studied the co-operation procedure, as it is delicately called, will have seen the joint interest that the Commission and the Assembly have in co-operating with one another.

Indeed, an almost corrupt deal has been struck between the Commission and the Assembly – a log-rolling or back-scratching arrangement between the two – whereby, if the Commission proceeds by way of the co-operation process, it can use the added power which has been attributed to the Assembly to strengthen itself and its intentions *vis-à-vis* the Council. Therefore, it is the Commission and the Assembly, jointly, which are given an accretion of power at the expense of the Council and, therefore, at the expense of this House – the Council being the only element which can be directly influenced and ultimately controlled by the Parliament and people of the United Kingdom. . .

Our parliament is a homogeneous body. It wills a single nation which elects the disparate Members who sit together in the House. It is the Parliament of a united kingdom. The Parliament which assembles at Strasbourg is an assembly of those who have been elected in different nations, and, incidentally, under different electoral systems, to congregate together. They do not come together as the representatives of a single self-recognising community. The nature of that assembly is different in kind from the nature of this Parliament.

We are performing a type of solecism in attributing the term 'Parliament' to that Assembly. What we should not do is create implications and hallow assumptions which attach to the word 'Parliament' when applied to the European Assembly. The European Assembly is not, in our sense of the term, a 'Parliament' and it is not the wish of the people of this country that it should ever be a Parliament in the sense of being the ultimate repository of the legislative and executive powers under which the people of the United Kingdom are to live.

DOCUMENT 9.8

'Europe 1992 – The Overall Challenge'

The following extract is from a European Commission resumé of the Cecchini Report of 1988. This analysed the likely benefits of the completion of the internal market by 1992, as proposed by the Commission in its White Paper in 1985.

The results
1.4.3. The total potential economic gain to the Community of implementation of the large market is estimated at some 200 000 million ECU or

more equivalent to approximately 5 per cent of the Community's GDP.

This calculation includes not only the results of a microeconomic evaluation of the savings made by removing the barriers which directly affect intra-Community trade (essentially frontier formalities and related costs and delays) but also, and more significantly, the lessons learned from a macroeconomic simulation designed to determine the benefits that will accrue from greater market integration, thereby encouraging competition and facilitating the exploitation of economies of scale.

Microeconomic evaluation

1.4.4. The study took particular account of the work on the cost of frontier formalities, on the existing barriers to both manufacturing industry and services and on the economies of scale and boost to competitiveness promised by completion of the internal market.

1.4.5. The direct costs of frontier formalities and the associated administrative costs to the public and private sector are estimated at around 1.8 per cent of the value of goods traded within the Community. To this must be added the costs to industry of other barriers on the internal market, such as technical regulations and the like, which industrialists questioned in opinion polls put, on average, at just under 2 per cent of their total costs. The combined total, then, adds up to about 3.54 per cent of the value-added by industry.

These figures reflect the specific costs of identifiable barriers. The total gains expected from a totally integrated competitive market in these products are far greater, particularly in the branches of industry where government procurement plays an important part, and in financial services and transport.

1.4.6. The study highlights substantial potential economies of scale unexploited by European industry. More than half the branches of industry on the Community market can support 20 firms of efficient size, compared with no more than four on each of the largest national markets. Only a truly European internal market can combine the advantages of technical and economic efficiency, since 20 firms operating Community-wide are more likely to produce effective competition than four firms on a national market. Comparing industrial structures today with a more rational, yet still not ideal, structure, an estimated one-third of European industry could see its costs fall by between 1 and 7 per cent, depending on the branch concerned. The aggregate saving from these economies of scale would be around 2 per cent of GDP.

The study confirms that for the full benefits of the internal market programme to be felt, all barriers to trade within the Community must be removed. In particular, European industrialists and businessmen must be convinced that the 1992 target will be achieved. Competition policy must be enforced effectively both by the Community and by the national administrations to ensure that the barriers removed are not replaced by other anti-competitive practices. Above all, both the benefits and the costs must be shared out fairly. Experience with the removal of customs barriers in the Community has shown that the moves have only a modest redistributive effect. Consequently, measures will undoubtedly have to be taken to assist the Community's less-favoured and declining regions and areas where restructuring has hit jobs.

DOCUMENT 9.9

Margaret Thatcher, 'The Bruges Speech', 20 September 1988

The speech of the British Prime Minister to the College of Europe on the subject of Britain and Europe stirred up considerable controversy. Though the language in which she presented her case was less diplomatic than the Foreign Office might have liked, its views differed little from that of preceding governments with the exception of Edward Heath's. Her 'guiding principles for the future' were interpreted by many as a response to Jacques Delors, President of the Commission who had prophesied in July 1988 that within ten years 80 per cent of economic, and possibly also fiscal and social policy would be European rather than national in origin. The principles were:

1)   . . .'willing and active cooperation between independent Sovereign States is the best way to build a successful European Community. To try to suppress nationhood and concentrate power at the centre of a European conglomerate would be highly damaging and would jeopardise the objectives we seek to achieve. Europe will be stronger precisely because it has France as France, Spain as Spain, Britain as Britain, each with its own customs, traditions and identity. It would be folly to try to fit them into some sort of Identikit European personality . . . I want to see . . . [the countries of Europe] work more closely on things we can do better together than alone . . . But working more closely together does not require power to be centralised in Brussels or decisions to be taken by an appointed bureaucracy. Indeed, it is ironic that just when these countries such as the Soviet Union which have tried to run everything from the centre are learning that success depends on dispersing power away from the centre, some in the Community seem to want to move in the opposite direction. We have not successfully rolled back the frontiers of the State in Britain only to see them reimposed at a European level with a European superstate exercising a new dominance from Brussels.

2)   'Community policies must tackle present problems in a practical way, however difficult that may be. If we cannot reform these Community policies which are patently wrong or ineffective and which are rightly

causing public disquiet; we shall not get the public's support for the
Community's future development. . .

3) 'If Europe is to flourish and create the jobs of the future, enterprise
is the key . . . The lessons of the economic history of Europe in the
1970s and 1980s is that central planning and detailed control don't
work, and that personal endeavour and initiative do, that a state-
controlled economy is a recipe for low growth, and that free enterprise
within a framework of law brings better results . . . Regarding
monetary matters, let me say this. The key issue is not whether there
should be a European central bank. The immediate and practical
requirements are to implement the Community's commitment to free
movement of capital. . ., to establish a genuinely free market in financial services, in banking, insurance, investment; to make a greater use
of the ECU (European Currency Unit). It is to such basic, practical
steps that the Community's attention should be devoted . . . When
these have been achieved and sustained over a period of time, we shall
be in a better position to judge the next moves. It is the same with
frontiers between our countries. It is a matter of plain common sense
that we cannot totally abolish frontier controls if we are also to protect
our citizens from crime and stop the movement of drugs, of terrorists,
and of illegal immigrants . . . We in Britain would fight attempts to
introduce collectivism and corporatism at the European level, though
what people wish to do in their own countries is a matter for them.

4) 'Europe should not be protectionist. The expansion of the world
economy requires us to continue the process of removing barriers to
trade, and to do so in the multilateral negotiation in the GATT
(General Agreement on Tariffs and Trade). It would be a betrayal if,
while breaking down constraints on trade to create the Single Market,
the Community were to erect greater external protection. We must
ensure that our approach to world trade is consistent with the
liberalisation we preach at home.

5) 'Europe must continue to maintain a sure defence through NATO.
There can be no question of relaxing our efforts even though it means
taking difficult decisions and meeting heavy costs . . . We must strive
to maintain the United States' commitment to Europe's defence . . .
NATO and the WEU have long recognised where the problems with
Europe's defences lie and have pointed out the solutions . . . We shall
develop the WEU, not as an alternative to NATO but as a means of
strengthening Europe's contribution to the common defence of the
West.'

DOCUMENT 9.10

Extract from Hendrik Brugmans 'Britain and Europe: A survey', 1991

Professor Brugmans, first Rector of the College of Europe, Bruges, comments from a federalist viewpoint on Mrs. Thatcher's 'Bruges Speech'.

'My first guideline', we read, 'is this: willing and active cooperation between independent sovereign states is the best way to build a successful European Community. To try to suppress nationhood and concentrate power at the centre of a European conglomerate would be highly damaging and would jeopardise the objectives we seek to achieve.'

First of all, one can only deplore her remark about 'suppressing' nationhood. The fact is that nobody, whether in or outside the EEC, has ever dreamed of such a doomladen scenario. Of course, nationhood will survive. Even at the end of the road. Italians will – thank God – still be Italians and Scots, Scots. To doubt this is gravely to underestimate the vitality of our historically formed nations. We hope that all of them will get rid of their chauvinistic delusions and the prejudices which do so much harm. But the sound essence of nationality itself will surely persist. It is regrettable, therefore, that the Prime Minister, in her carefully worded speech, should have introduced a remark that is so absurd, even as a polemical trick. It reminded us painfully of de Gaulle's remark that Europeans in the Community would be condemned to speak 'an integrated volapuk'. The main point of criticism however is that now we are no longer discussing methods of integration only in theory, as would have been the case in the 1940s, but in practice and with the experience of the 1980s behind us. In addition, Mrs Thatcher's ideas are nothing new. They have been expressed on several occasions and by more than one speaker, most notably de Gaulle. More important, they have been tried, and found wanting, at least four times: in the OEEC, the Council of Europe, the WEU and EFTA.

In the case of Mrs Thatcher she objects both to supranational action and to what she, with horror, calls 'Socialism'. In her remarks she made it plain that she did not want to see the Commission become more influential, or more like a Cabinet with 'limited functions but real powers' (the classical definition of a Federal Cabinet), while, at the same time, she was appalled by what President Jacques Delors said in Strasbourg about his plans for the future. Of course he wants to 'plan'; he is a Socialist after all! Above all, she clashed with him when he declared that, in ten years' time, eighty per cent of the relevant decisions about economic and social policy would be taken in Brussels rather than in the national assemblies. Finally, his proposal about social legislation in Europe, seemed to her unacceptable from both angles; it was too federalistic, but it was also creeping Socialism.

In this connection, a widespread misunderstanding has first to be cleared up. What does the word 'Brussels' mean as used by Mrs Thatcher? The implicit answer seems to be the 'eurocrats', a cosmopolitan bureaucracy, an uncontrolled group of so-called 'experts'. There is no doubt that this is a popular misinterpretation, and not only in Britain.

The reality is quite different. No important decision can be made in the EEC, no new orientation be introduced without the agreement of at least the majority, and in some circumstances even today, through the unanimous vote of all governments concerned. It is true that, with regard to the enormous mass of decisions that have to be taken, the Community administration is called upon to do fundamental preparatory work. But normally, the Commission does not submit proposals without first having weighed the foreseeable objections from this or that country and adapting its documents accordingly. Nor does it infrequently happen that a debate in the Council of Ministers leads to a decision to revise the entire proposal. Moreover, if a country should feel by-passed in the exchange of views, its elected members in Strasbourg have ample opportunity to attack the Commission. Consequently, whoever raises the bogus image of an 'all-powerful eurocracy', is guilty either of ignorance or of demagogy.

This having been said, it is clear that Mrs Thatcher, as a staunch Conservative, wanted to see a Europe where the political authorities interfered as little as possible with the economy. She, naturally, wanted to see her version of the market ideology which her Party had applied in Britain, extrapolated as a model for Europe as a whole. This is not an unpopular position, since we actually live at a time where Right-wing parties have the wind in their sails. But even taking this into account, is it imaginable that all Continental governments would follow the same path? Furthermore, is the process of integration as such, compatible with a policy of non-intervention? Let us first examine the economic aspects of this question.

Whether one likes it or not, we do live in a so-called mixed economy; that is in a world where economic decision-making is ceaselessly guided by 'the public hand'. That is the case within each of our countries and also in the EEC. The Single European Act of 1986, which defined '1992', stressed that areas such as scientific research or problems of the environment had to be brought into the sphere of Community tasks. It was also decided that the Social and the Regional Funds should be strengthened so as to pursue a more effective policy by means of which the less prosperous countries and regions of the Community could receive more generous help. The focus on ecology meant that 'Brussels' would be encouraged to intervene whenever industrial decisions were taken that might endanger our quality of life. In fact, it is unimaginable that the frontiers can be opened without such policies being in place, since the less ecologically-minded countries would then enjoy an unfair advantage over their more socially conscious competitors. Ecology, however, is expensive and the price we pay is that products from cleaner countries will cost more. As a result, once there is no question of any one country in the Community taking protectionist measures, the Commission (and who else could take on this task?) will have to ensure that minimum standards are introduced and applied in all member countries.

In conclusion, it is of the essence in the process of integration that the European authorities interfere more and more in the economic network that links our nations. To open frontiers means to introduce European-wide competition between countries and regions as well as individual firms. Such a development cannot be allowed to degenerate into chaos. There have to be rules for such a gigantic game.

Suggested reading

For the new economic initiatives L. Tsoukalis, *The New European Economy – The Politics and Economics of Integration* (Oxford, 1991) and G. Mackenzie and A. Venables, *The Economics of the Single European Act* (London, 1991). J. Pinder, *European Community: The Building of a Union* (Oxford, 1991) provides a very useful analysis of the development of the Community, seen from a federalist viewpoint. J. Lodge (ed.), *The European Community and the Challenge of the Future* (London, 1989) offers many insights. For the details of the later enlargements of the Community see F. Nicholson and R. East, *From the Six to the Twelve* (London, 1987). On the question of agriculture and the CAP, see M. Franklin, *Rich Mens' Farming* (London, 1985) and M. Tracy, *Government and Agriculture in Western Europe 1880–1988* (London, 1989). On monetary integration there are T. Padoa-Schioppa, *Financial and Monetary Integration in Europe, 1990, 1992 and Beyond* (Cambridge, 1988) and P. Ludlow, *The Making of the European Monetary System* (London, 1982). An interesting assessment of the integration process and its limitations, but one published before the SEA and SEM is P. Taylor, *The Limits of European Integration* (London, 1983). For the recent British role in the Community see S. George, *An Awkward Partner* (Oxford, 1990). For US views of current developments in the Community see G.C. Hufbauer, *Europe 1992 – An American Perspective* (Washington, 1990). An excellent handbook on the Single Market is R. Owen and M. Dyne, *The Times Guide to 1992* (London, 1990).

10 A new Pan-European order?

Introduction

The various forms of postwar European integration had as their context the Cold War division of the continent. Europe had undergone a process of partial and fragmented integration under the guidance and control of the Superpowers. Until the end of the 1980s the role of the Superpowers was ambivalent. On the one hand the division of Europe was a cause of tension. East and West Germany were the front line in the Cold War. On the other, under the supervision of the Superpowers, Europe, which had twice this century erupted in world war, achieved a kind of stability. As the Superpowers sought to manage and reduce the tension between them their participation in European affairs was further reaffirmed.

One of the main documents from the period of *détente* was the Helsinki Final Act of 1975 (see Document 10.1). This was a product of the Conference on Security and Cooperation in Europe. The Conference significantly included the Soviet Union and the United States and Canada. The implication that the organisation, or as it increasingly was to be called the 'architecture' of Europe necessarily included the North American States was not fully accepted by the Soviet Union. In spite of the recognition of their mutual interest in improving security through confidence-building measures, the Soviet Union still sought to use the idea of Pan-European organisation of the Continent to exclude the United States from European affairs. It was one of the several achievements of Mikhail Gorbachev's leadership of the Soviet Union that he came to accept not only the reality of the United States' presence but also its legitimacy (see Document 10.2 which combined elements of both the old and new approach). In itself this would not have sufficed to bring about any final redesigning of Europe's 'architecture'. It did, however, provide a forum for managing the impending transformation in Eastern Europe.

At the heart of the division of Europe lay the divided Germany. This fact was so central to the postwar order that, in spite of the earlier commitment to reunification, few in recent years had given serious consideration to the possibility that there might once again be a single German State.

When the authority of Herr Honecker's Government collapsed in the German Democratic Republic, the Federal Republic's Western allies reacted with visible consternation. But the initiative was quickly and skilfully seized by Chancellor Kohl. His 'Ten Point Plan' sought to reassure both sides of the postwar divide at the same time as laying the foundation for a single German State. The need for reassurance was clear. German reunification combined with the revolutions in the other East European States posed a threat not only to the disintegrating Eastern Bloc but also to the coherence and integrity of the Western organisations. How would the European Community cope with an expanded, and possibly Eastern-orientated Germany? What would happen to NATO? What would be the relationship of the European Community to the States to the east of Germany? How would answers to these questions affect the economic and security interests of the Soviet Union? These were but the main issues which were being forced on to the immediate agenda (see Document 10.3).

The pace of German reunification, the ratification of a Treaty on Monetary, Economic and Social Union followed in October by the entry of the East German Länder into the Federal Republic, necessarily brought rapid conclusions to some of the other problems. The Soviet Union had accepted that the unified Germany would be a member of NATO. The Allied Powers formally renounced their residual rights over German affairs. Equally important, an attempt was made to provide a more permanent framework for the new European order. In September 1990 the signatories of the Charter of Paris institutionalised the negotiations which had been conducted through the Conference on Security and Cooperation in Europe after the Helsinki Final Act.

The Charter of Paris created at most a framework of an international organisation. It lacked the powers and indeed the dynamism of the European Community. The Community, the strongest of the European organisations was being pushed forward on several fronts. Germany was arguing for the development of the Community's competence and institutions as a way of ensuring that the outcome of Germany's reunification would be the Europeanisation of Germany. The new Germany was to be contained within the Community. At the same time, longstanding negotiations with EFTA for the creation of a European economic area were nearing fruition. Agreement on both was reached at the end of 1991.

These two developments alone will impose considerable strain on the Community's ability to change, especially since the European economic area has actually increased the desire of EFTA members for membership of the Community, instead of delaying a new spate of applications, as was intended. But the Community has been called upon to do much more. The new regimes of the East European States have clearly set out their ambition of membership of the Community (see Documents 10.6 and 10.9). The European Commission has sought to hold back both sets of potential new members, suggesting that the European 'architecture' should consist of related pillars rather than a single structure (see Document 10.5). Its motive is clear: to protect and strengthen, the Community's institutional integrity and decision-making procedures. Different priorities are also voiced. Although the United Kingdom, consistent with her government's suspicion of federalism, has most frequently suggested that enlargement may be desirable even at the expense of tighter integration, enlargement has also been given priority by others, albeit sometimes for different reasons (see Document 10.8). The deepening and prospective enlargement of the Community is also being taken as an opportunity by the subnational regions of Europe to assert their role alongside the Community itself and the Member States (see Document 10.7).

While the Community is as yet unable to expand its membership and competence, to become itself the 'common European house', other organisations, including the Conference on Security and Cooperation in Europe (CSCE), NATO and even the United Nations are filling the gaps in a largely *ad hoc* fashion. This has given rise to a new problem. Europe is living with a number of different organisations whose relationships to one another are being defined as events unfold (see Documents 10.6 and 10.9). Whether these can be brought together to form the structure of a 'common European house' is open to question.

Documents

DOCUMENT 10.1

Conference on Security and Cooperation in Europe, Final Act, Helsinki, 1975

The Conference on Security and Cooperation in Europe (CSCE) can be traced back to Soviet initiatives in 1969. The Conference itself began in Finland in November 1972 and reached agreement with the Final Act signed on 1 August 1975. Although disarmament talks were conducted in a separate, more restricted, forum, the CSCE played an important role in redefining the basic concepts of security.

The participating States will respect each other's sovereign equality and individuality as well as the rights inherent in and encompassed by its sovereignty, including in particular the right of every State to juridical equality, to territorial integrity and to freedom and political independence. They will also respect each other's right to freely choose and develop its political, social, economic and cultural systems as well as its right to determine its laws and regulations. . .

133.   Having considered the views expressed on various subjects related to the strengthening of security in Europe through joint efforts aimed at promoting *détente* and disarmament, the participating States, when engaged in such efforts, will, in this context, proceed, in particular, from the following essential considerations:

134.   – The complementary nature of the political and military aspects of security. . .

135.   – The interrelationship between the security of each participating State and security in Europe as a whole. . .

DOCUMENT 10.2

Mikhail Gorbachev, '*Perestroika*'

Mikhail Gorbachev was elected General Secretary of the Communist Party of the Soviet Union in March 1985. Two years later he began to revise the Soviet approach to Europe.

Europe is indeed a common home where geography and history have closely interwoven the destinies of dozens of countries and nations. Of course, each of them has its own problem, and each wants to live its own life, to follow its own traditions. Therefore, developing the metaphor, one may say: the home is common, that is true, but each family has its own apartment, and there are different entrances too. . .

The concept of a 'common European home' suggests above all a degree of integrity, even if its states belong to different social systems and opposing military–political alliances. . .

One can mention a number of objective circumstances which create the need for a pan-European policy:

1.   Densely populated and highly urbanized, Europe bristles with weapons, both nuclear and conventional. It would not be enough to call it a 'powder keg' today. . .

2.   Even a conventional war, to say nothing of a nuclear one, would be disastrous for Europe today. . .

3.   Europe is one of the most industrialised regions of the world. Its industry and transport have developed to the point where their danger to the environment is close to being critical. This problem has crossed far beyond national borders, and is now being shared by all of Europe.

4.   Integrative processes are developing intensively in both parts of Europe . . . The requirements of economic development in both parts of Europe, as well as scientific and technological progress, prompt the search for some kind of mutually advantageous cooperation. What I

mean is not some kind of 'European autarky', but better use of the aggregate potential of Europe for the benefit of its peoples, and in relations with the rest of the world.

5. The two parts of Europe have a lot of their own problems of an East–West dimension, but they also have a common interest in solving the extremely acute North–South problem. . .

Our idea of a 'common European home' certainly does not involve shutting its doors to anybody. True, we would not like to see anyone kick in the doors of the European home and take the head of the table at somebody else's apartment. But then, that is the concern of the owner of the apartment. In the past, the Socialist countries responded positively to the participation of the United States and Canada in the Helsinki Process.

DOCUMENT 10.3

Speech by Hans-Dietrich Genscher, Minister for Foreign Affairs of the Federal Republic of Germany, 31 January 1991

Hans-Dietrich Genscher was Foreign Minister of the Federal Republic from 1974 to 1992.

The first joint act by the two freely elected German parliaments and governments must be a declaration guaranteeing the frontiers of our neighbours. The Federal Republic of Germany will then have to answer the question – what happens as far as its membership of the European Community and the Western Alliance is concerned if Germany is united? The answer is clear: Our membership of the European Community will remain irrevocable. So too will our determination to continue the process of integration, leading to political union. The same applies to our membership of the Western Alliance. We do not want a untied, neutralist Germany. . .

What NATO must do is state unequivocally that whatever happens in the Warsaw Pact there will be no expansion of NATO territory eastwards, that is to say, closer to the borders of the Soviet Union. This security guarantee is important for the Soviet Union and its conduct. It must also be the Western perception that the transformation in Eastern Europe and the process of German unification must not be allowed to impair Soviet security interests. . .

At this summit we shall have to discuss the future structure of Europe, whether it is to be structured in a confederate manner and whether this confederate order should ultimately lead to European federalism. President

Mitterand's call for a European confederation is an important and constructive contribution. What form should cooperative security structures take? We Germans will have to make it clear what shape German's future should have. The basic elements of a treaty on German unity in Europe should be defined by then. The CSCE summit can also contribute towards an East–West partnership for stability and a peaceful European order by dealing with the establishment of European institutions. Such as:

1. An institution to coordinate East–West economic cooperation. The European development Bank must also be seen in this context.
2. A Pan-European initiative for the protection of human rights. The application of the Council of Europe's human rights convention suggests itself.
3. A centre for the creation of a European legal area aimed at legal harmonisation.
4. A European environmental agency.
5. The extension of EUREKA cooperation across the whole of Europe.
6. Collaboration between ESA and corresponding Eastern institutions.
7. A centre to develop European telecommunications.
8. A centre to develop European transport infrastructure and policy.
9. A European verification centre.
10. A European conflict-management centre.

DOCUMENT 10.4

Charter of Paris for a New Europe, November 1990

The Paris Charter of the CSCE together with the Treaty on Conventional Forces in Europe and the Treaty on the Final Regulation in Relation to Germany set the seal upon the end of the Cold War division of Europe. The unification of Germany took place on 3 October 1990.

The era of confrontation and division of Europe has ended. We declare that henceforth our relations will be founded on respect and cooperation.

Europe is liberating itself from the legacy of the past. The courage of men and women, the strength of the will of the peoples and the power of the ideas of the Helsinki Final Act have joined a new era of democracy, peace and unity in Europe. . .

The 10 principles of the Final Act will guide us towards this ambitious future, just as they have lighted our way towards better relations for the past 15 years. . .

Freedom and political pluralism are necessary elements in our common objective of developing market economies towards sustainable economic growth, prosperity, social justice, expanding employment and efficient use of economic resources. . .

The participation of both North American and European States is a fundamental characteristic of the CSCE: it underlies past achievements and is essential to the future of the CSCE process. An abiding adherence to shared values and our common heritage are the ties which bind us together. . .

Although the threat of conflict in Europe has diminished, other dangers threaten the stability of our societies. We are determined to cooperate in defending democratic institutions against activities which violate the independence, sovereign equality or territorial integrity of the participating States. . .

Our common efforts to consolidate respect for human rights, democracy and the rule of law, to strengthen peace and to promote unity in Europe, require a new quality of political dialogue and cooperation and thus development of the structures of the CSCE.

The intensification of our consultations at all levels is of prime importance in shaping our future relations. To this end, we decide on the following:

(a) We, the Heads of State or Government, shall meet next time in Helsinki on the occasion of the CSCE follow-up meeting 1992. Thereafter, we will meet on the occasion of subsequent follow-up meetings.

(b) Our Ministers of Foreign Affairs will meet, as a Council, regularly and at least once a year. These meetings will provide the central forum for political consultations within the CSCE process. The Council will consider issues relevant to the Conference on Security and Cooperation in Europe and take appropriate decisions. . .

(d) A Committee of Senior Officials will prepare the meetings of the Council and carry out its decisions. The Committee will review current issues and may take decisions, including in the form of recommendations to the Council. . .

(h) In order to provide administrative support for these consultations we establish a Secretariat in Prague. . .

(j) We will create a Conflict Prevention Centre in Vienna to assist the Council in reducing the risk of conflict.

(k) We establish an Office for Free Elections in Warsaw to facilitate contacts and the exchange of information on elections within participating States.

(l) Recognising the important role parliamentarians can play in the CSCE process, we call for greater parliamentary involvement in the CSCE, in particular through the creation of a CSCE parliamentary

assembly, involving members of parliaments from all participating
States. . .

DOCUMENT 10.5

European Commission's Programme for 1991

*The Commission presents its programme to the European Parliament at the beginning
of each year.*

The Paris Charter has outlined the shape of a new Europe based on the
respect for human rights, democracy and the rule of law. In its proposals for
the 1992 Helsinki Summit the Commission will contribute all it can to
furthering progress along the new road of partnership and cooperation
opened up by the Charter. The Community is the first pillar of the new
European architecture. This means that the Community must find the right
formulas for its partnership with the rest of Europe. The Commission will
be delivering an opinion on Austria's application for membership. The aim
of the negotiations which it plans to bring to a satisfactory conclusion with
all the countries of the European Free Trade Association is to establish the
European economic area as the second pillar of the new Europe. . .
    Secondly, we must look to the East. The negotiations with Hungary,
Poland and Czechoslovakia must lead to European agreements. The third
pillar of the new Europe will have to be an association enabling these
countries to take part in the wider process of European integration and
serving to consolidate the reforms that have been set in train, assist them
in their transition to a market economy, help them to cope with the social
consequences of this structural adjustment and create a climate propitious
to the growth of trade and investment.

DOCUMENT 10.6

Address by Václav Havel, President of the Czech and Slovak Federal Republic, 1990

*Václav Havel, playwright and dissident under the Communist regime in
Czechoslovakia, was a founder member of Charter 77 which monitors the regime's
record on human rights in the light of the Helsinki Final Act. Under arrest as late
as February–May 1989 he became President of Czechoslovakia in December 1989.*

I think that the idea of a European Confederation has two dimensions.

I would call the first dimension a futurological one. Supposing that everything proceeds smoothly and all the major problems we are grappling with today are gradually resolved, we can . . . fairly easily imagine Europe emerging as one large confederated formation in fifteen or twenty years. . .

The most frequently expressed doubts or objections to the initiative of the European Confederation stem from the fear that, for some reason, a new institution is being planned or invented while there are already many other tested international institutions in Europe whose number would thus, quite uselessly, be enlarged, and whose fields of action would, quite uselessly, overlap the ambitions of the new institution.

. . .It is my opinion that contemplating at this stage any institutionalisation . . . of the idea of the European Confederation, is meaningful only if it is clear from the very beginning that such an institutional embryo by no means wants to take over the functions of the existing tested or viable institutions and organisations, but that, on the contrary, it wants to complement their activity. . .

Let me give a few examples in this respect:

(1) I think that the European Confederation should not, on principle, at least for the time being, deal with security issues. I believe that European security is a major theme of the Helsinki process and am convinced that, within the process, there are as yet unused, dormant potentialities for gradually creating an entirely new system of European security guarantees. . .

(2) In the many years of doing its important work, the Council of Europe has created and continues to create solid foundations for a Pan-European unification of the law, and the creation and development of a European political culture in general. Competing with the Council of Europe would be senseless. . .

(3) Then there are the European Communities, by far the most integrated European formation. I think that the idea of the European Confederation cannot overlook the existence of the European Communities or consider them something parallel that is unrelated to Europe as a whole, as an elite club that others have nothing to do with; it must rather view the EC as its motor, its standard bearer, the model of its own future. . .

I also think it would be wrong and even harmful to stability throughout Europe if the process of the creation of the European Confederation slowed down in any way the approach of the new Central and East European democracies to the European Communities. If it institutionalised, in any way, their position as second-class countries, for which belonging to the Confederation should constitute a satisfactory substitute, pacifying their higher ambitions.

DOCUMENT 10.7

Alfred Gomolka, Inaugural speech as President of the *Bundesrat*

Alfred Gomolka, Minister-President of Mecklenburg-Vorpommern, was the first East German to be elected President of the Bundesrat.

Through its unification Germany became the bearer of hope for East Europe, and precisely for this reason we must be conscious of our responsibility in connection with the integration of the East European states. That applies above all to our Polish neighbours. After a year of unity we have proved that we can live as good neighbours, that we Germans are Europeans. European Germans.

Thereby, the question arises: how, in a climate of uncertainty about the new European order, can the collapse of the compulsory associations in the East and the emergence of European Union in the West be brought into harmony. The answer lies in federalism, regionalism and in the principle of subsidiarity.

German federalism can be a very useful model for cooperation within the European Community and for the progressive integration of the European states. It has proved itself as a dynamic system, open to development and varied changes.

The 'Yes' to a federal Europe also means incorporating the Länder and regions as a 'third level' in the shaping of a political union. Crossborder cooperation between all the regions of Europe, especially in the political, economic, cultural and environmental fields is therefore a presupposition (of union). Failure to incorporate the Länder and regions into the process of European integration would mean automatically increasing centralisation of decision making and legal norms for ever more men. . .

The long repressed aspirations for autonomy in Central and Eastern Europe must not flow into a persistent nationalism. I see there, rather, the, perhaps necessary, first step on the way to a new European order, the first step under a common European roof.

DOCUMENT 10.8

Speech by Gerd Poppe of Bündis 90/Grüne in the German *Bundestag*

Gerd Poppe, a physicist and dissident under the Communist regime of the German Democratic Republic, is a member of Bündis 90/Grüne. Bündis 90 is an alliance of the citizens' movements which first opposed the Communist regime. Its support declined as the mainstream West German parties established themselves, forcing it to join with the Grüne.

I will limit myself today, however, to the consequences which result from the changes in the East. The possibility of a new Pan Europe should be the occasion for the EC to place in question its form and its concept of economic and monetary union. There is evidently no alternative to the EC as the core of Pan-European integration. However, the EC is not automatically the model of unification for the whole of Europe. A Pan-European community must be in a position to integrate widely different social and economic systems in a non-discriminatory way, to a greater extent than the EC has previously been.

Approximation of living standards must be the goal, not the presupposition of integration. Democratic participation in decisions affecting the whole of Europe, therefore, should not be dependent upon whether a country can keep up with the standards of the internal market of West Europe. . .

Moreover, it is necessary to open the West European market to East European products which are viable exports. That requires dismantling protectionism, to be sure on a timescale that is tolerable for West and East European industry. Just as significant would be limited protection, for a specific period, of the East European market against competition from Western products, so far as the latter pose a threat to economic units there. . .

Ladies and Gentlemen! We greet every act strengthening the European legislature. If, however, the fundamental question of the deepening or the enlargement of European structures is posed, we will reply giving precedence to enlargement.

DOCUMENT 10.9

J. Dienstbier, 'Priorities of Czechoslovak Foreign Policy', 1991

J Dienstbier, Foreign Minister of the Czech and Slovak Federal Republic, was a dissident under the Communist regime in Czechoslovakia. A founder member of Charter 77 and friend of Václav Havel, he became Foreign Minister in December 1989.

. . .what can Czechoslovakia do to ensure its security? Proceeding from our historical experiences, from our geographical situation, our vulnerability caused by a shortage of raw materials and energy and from the moral profile of our foreign policy . . . we have two possibilities to choose from. Either Central Europe will be fully included in conceptual considerations developing today at the most representative levels in connection with the shaping of a new European defence and security identity, or at least three Central European countries will have to start considering a closer cohesion of their security interests.

In the first case, the fact that advanced Europe includes in its defence and security identity the Central European area should be expressed by at least a minimum degree of concrete guarantees given to the states existing in this area . . . If we had to choose the other possibility as a result of lack of understanding of our position, i.e. the linking of our security interests with some of our former allies in the Warsaw Pact, which a certain part of the political forces in my country is in favour of, then such a solution could rather contribute to suspicion and tension in the former Soviet bloc. Quite logically the question would arise not 'why' such a solution but 'against whom' such a solution. . .

We are naturally aware that all our efforts to fully integrate in the European integration processes lead above all through the economic sphere. This is why after our very first foreign political step, which was the starting of negotiations with the Soviet government on the speedy withdrawal of Soviet occupation troops from Czechoslovakia, we immediately made the second one which was the message the Czechoslovak Prime Minister sent to Brussels expressing our decision to become as soon as possible a full-fledged member of the European Communities. . .

I would like you to understand that the system which existed for more than forty years in my country was a system that was functioning, functioning badly but functioning . . . Only when we manage to build again an administrative and economic structure compatible with advanced Europe, only then shall we have the right to say – we are again back in Europe. And for this we need the broadest possible collaboration on the part of this advanced Europe. . .

It seems to me that it is easier to speak in big declarations about the need for cooperation with the states of the former Soviet bloc than to start concrete negotiations on details. We negotiated our association agreements with the EC for more than eight months. When the talks reached the final stage we suddenly realised how many conditions and restrictions were put before us. We suddenly realised that the tough rules of the market and competition were being applied everywhere where solidarity should rule in the first place. And when we eventually reached compromises on our exports of textiles, steel and meat, the extent of which absolutely cannot threaten the EC markets, we had to face another condition – either you will allow the transit across your territory of a quite unbearable number of tractor trailers or one of the twelve participants will not sign the association agreement. . .

Within the economic renaissance of the Central European area we have decided to follow the path of even partial projects for the implementation of which regional groupings can be set up. These are projects exceeding the boundaries of individual states and aiming at a speedier modernisation of transport, the telecommunication network and power supplies, and improvement of the environment, and created a grouping, which we call

the Hexagonal and which may be renamed the Central European
Initiative. To some degree we are thus creating another axis of cooperation, that of North–South, but not a new bloc. . . In conceptualising our
new Czechoslovak foreign policy, we clearly set out on the path leading to
European integration, to those European institutions which are currently
preparing and forming the basis of this integration. We have made this
choice because we regard it as the only one which can save the nations of
Europe from becoming bogged down in old disputes and intolerances.

Suggested reading

The context and significance of the CSCE is explored by K. Dyson (ed.),
European Détente (London, 1986). Among the extensive commentary on the
impact of recent changes two articles stand out for their combination of
insight and synthesis: N. Malcolm, 'The "Common European Home" and
Soviet Foreign Policy', *International Affairs*, **65** (1989), pp. 659–776 and O.
Waever, 'Three Competing Europes: German, French, Russian', *International Affairs*, **66** (1990), pp. 477–93. In addition to *International Affairs*
regular assessments can be found in *Aussenpolitik* (an English edition is
available). On the impact of German unification see *The European
Community and German Unification, Bulletin of the European Communities*,
Supplement 4/90. A good survey of the problems and prospects of
integrating Eastern Europe is provided by Giles Merrit, *Eastern Europe and
the USSR* (London, 1991). See also, G. Bonvicini *et al*, *The Community and
the Emerging European Democracies. A Joint Policy Report* (London, 1991).
Among the numerous assessments of the security implications of the new
Europe see, for example, A. Hyde-Pryce, *European Security Beyond the Cold
War* (London, 1991).

Appendix A: The Institutions of the Community

The European Commission

This is the common executive arm of the three organisations of the Community. Its powers include:

1) upholding Community rules and defending Community interests;
2) initiating policies and proposals;
3) implementing the provisions of the treaties;
4) supervising the management of Community policies;
5) administering funds and drawing up budgets;
6) putting into effect the decisions of the Council of Ministers; and
7) mediation between the competing claims of the other institutions.

There are 17 Commissioners. Each of the five larger states have two and the other seven smaller states one. The Commissioners are appointed by the Member States, but undertake to act independently of their own countries. The Commission has a President and Commissioners are allocated specific responsibilities over the directorates-general. The Commission has a four-year term. The term Commission is also used to mean the 13,000, staff most of whom are located in Brussels though some work in Luxembourg.

The Council of Ministers

This brings together the ministers of the Member States of the Community, responsible for different areas of policy e.g., if transport is discussed the Transport Ministers are present. A separate arrangement exists for Ministers of Foreign Affairs, who technically meet within the framework of European Political Cooperation (EPC) when they are discussing the political as distinct from commercial and trade aspects of foreign policy. The Council of Ministers is the decision-making body of the Community. Under the SEA (see Appendix B) the Council now decides in some areas of Community policy by qualified majority. This means at least 54 votes out of 76 to pass a directive or regulation. The votes are weighted according to the population of Member States, with France, Germany, Italy and the United Kingdom having 10 votes each. The Council has the authority to issue:

1) regulations which are applicable to and binding on all Member States;
2) directives, which allow the states affected to choose the means to achieve the specified end;
3) decisions which oblige the parties concerned, either governments, enterprises or individuals; and
4) recommendations and opinions which are not binding.

The Committee of Permanent Representatives (COREPER)

This consists of the ambassadors of the Member States to the Community, together with their advisers. It prepares the work of the Council of Ministers and constitutes the main link between national governments and the Commission.

The European Council

Not to be confused with the Council of Ministers, this consists of the Heads of State or government, their ministers of foreign affairs and the President plus one Vice-President of the Commission. It meets at least twice a year and sets the broad guidelines for Community policy on matters of major moment such as the budget, accession of new members and the monetary system. Through this and the Council of Ministers, Member States have retained a large measure of control over the direction of the Community.

The European Parliament

This has been directly elected since 1979 and now contains 518 members (MEPs). The numbers of MEPs for each country is determined by their respective populations. The Parliament meets alternately in Strasbourg and Luxembourg and MEPs are grouped transnationally. It was originally conceived as an advisory and consultative body and known as the 'European Assembly', though it had the right by a two-thirds majority to demand the resignation of the Commission. Its role has significantly increased over the last decade. It has sometimes exercised its powers over the Community budget to considerable effect. The SEA (see Appendix B) has given it the power of assent in matters concerning the expansion of the Community. It also introduced a cooperative procedure which gives the Parliament an influence on qualified majority decisions. The Maastricht Treaty (see Appendix C) has also proposed a procedure of co-decision-making between Council and Parliament which will further enhance its role.

The European Court of Justice

This consists of thirteen judges and six advocates-general and is the supreme judicial authority of the EC. It is not to be confused with the European Court of Human Rights. The European Court of Justice has the authority to interpret and apply Community law. Its major contributions have been in the field of commercial law, though it has also developed case law in other areas, such as social welfare. Two fundamental principles have been established. First, Community law is directly applicable to individuals in Member States and, secondly, it is supreme over national law. In 1989 a Court of First Instance was created to hear cases dealing with matters of commercial competition. Judgements given there may be appealed against to the Court of Justice.

The Economic and Social Committee (ECOSOC)

ECOSOC is organised in specialised groups dealing with different subjects. Based in Brussels, it acts in an advisory capacity, bringing together representatives from employers, trade unions and other organisations such as local authorities and consumer groups. It gives its opinions on proposals made by the Commission.

Appendix B: The Single European Act

This came into effect on 1 July 1987. Its major points were:

1) the progressive establishment of the internal market by 31 December 1992, 'an area without internal frontiers in which the free movement of goods, persons, services and capital is ensured. . .';
2) the introduction of qualified majority voting for most 1992 measures, to replace unanimity. There were exceptions entered for measures affecting taxation, free movement of persons, rights of employed persons;
3) the introduction of a 'cooperation procedure', increasing the power of the European Parliament;
4) the establishment of a Court of First Instance under the European Court of Justice;.
5) an increase in cooperation in economic and monetary policy. The preamble referred to monetary union as a goal to be 'progressively realised';
6) new measures for health and safety of workers; disparities between richer and poorer areas of Community to be reduced ('cohesion') through the use of 'Structural Funds';
7) an emphasis on cooperation in research and technological development;
8) that the Community preserves, protects and improves the quality of the environment, protects human health and ensures prudent utilisation of natural resources;
9) the introduction of 'European cooperation in the sphere of foreign policy' through consultation

Paragraph 6a specified: 'The High Contracting Parties consider that closer co-operation on questions of European security would contribute in an essential way to the development of a European identity . . . They are ready to coordinate their positions more closely on the political and economic aspects of security'. A foreign policy secretariat was to be established in Brussels. The President of the Commission was to initiate action and coordinate and represent the positions of the Member States in relation to third countries.

Appendix C: The Maastricht Treaty, 10 December 1991

The Treaty

1) committed the EC to launching a common currency by 1999. Britain and Denmark are to be allowed to opt out if they so decide (see a) below);
2) sought to establish common foreign policies for the Twelve;
3) laid the groundwork for a common defence policy under the Western European Union;
4) added to the policy issues in which the EC would have a voice;
5) gave the EC a role in social policy – the 'social chapter' (from which Britain excluded herself, see b) below);
6) pledged increased aid for the four poorest nations of the Community: Greece, Ireland, Portugal and Spain;
7) somewhat increased the powers of the European Parliament, for instance through the procedure of co-decision-making.

a) Protocol on the transition to the third stage of economic and monetary union

The High Contracting Parties. . .

declare the irreversible character of the Community's movement to the third stage by signing the new Treaty provisions on Economic and Monetary Union.

Therefore all Member States shall, whether they fulfil the necessary conditions for the adoption of a single currency or not, respect the will for the Community to enter swiftly into the third stage of Economic and Monetary Union, and therefore no Member State shall prevent the entering into the third stage.

If by the end of 1997 the date of the beginning of the third stage has not been set, the Member States concerned, the Community institutions and other bodies involved, shall expedite all preparatory work during 1998, in order to enable the Community to enter the third stage irrevocably on 1 January 1999 and to enable the ECB and the ESCB to start their full functioning from this date on.

This Protocol shall be annexed to this Treaty.

b) Protocol on social policy

The High Contracting Parties,

noting that eleven Member States, that is to say the Kingdom of Belgium, the Kingdom of Denmark, the Federal Republic of Germany, the Hellenic Republic, the Kingdom of Spain, the French Republic, Ireland, the Italian Republic, the Grand Duchy of Luxembourg, the Kingdom of the Netherlands, the Portuguese Republic, wish to continue along the path laid down in the Social Charter of 1989; that they have adopted among themselves an Agreement to this end; that this Agreement is annexed to this Protocol: that this Protocol and the said Agreement are without prejudice to the Chapter of the Treaty establishing the European Community (hereinafter referred to as 'the Treaty') which relates to social policy, and whose provisions constitute an integral part of the *acquis communautaire*:

1. Agree to authorise those eleven Member States to have recourse to the Institutions, procedures and mechanisms of the Treaty for the purposes of taking and applying the acts and decisions required for giving effect to the above-mentioned Agreement.
2. The United Kingdom shall not take part in the deliberations and the adoption by the Council of Commission proposals made on the basis of this Protocol and the above-mentioned Agreement.

By way of derogation from Article 148(2) of the Treaty, acts of the Council which are made pursuant to this Protocol and which must be adopted by a qualified majority shall be deemed to be so adopted if they have received at least forty-four votes in favour. The unanimity of the members of the Council, with the exception of the United Kingdom, shall be necessary for acts of the Council which must be adopted unanimously and for those amending the Commission proposal.

Document list

1.1 Giovanni Agnelli and Attilio Cabiati, *Federazione europea o lega delle nazioni?* (Turin, Fratelli Bocca, 1918), *The Federalist*, Vol. 31 (1989), pp. 71–9.

1.2 Richard N. Coudenhove-Kalergi, 'Three years of Pan-Europe. Supplement', in Richard N. Coudenhove-Kalergi, *Pan-Europe* (New York, Alfred Kopf, 1926), pp. 197–8, 205.

1.3 Leon Trotsky, 'The Premises for the Proletarian Revolution' (1924), *Europe and America: Two Speeches on Imperialism* (New York, Pathfinder, 1971), p. 30.

1.4 Elemér Hantos, 'Der Europäische Zollverein', *Weltwirtschaftliches Archiv*, Vol. 23 (1926), pp. 229–30, 235–8.

1.5 A. Briand, 'Memorandum on the Organization of a Regime of Federal Union', *International Conciliation*, Special Bulletin June 1930, pp. 327, 329, 333, 335, 337, 339, 341, 343, 345, 353.

1.6 Edouard Herriot, *The United States of Europe* (London, Harrop, 1930), pp. 152, 286–7.

1.7 Hans-Helmut Dietze, 'Die Problematik der europäischen Rechtseinheit', *Geist der Zeit*, Vol. 16 (1938), pp. 314–15.

1.8 R.W.G. MacKay, *Federal Europe* (London, Joseph, 1940), pp. 23–4, 48, 51, 59, 63.

1.9 R.N. Coudenhove-Kalergi, *Pan-Europe* (New York, Alfred Kopf, 1926).

2.1 'Meeting at the Reich Ministry of Economics 22 July 1940', W. Lipgens (ed.), *Documents on the History of European Integration*, Vol. 1 (Berlin, Walter de Gruyter, 1984), pp. 62–5.

2.2 'Gustav Schlotterer and Wilhelm Zangen at the Grand Council of the Reich Group Industry' 3 October 1940, J. Noakes and G. Pridham (eds), *Nazism 1919–1945*, Vol. 3 (Exeter, University of Exeter Press, 1988), pp. 894, 897.

2.3 'Record of Vollrath Frhr, von Maltzan of 7 May 1941', Ludwig Nestler (ed.), *Die faschistische Okupationspolitik in Frankreich* (Berlin, VEB, 1990), pp. 160–1.

2.4 'Martin Bormann, Record of Meeting on Nazi Aims in Eastern

Europe, 16 July 1941', W. Lipgens (ed.), *Documents on the History of European Integration*, Vol. 1 (Berlin, Walter de Gruyter, 1984), pp. 85–6.

2.5   Comments on the General Plan East by Dr Erhard Wetzel, J. Noakes and G. Pridham (eds), *Nazism 1919–1945*, Vol. 3 (Exeter, University of Exeter Press, 1988), pp. 977–9 and H. Heiber, 'Der General-Plan Ost', *Vierteljahreshefte für Zeitgeschichte*, Vol. 6 (1958), p. 309.

2.6   Léon Blum. W. Lipgens (ed.), *Documents on the History of European Integration*, Vol. 1 (Berlin, Walter de Gruyter, 1985), pp. 281–2.

2.7   Helmuth von Moltke, 'Initial Situation, Aims and Tasks'. W. Lipgens (ed.), *Documents on the History of European Integration*, Vol. 1 (Berlin, Walter de Gruyter, 1985), pp. 385–6.

2.8   Altiero Spinelli and Ernesto Rossi, *The Ventotene Manifesto* (London, Altiero Spinelli Institute, n.d.), pp. 26, 31.

2.9   'Memorandum by Hugh R. Wilson', Harley Notter, *Postwar Foreign Policy Preparation 1939–1945* (Westport, US Department of State, 1975), p. 458.

2.10 Churchill to Roosevelt, 2 February 1943, *Roosevelt and Churchill. Their Secret Wartime Correspondence* (New York, Dutton, 1975), p. 311.

2.11 *The Memoirs of Cordell Hull*, Vol. 2 (London, Hodder and Stoughton, 1948), pp. 1642–6.

2.12 Yalta Conference, 11 February 1945, *Foreign Relations of the United States. The Conferences at Malta and Yalta. 1945* (Washington Department of State), pp. 971–2.

2.13 David Mitrany, *A Working Peace System* (London, Oxford University Press for the RIIA, 1943), pp. 31–5, 54–6.

3.1   Winston Churchill's Speech at Zürich, 19 September 1946, in A. Boyd and F. Boyd, *Western Union* (London, Hutchinson, 1948), pp. 110–11.

3.2   European Union of Federalists, Resolutions of the Montreux Conference, in A. Boyd and F. Boyd, *Western Union* (London, Hutchinson, 1948), pp. 141–2.

3.3   Summary of Discussion on Problems of Relief, Rehabilitation and Reconstruction of Europe, US Department of State, 29 May 1947, *Foreign Relations of the United States 1947*, Vol. 3, pp. 234–5.

3.4   Andrei Vyshinsky, A Criticism of the Truman Doctrine and the Marshall Plan, in United Nations, General Assembly, *Official Records*, Plenary Meetings, 18 September 1947, pp. 86–8.

3.5   US Economic Cooperation Act, Public Law 472, 80th Congress, 3 April 1948. Henry Pelling, *Britain and the Marshall Plan*, (London, Macmillan, 1988), p. 129.

3.6   Ernest Bevin, Speech on Western Union, 22 January 1948. A. Boyd and F. Boyd, *Western Union* (London, Hutchinson, 1948), pp. 117, 123, 125, 131.

3.7 The Secretary of State to the United States Political Adviser for Germany (Murphy), 6 March 1948. S. Everett Gleason and Fredrick Aandahl (eds), *Foreign Relations of the United States 1948*, Vol. 3 (Washington Department of State, 1974), p. 389.

3.8 The Ambassador in France (Caffery) to the Secretary of State, 23 March 1948. S. Everett Gleason and Fredrick Aandahl (eds), *Foreign Relations of the United States 1948*, Vol. 3 (Washington Department of State, 1974), pp. 401–2.

3.9 Carlo Schmid, 'Das deutsch-französische Verhältnis und der Dritte Partner', *Die Wandlung*, Vol. 2 (1947), pp. 792–805, in W. Lipgens and W. Loth (eds), *Documents on the History of European Integration*, Vol. 3 (Berlin, Walter de Gruyter, 1988), pp. 503–6.

3.10 Committee of European Economic Cooperation, *General Report*, Vol. 1 (London, HMSO, 1947), pp. 18–20.

3.11 Public Law 47, ECA of 1948 Amendment, 81st Congress, 19 April 1949. Foreign Economic Assistance Program, p. 592.

3.12 Statute of the Council of Europe, London, 1949.

3.13 Memorandum for Ernest Bevin, 19 October 1950. R. Bullen and M. Pelly (eds), *Documents on British Policy Overseas*, Series 2, Vol. 1 (London, HMSO, 1986) pp. 315–18.

4.1 Jean Monnet, Memorandum to Robert Schuman and George Bidault, 4 May 1950, R. Mayne in R. Vaughan (ed.), *Postwar Integration in Europe* (London, Edward Arnold, 1976), pp. 51, 53–5.

4.2 Robert Schuman, Declaration of 9 May 1950. Pascal Fontaine, *Europe – A Fresh Start. The Schuman Declaration 1950–90* (Luxembourg, Commission of European Communities, 1990), pp. 44–6.

4.3 Letter from Jean Monnet to E. Plowden, 25 May 1950. R. Bullen and M. Pelly (eds), *Documents on British Policy Overseas*, Series 2, Vol. 1 (London, HMSO, 1986) pp. 94–6.

4.4 Dirk Stikker, *Men of Responsibility* (London, John Murray, 1963), pp. 187–9.

4.5 Extract from the conclusions of a meeting of the British Cabinet, 22 June 1950. R. Bullen and M. Pelly (eds), *Documents on British Policy Overseas*, Series 2, Vol. 1 (London, HMSO, 1986) pp. 210–13.

4.6 André Philip, *Der Sozialismus und die europäische Einheit* (Gelsenkirchen, Ruhr-Verlag, 1950), pp. 10–15.

4.7 The Secretary of State, Dean Acheson, to the Acting Secretary of State, 10 May 1950. S. Everett Gleason and Fredrick Aandahl (eds), *Foreign Relations of the United States 1950*, Vol. 3 (Washington Department of State, 1974), p. 695.

4.8 The Acting Secretary of State to the Secretary of State, 10 May 1950. S. Everett Gleason and Fredrick Aandahl (eds), *Foreign Relations of the United States 1950*, Vol. 3 (Washington Department of State, 1974), pp. 695–6.

4.9   The Ambassador in the United Kingdom, Douglas, to the Secretary
        of State, 6 June 1950. S. Everett Gleason and Fredrick Aandahl
        (eds), *Foreign Relations of the United States 1950*, Vol. 3 (Washington
        Department of State, 1974), pp. 722–3.

4.10   Report by the Department of State to the Council on Foreign
        Economic Policy, 16 March 1955. William Z. Slany (ed.), *Foreign
        Relations of the United States 1955–1957*, Vol. 4, (Washington Depart-
        ment of State, 1986), pp. 226–7.

4.11   Fritz Baade, *Probleme des Schuman-Plans*, Kieler Vorträge, New Series
        2 (1951), pp. 21–2.

4.12   Chancellor of the Federal Republic of Germany, Konrad Adenauer,
        in the Bundestag, 12 July 1952, in C.C. Schweitzer, D. Karsten, R.
        Spencer, R. Taylor Cole, D. Kommers and A. Nicholls (eds),
        Politics and Government in the Federal Republic of Germany: Basic Documents
        (Leamington Spa, Berg, 1984), p. 291.

4.13   From the Paris Treaty establishing the European Coal and Steel
        Community, Paris, 1951.

4.14   Telegram sent on behalf of the British Foreign Minister, A. Eden,
        20 March 1952. R. Bullen and M. Pelly (eds), *Documents on British
        Policy Overseas*, Series 2, Vol. 1 (1, HMSO, 1986), pp. 855–6.

5.1   The North Atlantic Treaty, 4 April 1949, *NATO Facts and Figures
        270–3*, Brussels, 1971.

5.2   The Pleven Plan (EDC), announced in the French National
        Assembly, 24 October 1950, S. Patijn (ed.), *Landmarks in European
        Unity*, (Leiden, Europa Institute, 1970), pp. 73–85.

5.3   Ernest Bevin, British Labour Foreign Secretary to the House of
        Commons, 29 November 1950, HC Debates, Vol. 481, Cols. 1172–4.

5.4   General Eisenhower to the North Atlantic Council, 26 November
        1951.

5.5   Winston Churchill, Conservative Prime Minister, to the House of
        Commons, 6 December 1951, HC Debates, Vol. 494, Cols. 2594–6.

5.6   Communiqué issued after the Six-Power meeting on a European
        Army, Paris, 30 December 1951.

5.7   Article 38 of the Treaty Establishing the European Defence
        Community, 27 May 1952.

5.8   Konrad Adenauer, *Memoirs 1945–53* (London, Weidenfeld and
        Nicolson, 1966) pp. 416–17.

5.9   From the debate in the French National Assembly on the EDC, 29-
        31 August 1954, W. Rossenberger and H. Tobin (eds), *Keesing's
        Contemporary Archives 1954*, Vol. IX (London, Longman Group,
        1957) pp. 13751, 13754–5.

5.10   Statement by John Foster Dulles, Secretary of State, 31 August
        1954, *Department of State Bulletin 13*, September 1954.

6.1   Resolution adopted by the Foreign Ministers of the Member States of the ECSC at the Messina Conference, 1 and 2 June 1955, HMSO Cmnd. 9525, 1955, pp. 7–9.

6.2 Resolution and Joint Declaration of the Action Committee for the United States of Europe, 18 January 1956, *Action Committee for the United States of Europe, Statements and Declarations 1955–67* (London, RIIA, 1969) pp. 12–16.

6.3 Telegram from the US Ambassador to France, Dillon, to the State Department, 19 November 1956, Department of State Central Files 840.1901/11–1956.

6.4 From the debate in the French National Assembly on the ratification of the Common Market and Euratom Treaties, 2–9 July 1957, W. Rossenberger and H. Tobin (eds), *Keesing's Contemporary Archives 1957*, Vol. XI (London, Longman Group, 1957), p. 15957.

6.5 From the treaty of Rome 25 March 1957.

6.6 *The Seventeen Theses on the Common Market* from the Institute of World Economics and International Relations, Moscow 1957, translation from B. Dutoit, *L'Union Sovietique face a L'Intégration Européene*, (Lausanne, 1964) by R. Vaughan, *Post-War Integration in Europe* (London, Edward Arnold, 1976), pp. 156–8.

6.7 Anthony Nutting, *Europe Will Not Wait* (London, Hollis and Carter, 1960).

7.1 Bela Balassa, *The Theory of Economic Integration* (London, Allen and Unwin, 1962) pp. 2–3.

7.2 Extract from the first memorandum from the Commission of the EEC to the Council of Ministers, Brussels, 26 February 1959. Commission of the European Communities.

7.3 Speech by US Under-Secretary of State, George W. Ball, 2 April 1962.

7.4 Extract from interview with Jean Monnet – 'Prospect for a New Europe', *Bulletin from the European Community*, Vol. 2, Supplement 2 (Brussels, Commission of the European Communities, 1959), pp. 3–4.

7.5 'Russia – Hallstein answers Soviet Attacks', *Bulletin from the European Community* (Brussels, Commission of the European Communities, 1962) p. 4.

7.6 Extract from Walter Hallstein, *A New Path to Peaceful Union*, Indian Council for Cultural Relations (New York, Asia Publishing House, 1962).

7.7 The British Prime Minister, Harold Macmillan, to the House of Commons, 31 July 1961, HC Debates, 5th Series, Vol. 645, Col. 928 ff.

7.8 Press release from The National Committee for an Effective Congress, Washington, 27 December 1961.

7.9 Extract from speech by the French President, Charles de Gaulle, at a press conference at the Elysée Palace, Paris, 14 January 1963, Assembly – WEU 1963, *A Retrospective View of the Political Year in Europe* (Paris, March, 1964), pp. 20–2.

7.10 Paul-Henri Spaak, *The Continuing Battle: Memories of a European 1936–66* (London, Weidenfeld and Nicolson, 1971).

7.11 Extract from speech to press conference by President de Gaulle, Paris, 15 May 1962.

7.12 The Luxembourg Agreement, 29 January 1966, *Bulletin of the EC*, March 1966, No. 3. Commission of the European Communities.

7.13 Sicco Mansholt, 'The Promised Land for a Community', *European Community* (Brussels, Commission of the European Communities, November 1970).

8.1 From the Declaration by the European Commission on the occasion of the achievement on the Customs Union on 1 July 1968.

8.2 Communiqué from the meeting of the Heads of State or Government at the Hague, 1 and 2 December 1969, press release from the Dutch Ministry of Foreign Affairs.

8.3 The conclusions of the Werner Report on Economic and Monetary Union, 11 October 1970.

8.4 Extract from *The United Kingdom and the European Communities*, HMSO Cmnd. 4715 (London, 1971).

8.5 A Comparative Poll on the EEC 1970, European Commission, Brussels.

8.6 Labour Party Conference resolution, passed October 1972 – Report of the 71st Annual Party Conference of the Labour Party, Blackpool.

8.7 Extracts from *Why You Should Vote Yes*, Referendum leaflet from *Britain in Europe*, May 1975, London.

8.8 Extracts from *Why You Should Vote No*, Referendum leaflet from the *National Referendum Campaign*, May 1975, London.

8.9 Giuseppe Saragat, Italian Foreign Minister, on the question of direct elections to the European Parliament, April 1964.

8.10 Extracts from David Marquand, *Parliament for Europe* (London, Jonathan Cape, 1979) pp. 77–81.

9.1 The Tindemans Report on European Union, 1975–76 Questionnaire.

9.2 The conclusions of the European Council of 30 November 1976 on the Tindemans Report.

9.3 Extract from *The Enlargement of the Community: General Considerations* – a communication from the Commission to the Council, 20 April 1978. Commission of the European Communities.

9.4 Extract from *The European Community from the First Enlargement to the Second* by Roy Jenkins, President of the Commission, Montague Burton Lecture, University of Edinburgh, 1978.

9.5   Extract from *The European Community: What Kind of Future?* by Emile Noël, Secretary-General of the European Commission – lecture to the Belgian Royal Institute of International Affairs, 20 November 1984, Printed in *Government and Opposition* Vol. 20, No. 2, Spring 1985 (London, 1985), pp. 147–55.

9.6   United States–European Economic Relations 1981: an address by the Assistant Secretary of State for Economic and Business Affairs, Joseph Hormats, to the Mid-America Committee, Chicago, 16 December 1981.

9.7   Enoch Powell on the European Parliament: extracts from a speech in the House of Commons, 26 June 1986, *Hansard* 26 June 1986, c. 495–8.

9.8   *Europe 1992 – The Overall Challenge.* Extracts from article on the Cecchini Report, *Bulletin of the EC*, March 1988. Commission of the European Communities.

9.9   Extracts from *The Bruges Speech*, 20 September 1988, by the British Prime Minister Margaret Thatcher, Conservative Central Office.

9.10   Extracts from Hendrik Brugmans, *Britain and Europe: A Survey* (Hull, Benedicta Press, 1991), pp. 66–71.

10.1   Conference on Security and Cooperation in Europe, Final Act, Helsinki, 1975.

10.2   Mikhail Gorbachev, *Perestroika* (London, Collins, 1987), pp. 195–6.

10.3   Speech by Hans-Dietrich Genscher, Minister of Foreign Affairs of the Federal Republic of Germany, at a conference of the Tutzing Protestant Academy on 31 January 1990. Source: Embassy of the Federal Republic of Germany.

10.4   'Charter of Paris for a New Europe', *Bulletin of the European Communities*, 11–1990. Commission of the European Communities.

10.5   'The Commission's Programme for 1991', *Bulletin of the European Communities*, Supplement 1/91. Commission of the European Communities.

10.6   'Address by the President of the Czech and Slovak Federal Republic, Václav Havel, at the opening session of the Assembly on the European Confederation', Embassy of the Czech and Slovak Federal Republic, 1990.

10.7   Alfred Gomolka, 'Inaugural Speech as President of the *Bundesrat*', *Das Parlament*, 15–22 November 1991.

10.8   Speech by Gerd Poppe of Bündnis 90/Grüne in the German *Bundestag*, *Das Parlament*, 15–22 November 1991.

10.9   J. Dienstbier, 'Priorities of Czechoslovak Foreign Policy', lecture, 11 December 1991. Embassy of the Czech and Slovak Federal Republic.

The editors would also like to acknowledge the following publishers who hold U.S. rights: Harper Collins (extract 10.2); Pantheon Books (extracts 2.2 and 2.5); Librairie Hachette (extract 5.8); and Librairie Fayard (extract 7.10).